Stelios Contogoulas is a Greek finance professional who turned to writing in 2018, following a career in IT consulting and subsequently in derivatives trading.

He was born in Greece but has lived a big part of his adult life abroad. He studied computing at Imperial College London, and then obtained an MBA at Manchester Business School. Having spent ten years working as an interest rate derivatives trader in London, Stelios was caught up in the LIBOR 'scandal' in 2014 and was acquitted three years later.

This is Stelios's first authoring effort, inspired and driven by his multi-year legal battle.

To my wife, Semiramis:

You kept our family united and strong in the face of great adversity. You never stopped reminding me that things happen for a good reason. You are my best friend, my partner, my inspiration. You are the love of my life. I will love you, always.
"One step at a time, baby."

To my parents, Dimitri and Kallirroi, and my brother, Constantine:
I cannot thank you enough for everything you've done for me. You loved me and raised me in a healthy environment, with all the right ethics and principles. You taught me to help others and share the wealth. You allowed me to become the man that I always wanted to be. I could not have asked for better parents or brother; you are all my role models.
"Family is not an important thing. It's everything."

Stelios Contogoulas

TRUTH & LI(E)BOR

Sometimes the real conspiracy is where
you least expect it

AUSTIN MACAULEY PUBLISHERS™

LONDON • CAMBRIDGE • NEW YORK • SHARJAH

A CIP catalogue record for this title is available from the British Library.

ISBN 9781528946513 (Paperback)
ISBN 9781528946537 (ePub e-book)

www.austinmacauley.com

First Published (2021)
Austin Macauley Publishers Ltd
25 Canada Square
Canary Wharf
London
E14 5LQ

Writing your first book is a lot tougher than you might imagine. My story is based on true events and should theoretically have been easy and straightforward to write, but it often seemed like a monumental task. This task would certainly have been a lot tougher if it wasn't for a few people who greatly helped me along the way.

I want to thank my friend, classmate, and very successful author, Vish Dhamija, for his insights and vital tips. I am also grateful to my good friends, Elda, Christina and Stephanos, for reading the early versions of the book and giving valuable feedback. Thank you Harry, Nick and Georgia, for agreeing to provide character references for me in court, without any hesitation whatsoever. You were one of the reasons why the jury was able to see the truth.

Thank you, John Ryder – your skills in court captivated everyone. I owe my freedom to you and the rest of the legal team.

I also want to thank all the people who stood by me during the continued years of stress and adversity. You didn't disappear like some others did. You stuck with me. Even the ones among you whom I'd only known for a relatively short period of time. You know who you are, I love each and every one of you.

Finally, I want to thank my publisher for showing immediate and consistent enthusiasm and support for this book. Your attitude throughout the process has been incredible.

I am humbled by all your support – I will never forget it. Thank you.

Table of Contents

Prologue

'Conspiracy to defraud', is an offence under the common law of England and Wales, and is defined as follows:

'It is clearly the law that an agreement by two or more by dishonesty to deprive a person of something which is his or to which he is or would be entitled and an agreement by two or more by dishonesty to injure some proprietary right of his, suffices to constitute the offence of conspiracy to defraud.'

***

Sometimes life can be truly amazing, and other times it can royally suck. Most people experience highs and lows in their lives, tasting in turn success and bitter disappointment. One day you're living the dream, with more money than you can spend and countless friends, and the next you're penniless and lonely. From supercars and luxury holidays, to trying to scramble enough change for the bus ride home.

William Shakespeare famously said, *'It is not in the stars to hold our destiny but in ourselves.'*

That may be true, but there's always the other side of the coin, as expressed by the fictional character Forrest Gump: *'Life is like a box of chocolates. You never know what you're gonna get.'*

So, where does the truth lie?

Money, greed and hunger for power have traditionally been some of the main drivers for the majority of humans, and as a result people will do whatever it takes in the pursuit of their goals. As the world becomes more materialistic, so the moral fabric of our society gets eroded. Power gets progressively concentrated within corporations, guided by ruthless and merciless Chief Executives and Directors. Employees become expendable pawns, readily sacrificed in the name of profits.

Growing up in this world means negotiating a multitude of complex situations and events. Obviously, some situations we can influence, but others are far beyond our control.

This is a story which describes my personal journey. I was brought up in a healthy environment, with what I considered to be all the right values and ethics. I worked hard to become a useful member of society, always helping others and playing by the book. However, the universe was about to throw me a curve ball and turn my life upside down. I would become the proverbial fly, accidentally tangled in what appeared to be a vicious web of lies, deceit and back-stabbing.

You may have already heard of the LIBOR 'scandal' from the press; I always felt that it had been heavily reported from the prosecutorial side, with the defendants' side being vastly overlooked. In this book, I attempt to address this balance, putting all the pieces of the puzzle together and showing what I think the real truth behind it is. I also try to make the important link between the banks, regulators, politicians and the media, and how they can work together towards a common goal —I think that the LIBOR case is a perfect example of that.

As you read on, try to answer the following questions, based on the information you are seeing:

- What would you do in my situation?
- How would you handle the adversity?
- As you read the courtroom exchanges and see the evidence unfold, how does the big picture evolve in your mind?

(*Disclaimer: the events and dialogues in this book have been written as I remember them, so although some may be exactly as they actually happened, others may not. This shouldn't matter, as all the main points and concepts remain the same.*)

Have no doubt, this story could happen to anyone, from all backgrounds and social classes. These are situations that can truly break a person – how would *you* react?

***

London, 28th January 2001

I looked down at my hands, holding the small white envelope. I was in my early thirties, with clear signs of fatigue after all the hard work of the past decade. My once full head of hair had thinned and receded, revealing a round bald spot at the top of my head. My once athletic body, crafted by a wide range of demanding sports, had become soft and distinctly unfit. My belly visibly attested to an unhealthy lifestyle of long work hours, bad nutrition and zero exercise. I closed my eyes for a few seconds and then opened them again to glance at the envelope. It was blank apart from my name handwritten on the outside, and its contents were destined to completely change my life. I felt my hands shaking slightly, so I took a deep breath and steadied myself.

I looked around the big conference room, which was located in the middle of the seventh floor of the bank's headquarters. It was a bland, white-walled room with a garish blue carpet, and virtually nothing in it except a long rectangular table where the envelopes had been initially placed. A bunch of nervous people like myself were anxiously pacing around the room. It was a Sunday evening and we had just gone through a gruelling "assessment weekend" that the bank had organised for prospective summer interns. I was standing near the edge of the room, away from everyone else, one of around two hundred business school students fighting for a few dozen elusive summer internships. It was the early 2000s after all, so those investment banking positions were possibly the best jobs on the planet at the time. For each one of those internships, there were thousands of people who would do whatever it takes to secure them, and we were now down to the last few candidates.

People were scattered around the room, trying to find a suitable spot and preparing themselves mentally to open their own envelope. Throughout the weekend we had all mostly worked in teams, as we tried to successfully negotiate each task that had been given to us by the organisers. At this moment, however, we were all once again individuals – you could even say that we were enemies – and the room was eerily quiet. Each envelope contained a piece of paper that would indicate whether you had got the internship position or not. That's what it had all come down to a single piece of white paper with a couple of sentences written on it. Somehow, I had always thought that the moment of landing a lucrative high-profile job would be much more glamorous than that.

I stopped for a few seconds to think about my own personal journey, briefly considering the long road I had taken to reach that particular place in Canary Wharf. It was the culmination of decades of hard work, starting from school and evolving through university, my first career in IT and finally the MBA. I thought of my parents, Kallirroi and Dimitri, and how they had guided and supported me throughout my life. My older brother Constantine, who had often used me as a punching bag when we were kids, but who later turned out to be a great friend and mentor. I glanced across the room at Markus, with whom we were classmates but also flatmates and good friends. Markus was too concentrated to look at anything other his own envelope; that was understandable.

I closed my eyes and took one final deep breath. I told myself that no matter what the outcome, I'd be OK. I was a hard-working and motivated person and if this job didn't materialise, another one probably would down the road.

My mind wandered for a few more seconds, but then I thought, *Screw this. This job is MINE.*

I could never in a million years have imagined what a colossal life-changing point it would prove to be.

Chapter One
The Early Years

At this point, it's important to briefly describe my life, from the early years up until my big break as a City trader. My life leading to university was a rollercoaster ride with many twists and turns. It was a succession of events that built my character, and a wide range of experiences that made me the man I grew up to be.

As a kid, I was always relatively quiet and shy. Born into a middle-class family, I was brought up to respect my elders and my parents in particular.

My mother, Kallirroi, was a typical Greek stay-at-home mom; taking care of the house and her two boys. As a stay-at-home dad myself many years later, I eventually came to realise just how complex and demanding that job was. Kallirroi was the voice of reason, and annoyingly whenever there was an argument, she'd almost always turn out to be right. A tall slim woman with long black hair and typical Greek characteristics, she was firm but fair.

My father, Dimitri, was a banker himself – although on the retail side of the business – and he had always been my role model. He was a true professional, working endless hours each day wholly dedicated to providing a stable environment for himself and his family. Dimitri made many sacrifices in his desire to give his two sons all the opportunities that he himself never got, having grown up in a poor Greek family.

As a kid, I rarely saw my father on weekdays, due to his extensive working hours. We tried to make up for that on the weekends, but I always felt it wasn't quite enough. My father was the man I aspired to be; I always told him that if I managed to achieve half of what he had achieved in his life, I'd consider myself to be a great success.

My father was also my teacher and my mentor in many aspects of life. Dimitri was exceptionally nice to people, even towards strangers or people he'd only just met. His constant desire to help others was one of the most beautiful things I had ever seen in a person. It was no surprise that he was liked by everyone and people only had the best things to say about him. Dimitri was also the first to recognise and reward actions that he thought were worthy of acknowledgement by frequently writing letters to companies whenever he had a good experience.

'Son, people always write to companies when something goes wrong and they rarely give praise when something goes right,' he would typically say, 'I want to try and balance out that unfair behaviour.'

A perfect example of my father's character was when he oversaw the opening of the bank's new branch in a trendy area of Athens. It was a sleek new building, way ahead of its time in terms of design and facilities, and he was particularly proud of it. One Sunday morning, our family was out and about with friends and we happened to walk right outside the building. It was closed on Sundays, but Dimitri managed to spot the cleaning lady working inside.

'Wait right here!' he enthusiastically exclaimed to the family, 'I'm going to get the cleaning lady to open up and I'll give you all a private tour of the offices.'

The excitement was clearly visible in his eyes as he couldn't wait to show everyone his new pride and joy. He knocked on the glass door and gestured at the lady, dressed in her white cleaning uniform, who in turn walked slowly to the door and asked how she could be of any assistance. He eagerly informed her that he was the bank's Country Head and asked her to let him in so that he could show his friends the building. Her response was shattering:

'I'm sorry sir, but I don't know you and I cannot let you in.'

Dimitri was suddenly like a kid whose ice cream had just been taken away. We all slowly walked on, and I thought that this was the end of it. The next day, Dimitri went to work in the morning and the first thing he did was to find out who that cleaning lady was. He spoke to an employee from personnel and quickly identified her, but his next action was astonishing.

'Give that woman a raise, no questions asked!' he said. 'Not only does she do an excellent job cleaning, but she was not afraid to put the building's security above her own job. No doubt many people in my position would have got angry and perhaps even punished her. What she did took guts and discipline.'

That's the kind of person Dimitri always was, and the person I wanted to be when I grew up. No matter what problem or obstacle they came across in life, he always had a friend or acquaintance who would go out of their way to help – simply because this was exactly what he did for others as well. This aspect of his character got deeply ingrained within me, and from a very young age I realised that the best attitude in life is to have a single-minded desire to help and be nice to others. Not because you expect something in return down the road, but because it's the right thing to do. It may sound like a terrible cliché, but this is exactly how I was brought up. I sometimes considered it to be akin to brainwashing – but brainwashing of the best possible kind.

***

Thessaloniki, August 1971

I was born in Thessaloniki, Greece's second largest city, in a hospital only a few steps from the beach. Maybe it was the abundance of sunlight or the smells and sights of the sea, but I developed a deep love for my country that would stay deeply rooted within me even when I spent prolonged periods of my life abroad.

My father had got a promotion at the bank and was stationed in Thessaloniki when my brother Constantine and I were born in the early seventies. I was too young to remember those three particular years but from the surviving family photos – and the joyous moments my parents spent reminiscing them – I could tell that they were happy times.

In the mid-seventies, my parents took a big risk. An important opportunity materialised within the bank, where the need arose for someone to head their troubled Saudi Arabia operations. Dimitri, forward thinking as usual, grabbed it with both hands. The classic family story that my father has told over and over again throughout the years, was when he called his wife from work to tell her.

'Go to the study and grab the globe, GOT it?' asked Dimitri.

'Got it,' responded Kallirroi shortly after.

'OK, now find Saudi Arabia – it's a country broadly south east from Greece. Found it?' he continued excitedly.

'Yes.'

'Now find a city called Jeddah, OK?'

'Found it.'

'Great. Start packing because we leave in two weeks and we're going to live there for the next couple of years.'

Following the initial shock, to her credit, Kallirroi was immediately on board with the idea. By doing so, she showed the boys that a family is strongest when it cooperates and works together united as a team towards a common goal. She knew that it wouldn't be an easy place to live in, but Dimitri's career progression and compensation would be excellent.

What the hell, she thought, *there must be a decent ex-pat community there. We'll be back home before we know it.*

She was right.

A mere two years later, we were all back home in Athens with some great memories and film reels that we still watch to this day. I distinctly remember the house we lived in; a big square white house with wooden doors and windows, and lots of space to play outside. I spent endless hours with my brother riding our bicycles outside, just doing countless laps around the house while our dogs gave chase. One of the family's favourite funny stories is how one day – even though the outside area was particularly vast – Constantine and I managed to crash into each other with such force that my bicycle was nearly ruined.

Upon our return to Greece, the following few years were relatively uneventful. We lived a typical suburban family life, complete with a big green garden, childhood friends and two dogs. However, once again Dimitri seemed to have other plans. In the mid-eighties, the bank offered him a position he simply couldn't refuse – a senior role based in France.

***

Paris, September 1984

Our family moved to Paris in 1984, and this time Kallirroi was absolutely thrilled with the prospect. We spent three amazing years there, taking in the beautiful city and French culture. I wasn't particularly excited about all the museums, restaurants and other glamorous aspects of living in the "city of light", although the visits to Moulin Rouge and Lido will be forever engraved in my memory – as they would be of course, for most teenage boys in my position.

One aspect of living in Paris that was most beneficial for my brother and I was school. We enrolled at the British School of Paris and that was a truly eye-opening experience for both of us. Around half of the students were non-British, spanning over twenty different nationalities. For the first time in our lives, we interacted on a daily basis with people from various countries, backgrounds and cultures. There were some aspects that I would rather forget – *cough* rugby training *cough* – but decades later I still remain friends with many of my former classmates and always feel blessed to have met them. I genuinely felt that I was growing up and maturing as a person from all those new experiences. I learned about the English culture (shepherd's pie, WH Smith and Samantha Fox somehow managing to stick out more than others) and that was probably where my love for England really kicked off.

After three glorious years Dimitri's stint was over, and our family took the road home to Athens.

***

Athens, September 1987

In late 1987 I enrolled on a two-year GCE A-Level programme in a Greek private school, the ultimate goal being to study in a UK university. Three things dominated those two years for me: *studying, studying* and *yet more studying*.

I had been fascinated with computers from a very young age, ever since the day my father unexpectedly brought home a strange-looking rectangular black device. That machine was the Sinclair ZX81, my first computer and the first machine I ever programmed. From that point on, I was absolutely hooked. After a succession of increasingly powerful machines, I had become convinced that I wanted to study Computer Science and make it my profession.

When I started the A-Level programme, my goal had become crystal clear: I was determined to obtain a Computer Science degree at Imperial College in London. It was one of the most innovative and exciting universities on the planet and I spent hours studying every day, never losing focus of that exact goal. I had even printed out the university logo on a sheet of paper and stuck it on my bedroom wall; it was the first thing I saw when I woke up and the last thing I saw before I went to sleep.

I was extremely comfortable with mathematics, my teachers frequently telling me that I had a natural talent in the subject. I often found myself being taught new concepts and instantly seeing exactly how they fit together with other related principles. I was also lightning-quick while performing mathematical calculations in my head, a skill that would prove particularly useful in my subsequent trading career.

I took my A-Levels in June 1989 and having been thoroughly prepared for them, I was feeling supremely confident as I entered the examination room. Sure enough, I blitzed through each question in what felt like one of the best days of my life. I had that feeling where I just *knew* that no matter what the obstacles (or in this case, questions), I would easily overcome them. As the Mathematics exams finished and all the candidates gathered outside the examination room to discuss the questions, the broad feeling was that they had actually been particularly tough. I was convinced that I had done very well, but I tried not to sound like a smart ass.

'Those questions were really tough, especially question two,' said one of the other candidates.

'Yeah, dammit, I didn't even have enough time to answer all the questions,' said another.

'They were definitely tough questions,' I said, trying to play along and not make them feel bad, while avoiding commenting on how well I thought I'd done myself. I had a very good feeling about my prospects, hoping that the endless hours of studying were worth it.

***

London, September 1989

When the results were announced a few weeks later, I had been accepted at Imperial College, following in my older brother's footsteps who had also been accepted in the Mechanical Engineering department a year earlier. The immense sense of relief made me realise just how much pressure I had put on myself to succeed. But that was me – set the goal, visualise it, and work like hell to achieve it.

Years later, Dimitri sat down with his two sons to have a talk, his words literally bringing me to tears.

'Now that you've both graduated from Imperial College, there's something I need to say,' he told us.

'For years it had been my dream to study at Imperial, but I didn't make it. I didn't want to tell you this during your preparation or while you were studying there, because I would be putting pressure on you, and that was the least of my intentions. But now I can tell you this, and I feel extremely proud of you both. You have put a solid foundation for your future careers, and your mother and I will be fully supporting you every step of the way.'

I realised that very few parents would have done what my father did, instead they would have most likely exerted pressure, in order to finally realise their own dream through their children. Being the great man, Dimitri approached that particular situation in his own amazing way.

I spent three years studying Computer Science, where I met dozens of extremely intelligent and talented people. I remained good friends with many of them and closely followed several of my classmates in their chosen professions. There were businessmen, scientists, bankers, politicians – you name it.

I completed my bachelor's degree with Upper-Second class honours, missing out on a better result due to my obsession with snooker. I may not have achieved the top-class honours, but I had made the university's snooker team and participated in inter-university tournaments. For me, that was probably a more difficult and satisfying achievement.

After completing the Computer Science course, I went on to take a master's degree in Biomedical Engineering, at the same university. In hindsight, I was never quite sure what I was thinking with that decision, as it was a highly specialised degree and not suitable at all for a career in Greece at the time. Hey, I never said I was perfect.

Athens, August 1993

I returned to Greece in 1993, happy to be finally done with studying and eager to get started with my professional career. That excitement was brought to a screeching halt upon realising that I first needed to deal with the small matter of the Greek military service. A compulsory service, typically lasting for around one and a half years, and one of the major headaches adult Greek men had at the time.

There were a plethora of tricks and methods employed by Greeks in their attempt to avoid serving, some more creative than others. Some people moved abroad and lived there for decades, until they reached an age where they could simply pay a small financial penalty instead of serving. Others were much more creative, utilising a Greek law that relieved people from military duty if they were judged to be mentally ill.

I remember vividly the entry interview at the Greek army, where everyone was asked some basic background questions. This process was done concurrently for many new recruits, all grouped together in a big room, and one guy next to me was giving the following answers:

'What's your name?'

'Genghis Khan.'

'When were you born, and where?'

'February 1162, in Boldog.'

Another guy had stuck two pencils up his nostrils and made weird beeping noises, claiming that he was an extra-terrestrial being.

You get the broader picture.

I chose not to go down that route, mainly because I felt it was my duty as a Greek citizen to serve my country, but also because I didn't want to look like a total imbecile in front of a bunch of complete strangers.

I joined the armoured corps and spent the first seven months in the main training base an hour's drive from Athens. Surprisingly, it wasn't a total waste of time as I originally thought it might be. The armoured corps was considered to be one of the toughest in the Greek army, and so people with power and connections did everything they could to avoid being drafted there. Contrary to every other person there, I didn't actually care. I was determined to see it through and gain as many positive experiences as possible in the process.

The first three months were quite tedious, consisting mainly of basic military training, but then the 'fun' started. From a couple of thousand recruits, I was selected to be one of roughly two hundred who would go through military school and become Petty Officers. It was two months of discipline, studying and tough physical activity, during which I lost a full seven kilos of weight.

Upon completion I was made Sergeant and was handpicked to be one of fifteen individuals who would be in charge of training the next batch of recruits. We had gone through sixty days of hell and this was – in theory at least – my chance to get revenge on some new and unsuspecting recruits. And yet, that's not quite how it played out. I found myself constantly helping the new recruits, giving them hints and tips on how to make those days a little more bearable. My father's mentality was clearly already embedded deep within me – and I wouldn't have it any other way.

Chapter Two
First Career

Athens, June 1995

My military service was complete in the summer of 1995 and I was eager to start my professional career. I had felt like a caged lion, trapped for nineteen months, waiting to be released into the corporate jungle. I went on to find a job within only a few weeks of searching, a time period that was quite typical in mid-90s Greece. The economy was doing well and there was plenty of demand for skilled individuals, especially in the booming IT industry.

My first job was with a Machine Vision firm, which involved designing and implementing complex systems for industrial applications. These systems used cameras and some clever computer code to perform crucial tasks such as quality control, robotic guidance, and precision placement. The first months were incredibly exciting, as I got deeply immersed in a brand-new world and gained substantial technical knowledge. I went through an intensive ten-day training course in the United States and started travelling to client sites, as I got more involved in high-profile projects involving big clients, such as Nestle and Rolex. It was exciting for the first year, but it became bit repetitive the second year. By the third year, I was desperately looking to make a change.

In 1998, I saw an advertisement for a position in the Greek office of the world's biggest IT consultancy firm at the time, Accenture. Their Greek offices were still relatively small, so I thought it would be a smart move to get in early and eventually be part of something much greater. A few days later, I was interviewed and particularly impressed the senior partners, promptly earning myself the position. Soon after, I was assigned to a major project which involved developing a centralised system for a large Greek state-owned bank. I stayed in that project – and the firm – for two years. This was more than enough time for me to figure it out once and for all: I needed a complete change of career. *FAST*.

One day, I woke up in the morning and something quite peculiar happened. Still half-asleep, I washed my face and took a long look at myself in the mirror. My uneven haircut and two-day stubble gave me a particularly scruffy look. The dark circles under my eyes betrayed the fact that I had been going through a particularly tiring stretch at work, with fourteen-hour workdays and junk food dinners. I paused for a few seconds and then spoke out loud:

'*I hate my job.*'

It was as if I had to hear myself say it, so that I could finally accept it. Programming and IT consulting were just not for me, as I found myself getting bored quite easily and needed a challenge. I wanted something more exciting, more fast-paced and less repetitive. In fairness, those past two years were not a waste of time as I thought about it; as it turned out, that job was the first link of a chain of events that led me to meet the love of my life (more on this later).

I had concluded that I needed to change career, but I had absolutely no clue how to go about it. I came from an MBA family, my father having completed his at INSEAD in the eighties and my brother his at London Business School two years earlier. Naturally, when I went to them for advice, they both strongly recommended I do the same. It would be a substantial investment financially, but the potential upside convinced me that it would be a no-brainer decision.

After some tests and interviews, I got admitted at Manchester Business School and started the course in late 2000. As I set foot in the business school for the very first time, I remembered the words I had told myself when I finished my master's degree in 1993:

'That's it, no more studying for me, *ever*!'

Meanwhile, the destiny stared at me with a sarcastic smirk on her face, 'Yeah. Good luck with that one, mate.'

***

Manchester, September 2000

The MBA was a thoroughly overwhelming experience for me. The sheer volume of reading, assignments and group projects made it a truly daunting task. In hindsight, I realised that it was probably purposely done in such a way; this was essentially intense training in time-management and organisational skills.

My MBA class consisted of just over one hundred individuals, many of which were quite exceptional people. The sheer variety in my classmates' nationalities, professions, and general backgrounds made it an astonishing place to study. I got to be friends with many of them, but at some point, the classmates eventually found out that they would soon be competing against each other in search of jobs.

It wasn't long before a number of major global firms started making on-campus presentations, trying to attract top talent. On a typical rainy Manchester Monday, a Barclays employee came to the business school to make a presentation of the bank and his job in particular.

Let's take a moment here and describe something important about me: I always loved driving and had been obsessed with cars and motorsport for as long as I can remember. When I was a little boy, my most cherished toys were cars, and I'd spend countless hours dreaming I was a racing driver. I took my driving test soon after my eighteenth birthday and always thoroughly enjoyed even the shortest and most mundane car journeys. My friends gave me the nickname 'taxi driver' because of my frequent desire to drive people around, but that didn't stop me or annoy me at all. I used to read all the popular car magazines and had full encyclopaedic knowledge of all major cars in production. If you asked me for a particular make and model, I could tell you all the engine and body variants, complete with statistics such as horsepower, 0-100kph acceleration time, top speed, and many others. I knew from a young age that I would never lose this love for cars, being totally uninterested in things like having flashy clothes or going to wild parties like other kids did. I would have gladly given up every other luxury to pursue my love of cars and anything that had to do with motor racing.

So why mention all this? The reason is that, despite his bland attire, the man from Barclays giving the presentation was in fact a trader who also had a love for cars. Following a pretty standard and rather dull thirty-minute presentation, he closed with this:

'So, do you want a job that's exciting, fast-paced and very rarely repetitive? Do you want to buy that Ferrari that you always dreamed of? Then come work for Barclays and become a trader.'

The man had just spoken two sentences that resonated with every single bone in my body. I knew right there and then that I was going to go after a summer internship in trading, hopefully leading to a full-time job.

Barclays was the first bank to make a presentation at the business school, so it was also the first bank to outline their internship application process. It was not a simple or easy process, as I later found out, the first step being an aptitude test that consisted of three parts – Mathematics, English and a Psychometric evaluation. The first two were GMAT-like tests with relatively simple questions individually, but with two major pitfalls: the wording was often purposely tricky and there were way too many questions for the allowed time to answer them. As a result, this test was effectively yet another way of assessing how individuals handled stress and time pressure. Apparently, roughly eighty per cent of the internship applicants were cut based on those test results, making it a crucial initial filtering phase.

The next round consisted of on-campus interviews conducted by Barclays senior staff. I had heard about aggressive investment banking interviews and how they sometimes tried to break applicants, and I was about to get a taste of it myself.

The first interview was with a quantitative analyst who spent the best part of an hour asking mathematical and numerical questions, attempting to draw out a mistake. The mistake never came, boosting my confidence and hopes, but the second interview was a very different affair.

The follow-up interview was with a senior salesman who started asking all the typical interview questions. I was in the middle of answering a question when I noticed him leaning back in his chair, seemingly falling asleep. This was a classic example of interviewers trying to provoke a reaction to an unexpected situation, and surprisingly, it was a relatively common tactic in banking interviews. I politely spoke to him, asking if he needed some rest and would prefer me to leave. There was no answer. I then calmly got up and walked over to the interviewer's desk, noticing a pack of post-it notes and a pen lying on it. I quickly wrote a message:

'You've probably had a very long week and need some rest. I'll let you recuperate and will be available to meet again, should you wish to do so. You have all my contact details if needed. Regards, Stelios.'

Following those two interesting – if slightly surreal – interviews, I was informed that I had made it to the final phase of the internship process. This final round was the 'Assessment Weekend' that Barclays held on an annual basis. Summer internship candidates were flown to the Barclays headquarters in Canary Wharf, where they would undergo a series of tests over two full days. Those were probably two of the toughest days of my life. All the tests were extremely well thought out and beautifully executed – kudos to Barclays for that.

One test involved a scenario where you had to sell a car to prospective clients. I was terrible at that and quickly realised that I couldn't be a salesman to save my life. In fact, I wasn't even a competent salesman selling my favourite product in the whole world.

Another test was one that really shocked most candidates, and one which required total out-of-the-box thinking. We were placed in round tables of eight people – seven candidates and one bank employee who was assigned to supervise. Each candidate was given a sheet of paper with instructions, and we were told that they had to work as a team to complete this assignment.

The instructions were relatively simple. There were seven candidates and seven specific letters of the alphabet, each one written on a sticky piece of paper. Each candidate would stick one letter on their chest and the goal was to form as many words as possible by standing side-by-side. We simply needed to arrange ourselves in line, form the selected word, and move onto the next one. Each group had three minutes to make as many words as possible, a task that sounded simple at first. Naturally, however, there was a catch. There were three little details which made the task infinitely harder:

- Candidates knew all seven letters, but they only knew which letter had been assigned specifically to them.
- Candidates were not allowed to speak during the task.
- Candidates were blindfolded during the task.

As I read those final three details, I felt cold sweat running down my face. I might as well have been asked to climb mount Everest, barefoot, with no equipment.

As the instructions were handed out to us and we began reading them, there was complete silence in the room. Everyone was frantically trying to find a way around the obvious obstacles, but it seemed like an impossible task. Suddenly, I had an epiphany. This task wasn't about making ten or twenty words to win; it was about making two or three at most. I took the lead and spoke to the group.

'Right everyone, I have a thought. I think that if we manage to make three words, we'll win this task. It's probably going to be very difficult for another team to somehow make more. So, let's decide on three words, since we know what the seven available letters are, and let's all memorise them. When we start the task, we will each know in which position we are placed within each specific word.'

I felt more and more confident as I was speaking, realising that I was partially making it up as I was going along. Never mind, it was all making sense so far and the other team members were nodding in approval.

'The big problem is that we'll be blindfolded and not allowed to speak,' I continued. 'That's OK, we will communicate by making other sounds. The person with the first letter in the word will stand up and clap once. The person with the second letter will hear the clap and stand next to that person, and clap twice. And so on, and so forth. When the word is complete, we all clap seven times and we move onto the next word. Agreed?'

That last question was mostly rhetorical, since our time for formulating a strategy was up and the task was about to begin.

'OK let's do that!' they all approved.

Each candidate was blindfolded, and a bank employee announced that the time had started counting down.

Three very quick and unusual minutes later, the task was over – much to the relief of the candidates. I took my blindfold off and sat down on a chair, exhaling loudly. I looked around and couldn't help giggling when I realised that one of the team members from the adjacent table had somehow wandered all the way to the other end of the room.

The scores were recorded, and I was absolutely chuffed to see that the two words my team had managed to form made it the joint-highest score out of the whole room. The team celebrated by fist-bumping and hugging, but the celebrations were cut short – it was already time to move onto the next test.

The last test I took was a card-based game that mimicked a trading situation where candidates started with partial information and were then gradually fed the rest. As more information was revealed, the trading strategy would change in order to adapt to the new parameters. I immediately felt at ease with the situation, figuring out a robust strategy from very early on in the game. In the end I blitzed it, registering the second highest score out of roughly two hundred candidates. Harry Harrison was the Barclays manager who was assigned to observe our table and that's where I first caught his attention. Harry would later turn out to play a big role in my career and subsequent adventure.

***

At the end of the two days, the candidates were all asked to assemble in the conference room on the seventh floor, and this brings us back to the precise moment where I was nervously holding the white envelope in my hands.

As I took the piece of paper out of the envelope and slowly unfolded it, a single word caught my eye: "*Congratulations*". That's all I needed to read, as I finally let myself go and felt my legs getting weak. I sat down on the floor of the room, with the piece of paper still in my hands, and the emotions finally started flowing. Relief, elation, satisfaction all rolled into one. I felt two days of immense stress suddenly leaving my body and the feeling was incredible. After nearly two decades of hard work I had finally made it – the first step to becoming a trader in the City of London.

***

October 2010, London

It was a cold Friday evening and I had just returned home from the gym. My busy life as a derivatives trader had taken a toll on me and I had recently decided to make a change in my personal life, in terms of exercise and nutrition. For the past few years, every time I had looked at myself in the mirror, I really didn't like what I saw. I had let myself go, spending most of my day sitting on my trading desk and getting practically no exercise at all. I ate at random times of the day and the nutritional value of my meals was typically very poor.

My recent girlfriend – a young fitness enthusiast in her late twenties – frequently reassured me that I looked handsome. I wanted to believe her, but I was sure that her judgement was severely influenced by the size of my wallet. I didn't care.

Two months before, I had decided to make a change and had started going regularly to the gym. After only a few weeks of weight training, Pilates and indoor cycling, the difference was already visible, and I felt more energised and upbeat.

That evening I was driving my brand-new Audi R8, a car I adored and which I had taken a particularly long time to select when looking to make my purchase. It had to be the perfect colour combination: 'Phantom black' exterior colour, carbon side-blades, black leather interior and dark grey titanium wheels. No matter which angle you looked at it, the combination of the dark colours and the aggressive lines made it look really menacing. I called it my *Batmobile*.

The King's Road in Chelsea was uncharacteristically empty that evening, so I was slightly more heavy-footed than normal. The car's open-gate metallic gearbox made the characteristic 'clunk' every time I manually changed a gear, while the rear-mounted V8 engine's deep rumble provided a resounding background soundtrack situated at a mere inches behind the driver's seat. It had a particularly powerful Bang & Olufsen twelve-speaker sound system, but that was largely unused. To me, the mechanical sounds coming out of the car were more intricate and melodic than Chopin's infamous 'Black Key' Etude, and more powerful than Beethoven's thunderous Third Movement of the legendary 'Moonlight Sonata'. That car was not only gorgeous from the outside, but it was also deeply satisfying to drive even at low speeds.

I had nearly arrived home when the symphony of mechanical sounds was abruptly interrupted by my phone ringing.

'Mr Contogoulas, it's Johnny, the porter from your building,' said the familiar voice on the line.

'Hey Johnny, good evening, what's up?' I replied cheerfully.

'A courier just passed-by and left an envelope for you marked "Urgent" and "Confidential". I thought about waiting to give it to you when you returned home, but then I changed my mind. I hope you don't mind,' he said hesitantly.

'Not at all, Johnny, you did the right thing. I'm on my way now.'

Barely a few minutes later, I was entering the building's underground garage and carefully proceeded to park the sleek supercar in my allocated space at the far end. I hastily walked to the elevator and, wasting no time, made my way to the ground floor. As soon as the elevator doors opened, Johnny stood up and greeted me.

'Mr Contogoulas, here is your envelope,' he said and handed it over.

As I was opening the envelope, I could feel Johnny stare at me with anticipation, almost as if he was anxiously waiting for me to tell him what it was all about.

Within the plain white envelope there was a single piece of paper. It was from a man called Ron, a lawyer at one of the biggest law firms in the UK. The letter read as follows:

"Dear Mr Contogoulas

We represent Barclays Bank in the matter of an ongoing investigation regarding events that happened around five years ago. The investigation has been active for some time and you are one of many current and former Barclays employees that we need to talk to.

We are not at liberty to disclose any details in writing, due to the high sensitivity of the case. We would like to arrange a meeting at your earliest convenience and would appreciate it if you could contact us on the numbers provided below.

Please note that this is a top-secret investigation and you are not allowed to alert anyone to its existence or nature. Failure to do so could bring criminal charges against you.

Looking forward to your swift response. "

I read the message and then immediately proceeded to read it a second time. I always had a habit of doing this when particularly important documents were involved. I folded the paper, put it back in the envelope and placed it in my trouser pocket.

Having made my way to my flat, I headed straight for the living room, sat down on the sofa and laid my coat neatly beside me. I reached over to grab a bottle of 16-year old Lagavulin and took out one of my favourite Saint-Louis crystal whisky glasses. I always loved how those particular glasses somehow managed to extract the full aroma of the drink. I poured some of the whisky and then I slowly raised my glass, looking into the light through it and admiring its complex colours. Finally, I took a sip and slowly laid back on the soft white sofa. I had a bad feeling about this.

Chapter Three
The Summer Internship

London, June 2001

Having succeeded at the incredibly difficult 'Assessment Weekend' and being offered the internship position at Barclays, I returned to Manchester to resume my MBA. The vast amount of reading and assignments at the business school had left me no choice but to dive deep into it and work nearly round-the-clock in order to meet the various deadlines. However, as June 2001 arrived in a flash, I now needed to put a full-stop to the business school curriculum and concentrate on the summer internship. It was time to travel to London and spend twelve weeks at the bank; a prospect that excited me but also scared the hell out of me. Up to that point of my life I had succeeded in everything I had aimed for. This, however, was the proverbial jackpot.

It was early on a warm June morning when I made my way towards the Barclays building for the very first time. As I walked along West ferry Road, I observed the brand-new developments on the riverside of the Thames. They were tall, modern buildings with big glass surfaces, most of them having popped up like mushrooms over the previous years. They were right on the edge of the Thames, so it made perfect sense to build them in a way that reminded their wealthy tenants just how special they should feel. Walking by these buildings meant that most often than not, you could catch a glimpse of their garage and the exotic cars they invariably hosted. A red Ferrari 355 was visible from one particular building and I briefly stopped to admire it. A couple of minutes passed – they seemed like seconds – as I couldn't take my eyes off it.

Snap out of it, man, I suddenly thought to myself. *You will have plenty of time for this later. Get to work and don't be late.*

I quickened my pace and a few minutes later I arrived at my destination.

Barclays headquarters was actually quite different than most of the other surrounding buildings. It had only been built in the early 1990s, but the design was very traditional and old-fashioned. I liked that a lot.

I stepped through the main revolving doors and headed to the security office, where I was issued a temporary pass labelled "*Visitor*". I swiped it on the glass turnstiles and headed straight for the trading floor, two floors up. As I pushed one of the two big entrance doors to the vast trading floor, I felt my heart pounding.

The door opened, and a veritable barrage of information instantly overloaded my senses. The trading floor truly was like nothing I had ever seen before, with rows upon rows of desks arranged in parallel lines, one next to each other. On each desk there was a complicated communication system including phones, digital displays, speakers and microphones. Depending on each person's role, there were anywhere between two and eight computer monitors on each desk. Secretaries had two screens, sales people usually had four, and traders had as many as they could possibly fit in such a small amount of space.

I walked towards the Sterling Desk, as I had already been given directions to find its location within the trading floor. Upon arriving, I saw the familiar face of Harry Harrison and that certainly calmed me down a bit. Harry looked up and saw me standing next to him. He smiled, got up and shook my hand.

'Welcome to the Sterling desk,' he said cheerfully. He introduced me to the traders in the group, but I struggled to remember all the names. I'd always been exceptionally bad with names; it was almost as if my brain shuts down when I'm being introduced to someone, and their name instantly drops out of my memory. I was making a conscious effort to overcome that weakness, but I was once again failing miserably.

Harry introduced me to Nat and Kilian, the two Sterling swaps traders. They were senior and well respected, as they had been trading successfully for years. I also met the UK Gilt traders – Aiden, Nigel, Jason, Trevor – who were all very likeable and easy-going from day one.

The summer internship actually formed part of my MBA course and for this reason I had to be assigned a specific Internship Project. I was then required to submit a written report based on this project, which would subsequently be evaluated and count towards my overall degree result. Harrison soon assigned me a project, which would be based on an instrument called the *Gilt Basis*. The Gilt Basis trader happened to be Trevor, a trader with whom I would have to work closely and learn from throughout the internship. Trevor eventually turned out to be a good friend and greatly supported me during the dark times that came many years later. He was also a very good 9-ball pool player, which meant that we often spent some very enjoyable evenings battling over the pool table.

The summer internship was supposed to be a way for individuals to learn about investment banking and produce an end-of-term written report for the Business School. However, as the days went on, I realised that learning about the business or the Gilt Basis was only a small detail, as far as the people on the Sterling desk was concerned. Their main goal was to gauge what kind of person I was and whether I would fit well within the existing team. For them, I was obviously smart enough to be able to learn the business. After all, I had already successfully passed their elaborate intake process, beating hundreds of other candidates.

A few months back, I had asked an interviewer what type of people they were looking for when deciding whom to hire. His memorable answer was:

'We are looking for people who are not assholes.'

I was now starting to realise that this response wasn't just a bit of fun or banter – it was the actual truth.

Even though I was thirty years old at the time, I was effectively entering the trading world at a junior level. I soon discovered during the internship that I would be required to bring morning coffees to the other team members. Some people in my place might have got annoyed or offended, being asked to bring coffee – let's not forget that I was soon going to have two degrees and five years of substantial work experience behind me. However, I didn't mind at all and gladly did the morning coffee run for the team. I later realised that this was probably just an additional test, which would show Harry and the others yet another aspect of my character. It was also a simple money management task – I had to make sure I always had enough change in order to manage each day's order. I often planned ahead, ensuring that I had accumulated enough coins and notes of each denomination so that I didn't run into cash flow problems at a later stage. My single-minded aim during those twelve weeks was to be perfect at everything I was asked to do. No job was too small or insignificant. I was going to treat all my responsibilities as if they were of the most importance in my life.

The twelve weeks of the summer internship went by in a flash. Within that time, I got to know every member of the Sterling Rates Trading group and I was genuinely impressed with the sheer concentration of talent. Not only were these people excellent traders and amazingly fast with numbers, but they were also very knowledgeable on a wide variety of subjects. Sports, music, politics, arts, you name it. There was continuous joking, betting on all sorts of things, and general banter.

One evening the group arranged to have a dinner, which was a relatively common team-building event, and as the evening went on, the drinks kept coming. The casual chat progressively became more aggressive and people would bet with each other on anything that crossed their minds. Many of these people had the gambling gene buried deep in their DNA, and it became evident at every opportunity.

Dinner was followed by a visit to the nearby 'Secrets' strip club. While some of my colleagues were decent and respectable family men, others underwent some kind of metamorphosis as soon as they crossed the club's entrance. I looked at them and I was astonished by the transformation. Even some senior managers and reclusive individuals who were always serious and composed at work, became drooling animals.

The respect and admiration that I had built for many of the guys suddenly took a hit. There was a reason why the City Boy stereotype was that of loud, arrogant and sex-crazed aggressive men – it accurately described the vast majority.

At work, there was a lot of banter within the group, and that was fine with me. However, when something significant happened in the markets, it was as if someone flicked a switch and they all went into full-on 'trading' mode. Their complete and total focus turned to their screens, mouse in hand, shouting orders at their brokers and to each other. There were big amounts at stake and these guys had a lot to gain, but they also had a lot to lose. Have a bad trade and you could lose a big chunk of money. Have a bad month and your boss would take you aside and have a word with you. Have a bad year and you could easily get fired.

As I would later find out, very few people had the skills and instincts required to be successful traders. It was certainly not a job for the faint-hearted. One day during the internship, I saw one of my fellow interns, John, collapse to the ground and fall unconscious. John was one of those *brain-the-size-of-a-planet* PhDs, with four degrees and exceptional mathematical and numerical skills. As it turned out, he didn't have the stomach for the relentless ups and downs of trading, and his body eventually gave up. Not long after that day, I heard that John had quit and decided to go into academia.

***

September came, and I had reached the end of my internship. Those past three months had been a real eye-opener for me, having taken in vast amounts of information and learnt a great deal. I felt good with what I had achieved, but I was naturally nervous. Did Harry and the team think that I was cut out to be a trader? Did they think that, in fact, I was *not* an asshole?

As fate would have it, on the 11th of September 2001, Harry asked me to go for an early lunch. We exited the building and walked across the road to the nearby sushi restaurant, and as we sat down, I remember biting my fingernails in nervousness. Harry looked at me and couldn't help but notice the obvious anxiety. He said two calming words:

'Relax, Stelios.'

He paused for a little bit and then continued coolly.

'You've done very well and the team like you. You've shown very good character and eagerness to learn, and those were the two qualities I wasn't sure of when I picked you to be our summer intern. I knew that you had the numerical skills the minute I saw you demolish the opposition during that card game on the assessment weekend.'

I felt a huge weight off my shoulders and tried in vain to hold back a discreet smile.

'We'd like you to join our team full-time when your MBA course is complete, and we all think that you have a bright future ahead of you as a trader. Congratulations!' concluded Harry and took a sip of water.

I, for once, was lost for words. It took me a good few seconds to compose myself and get my thoughts together, before replying proudly.

'Thank you very much Harry. This means the world to me. It's the culmination of decades of hard work. I won't let you down.'

Upon our return on the trading floor, the plan had originally been that the team would congratulate me and spend some time chit-chatting. Instead, when Harry and I entered the floor, there was near-complete silence. Every person in the room was glued to a TV screen, watching the terrible 9/11 events unfold. I was well and truly part of the team, but there were going to be no celebrations on that day.

When I got home that evening, the first thing I did was call my parents and tell them the good news. Kallirroi was screaming with joy, in her typical booming manner. Dimitri was much calmer and collected, but I could sense the excitement and emotion in his voice. The kid had done well, and both parents were extremely proud.

***

Paulina was a Greek woman in her early twenties, whom I had met one evening in London during the summer internship. She was a good friend of one of my MBA Greek classmates, and we hit it off straight away. She was not my traditional 'type' when it came to women, however, it was evident from the first moments that we very much enjoyed each other's company, and that made me particularly happy. We had been seeing each other since the start of my internship in London and she had returned home to Athens a few days earlier. We were happy together, but the big problem was that Paulina lived in Athens, while my resolute goal was to live and work in London.

When I was offered the full-time job, I couldn't wait to call Paulina and tell her the good news. She was happy for me but also sad, because deep down she had wanted me to return to Athens and be with her. What I told her next really stunned her.

'I'll be going back to Manchester to complete my MBA and in April I'll move to London. Do you want to move in with me?'

There was nothing but silence down the other end of the line, until finally, I heard the one word I was looking for: '*Yes!*'

Upon my return to the MBA course, I realised that all the pressure had been lifted from my shoulders. I no longer needed to outperform or score highly in the various exams and assignments; I already had a great job offer after all. I took things easy and decided not to worry about grades any more. Funnily enough, that had the exact opposite effect to what one would expect. I found myself greatly enjoying every bit of the course and as a result my performance improved substantially going into the final stages of the MBA. I graduated in early 2002 with Distinction and successfully closed yet another chapter in my life.

Chapter Four
Sterling Swaps Trader

During the early 2000s, global business was booming. Banking was an incredible money-making industry and as such job demand was high. On the flipside, pay was also great as banks used a variety of tricks to attract top talent.

Barclays in particular offered online training courses to individuals like me, who had already secured a full-time job offer but still had a few more months of studying left. These courses would get individuals up-to-speed with some important theoretical aspects of the bank, and as a reward the bank would pay them for every course that they completed successfully. On top of that, there was a sign-on bonus that was paid to many new employees on their first day of work. I was understandably thrilled, and there was never any doubt regarding where I planned on spending the money.

My first day working full-time at Barclays was Monday 15th April 2002. Shortly after, there was a red 'Rosso Corsa' Ferrari 348tb sitting snugly in my garage, its clean lines visible through the red custom-made cover with the distinctive black prancing horse over the bonnet. It was a ten-year old car – not a particularly expensive one at the time, costing roughly the same as a brand-new Ford Mondeo – but it was sexy as hell. I would start the engine and simply sit in the car, just to hear the rumbling sound of the glorious V8 engine and to feel the soft texture of the cream Connolly leather interior. Every journey was an event, with the car producing all the sounds, vibrations and smells that a proper supercar should. I had used nearly all the money I had in my account to buy the car and had to live a very frugal life as a result, even arranging monthly payments for the monstrous car insurance premium. But I didn't really give a damn. It was one of the cars I had on my bedroom wall when I was a teenager, and it had the word 'Ferrari' over the engine bay. That's all that mattered.

***

London, April 2002

Following the completion of my MBA, I moved to London in April 2002 and Paulina moved in with me shortly after. It was never love at first sight, but we worked hard at it. From the early stages of our relationship we both found aspects that we may have otherwise considered unacceptable, but we tried hard to overcome them. Paulina didn't like the fact that my time was dominated by my work, even on weekends. She wanted more of my free time, but even then, she found herself 'competing' with the Ferrari for a sliver. On the other hand, I frequently got tired of her incessant desire to socialise and distressing money-spending rate.

Initially, I worked very long hours, so we rented a small one-bedroom flat in Canary Wharf, enabling me to walk to work every day. I really didn't care about what the flat was like, as long as it had a secure parking space for the Ferrari and Paulina was happy with it. The next few years were going to be all about building my career and I prepared myself for a period of very hard work, extremely long hours and very little sleep. Bring. It. On.

***

My first day at Barclays as a full-time employee was something of an anti-climax. I arrived at the building on Monday morning – 7:30am sharp – and proceeded to collect my ID pass. As a 'permanent staff' pass, it had the distinctive blue logo and my name written on it. I looked at it with satisfaction and used it for the first time to go through the glass turnstiles, taking the familiar route to the second floor. I found my way to the Sterling Trading desk and once again saw those familiar faces, who were now officially my new colleagues. I was all pumped up and felt like king of the world.

'Ah, Stelios!' said Harry and paused his traditional early-morning reading of the Financial Times. 'Great to finally have you full-time on the team. Here's a list of tasks that you need to get cracking on straight away. Firstly, you'll need to redesign and optimise all of the group's Excel pricing models. That should take you a couple of months. Then we have the really big project: a major redesign of the bank's yield curve algorithms – a very complex task that should require substantial time to complete. Andy, our desk's designated IT specialist, will get you started and help you with any questions you have.'

Suddenly, the 'king of the world' image came to a screeching halt. I had gone through the MBA in order to change my career from IT, and there I was, fully immersed into programming and systems again.

This isn't right, I thought, but decided to be patient as I realised that I didn't want to ruin my new career straight off the blocks. The people in the group obviously knew of my comprehensive programming skills and were clearly going to take full advantage. I spent the next two years deeply absorbed in systems projects and eventually that started to frustrate me deeply. Naturally, I wanted to help the group in any way I could, but I had been hired to be a trader and I hadn't actually traded yet.

I was physically located within the Sterling Trading group for those two years, so I had been in direct contact with all the other traders. Whenever I had spare time, I would speak to them and ask all the questions that came to my mind. I wanted to understand their job, what their thought process was, and all the mechanics of each financial product that they traded. Most importantly though, I was fascinated by human psychology and was particularly interested in how traders behaved in times of adverse market conditions. I tried to accumulate as much knowledge as I could, while working on the complex technical tasks that had been given to me by Harry.

My first assigned task was to redesign and optimise the group's swaps pricing models. This was no walk in the park, as there were numerous parameters involved.

It's crucial at this point to single out one of these parameters:

LIBOR (the 'London Inter Bank Offered Rate').

I never had specific training on LIBOR, but as I understood it at the time, it was a number which broadly showed at what rate a bank could borrow money in the markets. In fact, it was a *borrowing percentage rate*, just like a regular person borrows money from a bank.

LIBOR came in various maturities starting from overnight and going up to twelve months, and it was published on a daily basis on a range of popular platforms. In the major currencies such as the US Dollar ('USD'), the British Pound ('GBP') and the Euro ('EUR'), it was calculated in a very specific way:

- Sixteen designated 'panel' banks were polled every morning for their individual LIBOR rates on each designated maturity, and for all the required currencies. Their entries were submitted by 11am UK time.
- Once the full list of 16 numbers was collected, the top four and bottom four entries were discarded and the remaining eight were averaged – this was done to remove outliers and have a broadly representative final number of the average rates.
- The final calculated numbers for each currency and each maturity were published on the British Bankers Association (BBA) site, and on other platforms such as Reuters and Bloomberg.
- The BBA was the body responsible for overseeing LIBOR and its operation.

LIBOR rates were important numbers since they were referenced in a number of products, such as Interest Rate Swaps and loan payments and trillions of dollars of products used it as an index.

Going back to the swap pricing sheet, LIBOR was one of the inputs and it played a role in calculating swap rates and valuing trades. Kilian, the Short-Term GBP Swaps trader, took me through the basic concepts soon after I joined the desk.

'OK Stelios, listen carefully,' Kilian started.

'I'm all ears!' I replied, grabbing my notepad and pen.

'Three-month LIBOR is a number that's supposed to show where banks lend cash to each other for three months. Simple enough, right?'

'Roger that.'

'There is also an active and liquid cash market, where participants borrow and lend money to each other,' continued Kilian.

'Understood,' I confirmed, 'so is it a safe assumption to say that LIBOR and the cash market should be directly comparable?'

'They should be the same, in theory,' confirmed Kilian. 'In practice, however, things are a bit different.'

'How so?' I asked curiously.

'Well, it's been a constant phenomenon for years now, that three-month Sterling LIBOR is always roughly four basis points – in other words, 0.04% – above where three-month cash is trading,' explained Kilian. 'That's how it is, and how it's been for a while.'

'Understood,' I confirmed.

'So, in your pricing sheet,' carried on Kilian, 'the way to estimate three-month LIBOR is easy: take the three-month cash offered rate, add four basis points and hey presto! You've got it.'

I noted it down and went on to place that exact code within the Excel pricing sheet. I appreciated that there was an apparent four basis point discrepancy between the theoretical three-month LIBOR rate and the actual rate, but apparently this was how the market had always operated. [Note: This phenomenon would later be called '*Highballing*']

My 'to-do' list had dozens of unticked items, so I accepted this as fact and swiftly moved on.

***

One day in the autumn of 2004, I finally cracked, just like on the day I had decided to quit my job at Accenture. I realised that I could take no more, having finally had enough and needing to make a change. Soon after I had arrived at the office that morning, I found Harry and asked to speak with him. I took a deep breath, took Harry aside, and told him exactly what was on my mind.

'Harry, you hired me to be a trader and – damn – I'm not trading! It's been over two years of this, and although I want to help the team with my programming skills, I can't go on. I need to have a trading book and start trading. I want to know if I can do this!'

I realised that I had just said those sentences in one breath and my face had turned bright red from the effort. My frustration was evident. Harry leaned back and crossed his arms, reflected on this for a minute and replied in his typical calm manner.

'OK, I understand. I will give you a trading book to start, with a specific year-end target, and we'll see how that goes. You want to trade with the big boys? Here's your chance.'

Shortly after, I returned to the desk and I could barely believe the outcome of that conversation. I had been prepared for all sorts of responses, many of them negative, but the actual result was sweeter than I ever anticipated. I had managed to finally set myself up as a trader, after a long and arduous road. My father had often told me: '*If you don't ask you don't get*' – how right he was.

In the last quarter of 2004, I was given the Sterling Forward Rate Agreement (FRA) book to trade.

A FRA was another derivative product based on interest rates but much simpler than Swaps, the main difference being that FRAs consisted of one payment only, while Swaps had multiple payments and a wide range of customisation parameters.

My trading book was a small one, with limited customer flow and a comparatively puny year-end target. But it was a start, and I couldn't wait to get stuck in. I was assigned a number of Sterling brokers that I would use on a daily basis to execute trades. These were people that I had direct phone lines to, and I would be in constant communication with them for the duration of the day.

My first trade was one of the most nerve-racking events of my life up to that point, even though it was an admittedly minuscule trade.

'Ones-fours the tenth I offer small at five!' yelled a broker down one of the lines, in his distinct Essex-boy accent.

Most money brokers at the time were the stereotypical City boys; loud, aggressive and always after the next money-making deal. Many of them had no university degree and had been thrust into the business straight after school in the eighties and nineties. Most of the brokers couldn't trade to save their lives and didn't really understand much of the mechanics behind instruments, such as interest rate swaps and forward rate agreements. Their primary job was to relay information to and from their clients, using phone lines and messaging systems. Traders often referred to brokers as 'telephone monkeys' due to the simplicity of their job.

Their secondary – but probably just as important – job was to entertain their clients, offering pretty much anything in order to keep their traders happy, and thus ensuring that more trading business would be coming their way in the future. More business with their traders meant more commission for them, and that was the kind of language that all brokers understood. Ironically, brokers were usually compensated much better than traders, as they would typically get paid nearly half of their commission earned. Depending on the traders' monthly trading volume, brokers would offer them all kinds of gifts to show their appreciation and to keep the business going. Dinners at Michelin-starred restaurants, front-seat tickets to sporting events and concerts, and if you really were one of the big boys, first-class trips to all the nice places in the world.

During my trading career, I never felt like asking for much from my brokers in terms of entertainment, being content with seeing them once or twice a year over a beer and dinner. I did have one or two favourites whom I actually thought were genuinely pleasant and intelligent people, and I would arrange to see them a bit more often for a drink or the odd football match. I had heard stories about how lavishly other more demanding traders were treated by their brokers – first-class tickets to New York, ski trips in the Alps, or even all-expenses paid trips to the Monaco Grand Prix, on-board luxury yachts in the company of eager-to-please Eastern European models. Some traders often boasted about their broker-funded adventures, bragging about their exploits and sharing photos of naked women. I had always found all that excessive and never engaged in such events, preferring to draw a line between *business* and *pleasure*.

Ones-fours the tenth I offer small at five! I glanced at my pricing spreadsheet and identified what it was currently showing as the fair price. It showed five and a half.

That's good, I thought, realising that it was being offered at a better level than my theoretical mid-market price. I glanced at the Short Sterling futures, my hedge for that particular trade.

I can probably even get the futures hedge on the bid side, I thought, adding to my nervous excitement. That would be an extra half a basis point in profit.

'MINE!' I shouted quickly down the line, as I had seen my colleagues doing countless times in the past couple of years.

'Citi, one hundred million,' was the immediate reply from the broker, indicating the counterparty and amount offered.

'That's done,' I snapped back, and the trade was completed. My first trade was finally on the board and I was now officially one of the Sterling Group's traders.

***

Over the following weeks, the team watched me trade and started to increasingly engage with me. It was apparent that they liked me, as I also shared a similar sense of humour with them and was always eager to get stuck in whatever was needed on the desk. I would often volunteer to get the morning coffees, having memorised each trader's preference from my summer internship days.

I happened to have particularly good all-round knowledge when it came to sports and eighties pop music. Whenever there were quiet times in the markets, the team would joke around and test each other's knowledge in various subjects – and I was more than up to the task.

Naturally, as City traders usually do, at some point the team gave me a nickname. There had been nicknames such as 'Ketchup', 'Skippy', 'Lofty' and 'Bucket head'. The boys were definitely not short on imagination and neither did they worry about being offensive.

For me, it was 'Easy FRA' – one of their best efforts, actually. At the time, EasyJet was one of the up-and-coming companies that everyone was talking about, with a particularly flamboyant Greek founder. The combination of the Greek element, together with the FRA book that I traded, made it a catchy nickname that stuck.

Chapter Five
Dollar Swaps Trader

December, 2004

Year-end arrived in a flash, and by early December it was time to determine how well the group had performed. It had been a good year for sure, with most traders meeting or exceeding their targets. I didn't quite manage to reach my modest target, but I had been profitable and thus successfully followed rule number one: *Don't lose money.*

I was happy with my performance and pace of learning the business, and I could see myself improving as a trader in the future. However, there was one thing that was constantly nagging me in the back of my mind, a missing piece in the big-picture puzzle: I was never going to become the number one Sterling Swaps trader. Nat and Kilian were two very successful and established individuals and had successfully run the Medium-Term and Short-Term Swaps books respectively for a number of years. They were well-respected within the bank and the broader market, and they weren't going anywhere. I was fully aware that in order to progress, I would eventually need to make a move away from the Sterling desk. I decided to keep my eyes open for potentially good opportunities that might arise, and as it turned out I didn't have to wait very long.

***

A few weeks back, the bank had hired two individuals from a rival French bank. Fred Gourtay and Alex Pabon were Swaps traders with a big reputation and they had been brought in to build the practically non-existent Short-Term USD Swaps business at Barclays, based in the bank's New York office.

Building a strong franchise in a specific product always required the bank to be able to service its clients during all market hours. That posed a problem for Barclays, because there was currently no London-based USD Short-Term Swaps trader, and that's precisely where I would step in.

Jay Merchant was an established Euro Swaps trader at Barclays and had physically sat very close to me for a few months. The two of us had got to know each other and there was clear mutual respect between us. Jay was known to be an intelligent and sometimes aggressive character, a man of Indian origin in his late thirties. As a kid, he may have not had the same opportunities as many of his colleagues, he more than made up for it with hard work and determination.

When he was young, he discovered his love for tennis, which he pursued through his teenage years with unabated drive. He spent countless hours training and practicing, ending up as the hitting partner for one of the best players in the world at the time. Jay was driven by a desire for success and personal accomplishment, and he was a particularly bright guy with a definite knack for markets. He was very demanding as a person – particularly with juniors – but when he liked someone, he was a great manager and mentor. Jay had already seen me grow as a person and a trader, and when the opening for the London-based USD Short End Swaps trader materialised, he knew exactly where to go.

One day in December 2004, Jay approached me and told me all about the upcoming role, going on to explain the relevant details and showing his obvious excitement about the prospect. I briefly considered the situation and saw that it made a lot of sense. I would be trading a much bigger book, albeit effectively only during London morning hours. It would be a shared book, with Fred and Alex doing the vast majority of trading and risk management. But it was still a step forward towards the right direction for me. My response was just what Jay wanted to hear:

'I like it! When do I start?'

Jay arranged an informal meeting with myself, Fred and Alex, so that we could all get to know each other over a few drinks. When we met up in person that day, my immediate impression was that Fred was a calm, soft-spoken Frenchman in his late thirties, and Alex was a likeable but aggressive, gung-ho twenty-something American. It turned out to be spot on.

***

In January 2005, I started on my new role on the USD Swaps desk. I was genuinely excited, but I also never lost sight of my ultimate goal which was to be the primary owner and market-maker of a significant Swaps book in a major global bank.

'Stay focused,' I would often tell myself, *'You'll be effectively babysitting this book during London hours for the big boys in New York. You can do this for a year or two, and by that time you will get your chance to run your own book. Rome wasn't built in a day.'*

Fred was in London for a couple of weeks in early 2005, and that was a great opportunity to get to know him; after all, I still had a lot to learn. I was eager to soak up all the information that Fred had to give me. He was a very experienced and successful trader, and someone that I definitely looked up to.

One morning, Fred stood up from his chair and walked a few steps across to my desk.

'Come with me, there's someone I want you to meet,' he said.

The following two minutes were destined to change my life forever.

The two of us walked a few rows away on the trading floor and Fred stopped at the edge of the main corridor, right next to the last desk in that particular row. Sitting there was Peter Johnson, a slightly older-looking guy with a bit of excess weight and grey hair. He was an Englishman in his early fifties with already a long career at Barclays. He was an established, successful, and very senior trader.

'Stelios, this is Peter, but everyone calls him PJ,' said Fred. 'He is the USD cash trader here at Barclays and he's the person responsible for submitting LIBOR rates for the bank. Alex and I will be asking you on occasion to relay some information to him, relating to LIBOR rates and our preference on it. So, all you have to do is let him know, OK?'

Peter got up, holding his distinctive Barclays coffee mug in his hand, and smiled.

'Nice to meet you, Stelios. Just let me know whenever you boys need something, and I'll do my best to help out,' he said, taking a sip of his hot coffee.

'Will do, nice to meet you Peter,' I replied, and just like that Fred and I turned around, and started walking back to the Swaps desk.

From that day on, my main goal remained to gain experience and help the team in whatever way I could. I quickly established my daily early-morning routine, which I followed religiously. I would wake up at 5:30 a.m. and put the news on the television, in order to catch any major overnight events. After that it was a quick shower, some breakfast and straight onto the underground. I had always hated shaving and being a trader who rarely saw clients face-to-face, I almost never had to. I really, *really* liked that.

I was at the desk by 6:30 a.m., always feeling energised and ready to rumble. I would spend the first fifteen to twenty minutes starting up my systems and reading news items and research. Being still junior, I was frequently quizzed about various aspects of the markets, so I wanted to be as best prepared as I possibly could.

At around 7 a.m., after my brokers had come in to their offices, I would poll them for their estimates for LIBOR that day. This process was something that had been dictated to me by Fred and Alex, and the instructions were clear. Every morning, I would ask three or four brokers for their predictions on one-month, three-month and six-month LIBOR. I would then then average these numbers out and round them to the nearest quarter of a basis point, and those would be the LIBOR estimates for the day, until the time they were published shortly after 11 a.m. UK time.

I followed that procedure day in and day out. I often compared the published LIBOR rates with the cash markets, and unsurprisingly I found a similar 'Highballing' effect in the US Dollar market just like I had seen in Sterling. Initially, I found it interesting and deduced that it was simply a construct of the markets just like Kilian had told me all that time ago. However, upon further consideration, I realised that this practice was much more significant. 'Highballing' was in fact a robust money-making exercise for the cash desk, and here's why:

Every bank had dozens of desks which accumulated USD cash exposure, and which required funding. In many cases, the funding of each desk was only allowed – or was dictated – to be done via the bank's cash desk. On any given day, the cash desk would lend the required amount of cash to whichever trading book needed it, at the published LIBOR rate. However, the cash desk itself would borrow this cash via the market, at the prevalent rate. No wonder that the LIBOR rate was always a few basis points above the market cash rate – it was an explicit arbitrage by the cash desks. It sounded crazy to me, but it seemed that the cash desk made those three-four basis points of profit from most internal trading books *every single day*. For example, the cash desk could borrow at 1.00% but it would internally lend out cash at the LIBOR rate: 1.04%.

Easy money.

After completing my start-of-day routine, my duties would be quite straightforward for the remainder of the day. A post-it note stuck to one of my screens conveniently reminded me of them, even though I had already memorised them from the very early days.

- *One*: Make sure that the yield curves and pricing sheet are working properly.
- *Two*: Make markets on Short-Term USD Swaps to clients whenever they need them.
- *Three*: Make markets on Short-Term USD Swaps to the inter-dealer brokers, being careful not to make any wrong prices and get in trouble. I was expected to increase the bank's presence in those derivatives, and making markets to brokers was the best way to achieve that.
- *Four*: Speak to the bank's salesforce when they ask for market commentary and views on particular instruments.
- *Five*: Keep up-to-date with global developments and market movements, but most importantly *KEEP LEARNING*.

***

On one particular occasion, I walked over to the cash desk to relay yet another request from my New York bosses, but PJ's seat was empty, and all his computer screens were switched off. I hesitated for a few seconds and just stood there staring at the seat and looking momentarily confused. I couldn't spot PJ's trademark coffee mug, so I eventually concluded that he was away for the day. Seeing my hesitation, the man sitting next to his seat got up and moved across towards me.

'Morning, Stelios,' he said. 'I saw you talking to PJ the other day, but we didn't get introduced. My name is Jonathan and I'm PJ's junior. I cover for him whenever he's on holidays, just like he is this whole week. Pleased to meet you.'

He thrust his hand forward and I shook it firmly.

'Nice to meet you, mate,' I replied. 'Listen, my bosses at New York often ask me to pass on the book's LIBOR preferences, but since PJ is away today could you please help instead?' I continued.

'Sure thing mate, what will it be?' enquired Jonathan.

'They would like a low three-month LIBOR and a high one-month LIBOR please mate.'

'Consider it done.'

That was my first encounter with Jonathan, who was a very junior employee in his early twenties – just as junior as I was, in fact. He was one of the politest people you would ever meet in this business, always soft-spoken and kind. Throughout my time at Barclays, I would pass on the LIBOR requests to Jonathan whenever PJ was unavailable; it was business as usual.

As Fred and Alex increased their trading volume, the book naturally started accumulating positions in various instruments and maturities. One of the main instruments they traded were LIBOR fixed-vs-floating interest rate swaps. It's not worth going into the details or mechanics of how swaps work, but to simplify things this is the executive summary:

- An interest rate swap is an agreement between two parties to exchange payments for a specified period of time and on a specific notional amount.
- One counterparty pays a fixed percentage rate (the 'fixed' leg) and the other counterparty pays a floating percentage rate (the 'floating' leg, usually LIBOR).
- Each leg is paid at a specific interval, usually quarterly, and the payments are calculated using the relevant percentage rates and notional amounts.
- Interest rate swaps are a great way for clients to mitigate interest rate risk, and they had become very popular ever since the 1990s.

The Short-Term USD Swaps book eventually accumulated numerous positions and had a natural preference for where the various LIBOR rates would set. One evening before I left work, Fred spoke down their shared line.

'Stelios are you there?' he asked in his distinctive French accent.

'Hey Fred, I'm just about to close up and go home. What's up?' I replied.

'Right, tomorrow the book has a big three-month LIBOR fixing and it would really suit us if the number was high. Can you please tell PJ?'

'Sure, of course I will. Have a good evening,' I said and signed off.

The following morning, after completing my morning routine, I got up from my seat and walked over to the cash desk. I stopped by PJ's seat and greeted him.

'Good morning, Peter. Fred told me to let you know that a high three-month LIBOR rate today would really suit his book,' I said assuredly.

'Sure, not a problem, I'll see what I can do,' replied PJ, barely lifting his eyes from his screens.

'Thanks, appreciate it. Oh, and by the way, I'm going to get a coffee from downstairs – would you like one?' I asked politely.

'Skinny cappuccino please mate!' responded PJ in his typical English accent.

This process of expressing preference to LIBOR rates and making requests happened relatively infrequently at first – perhaps once every couple of weeks. It was initiated by Fred and Alex down the line and PJ's reaction to the requests was accommodative and receptive. I frequently offered coffee and the occasional takeaway lunch in order to show my appreciation, as I realised that PJ was a senior Director of the bank and many ranks above me. He could have easily said to me 'I'm busy kid, go away,' and then I would have to explain to Fred why the request hadn't been received.

One day, I noticed that even though Fred and Alex's request was for a high three-month LIBOR rate, PJ had actually submitted one of the lowest rates out of the sixteen contributor banks. It looked slightly unusual but was totally understandable, given that LIBOR submitters had their own trading books and often ran huge positions themselves.

I was aware of this fact and had seen it with my own eyes during my time on the Sterling desk. Pete, the Sterling LIBOR submitter, would sometimes come over and ask Kilian to execute trades for him. I had been particularly impressed by the size of those trades; billions in notional amount and much larger than the usual trades executed by the desk.

The first time that PJ submitted a rate opposite to Fred and Alex's stated preference, the immediate reaction was mighty.

'Stelios pick up!' Alex roared down the line in his strong American accent. He had a habit of becoming loud and aggressive when something displeased him, and by now I was very familiar with that tone.

'Hi Alex, good morning,' I replied in a steady voice, trying to guess what was coming next.

'*What the hell dude?*' screamed Alex. 'We told you that we preferred a high three-month LIBOR rate and PJ submitted one of the lowest numbers on the day. Did you not tell him of our preference?' came back the thundering reply.

'Of course I did,' I replied defensively. 'I always make a note of your preference as soon as you instruct me, and I make absolutely sure I pass on the right message.'

'You forgot! Otherwise he would have put a higher rate in!' Alex persisted.

'No, I didn't forget Alex.'

'Yeah, whatever man,' said Alex and slammed his phone. He was clearly annoyed with me and he made absolutely no attempt to hide it.

Following that brief but intense conversation, I felt distinctly upset. I had done nothing wrong, I had followed my superiors' instructions to the letter, and I was still being questioned about my actions.

That's not fair! No way will I let this ever happen again, I thought. From that moment on, I decided to make every such subsequent request in writing, via email. I was well aware that all company emails were recorded and stored for over five years, with extensive archive search capabilities. If there was ever any doubt again about my actions in the future, I would be able to instantly produce the proof.

For the following few months, I continued babysitting the book and gaining experience, while also regularly relaying LIBOR requests from Fred and Alex to PJ.

My relationship with Fred was fair, but we never got close. We talked about cars on occasion, and when I swapped seats with Alex on a few occasions – I would go to New York for a week while Alex would come to London in my place – I sat next to Fred and watched him trade. We went out to drinks or dinner with brokers a few times, so there was a limited social aspect to our relationship as well. Despite all of that, I never really managed to get close to Fred or get to know him more as a person.

On the other hand, my relationship with Alex was not good; Alex was too aggressive for my liking, both in terms of trading as well as on a personal level. Alex would frequently swear and curse, and his attitude was generally incompatible with mine. While Fred would make requests in a polite manner (*'...we need to have a low three-month LIBOR please'*), Alex would use much stronger language (*'...we need to fucking jam that shit down, you know? You gotta fucking get this shit done man!'*).

Alex was unpredictable, and he had a reputation in the market for being a bit of a loose cannon. He would often quiz me on certain aspects of trading and on technical details, some of which tested my knowledge and fell short of his expectations. Whenever that happened, Alex was not one to hide his frustration and disappointment.

'You understood what I just told you, right? *Right*??!?' he would often bark down the line.

I tried my very best to learn and get up to speed, but I was naturally annoyed by Alex's behaviour. I was never going to become friends with him, but we were colleagues and I had to find a way to work with him effectively and peacefully on a day-to-day basis.

***

Don Lee was another USD Swaps trader based in London. He was the market-maker for the Medium-Term book – covering Swaps from two years up to fifty years maturity – and his seat was immediately to the right of mine. The trading floor was arranged in parallel rows, where traders sat next to each other with no partitions or separators of any kind. As it happened, for the duration of my time at the Dollar Swaps desk, I had an empty seat on my left. There were some other traders immediately behind me, but they traded different products and although we would frequently chat, we never really got close.

For the following year, my main partner and companion would turn out to be Don. He was a South Korean man in his late thirties who had spent most of his life in the United States. He had been moved to his current position circa one year earlier and he was particularly happy that I had joined the desk. You see, he didn't like trading Short-Term swaps at all, as he never fully understood the mechanics involved and always concentrated on the Medium-Term side. Short-

Term products are usually affected by factors, such as Central Bank actions and economic developments in particular countries, while Medium-Term products are all about flow and customer orders. Don was exceptionally good at managing customer orders and handling flow, but he disliked the rest.

When I joined the Dollar desk, Don was visibly happy and excited; he could finally let go of the major headache he'd had for a while. Over the following year, Don and I would interact extensively and get to know each other well, eventually finding out that we were quite compatible characters with similar backgrounds. Don had also come from a middle-class family and had been an excellent student. He was married, a hard-worker, and he had a bright future ahead of him. He belonged to that rare breed of traders who were soft-spoken and modest; qualities that I always considered to be a great asset.

***

London, July 7th 2005

It was a dark day for London. A string of terrorist attacks on buses and underground trains shook the nation's capital and the damage caused was immeasurable. Up to that day, I had been taking the tube to work every morning, just like most of my colleagues did. On the day of the bombings, I thought about all those innocent victims and realised that it could have easily been me in their place. That day turned out to be the last one that I ever took the tube to work.

The next morning, I got into my car – a blue Mini Cooper – and drove to work. I had got rid of the vastly impractical and unreliable Ferrari a while ago, having had my fun with it but eventually realising that I was most happy when it was safely parked in the garage. I would often just stand and look at it, marvelling at its perfect curves, the air intakes and pop-up headlights. But this car had been a dream, not a car to drive on a daily basis. It had to go.

I commuted to work by car for a few weeks and really enjoyed it. No more long waits at the platform for the notoriously unreliable District tube line. No more getting squashed with a hundred, usually smelly, people in the narrow carriages. It had now become a comfortable ride with some soft music and the air-conditioning for the admittedly rare warm London days.

Coincidentally, Don and I both lived in South West London and his home was literally on my route to work. It wasn't long before I started carpooling with Don, picking him up every morning at 6:15 a.m. and driving him into work. It was a win-win situation for us both: Don would get a free ride to work and I would have someone to chat with during those mundane early morning trips.

The subject matter would range from sports and music to markets and world affairs. At some point, I discovered a popular TV series which was aired on a subscription channel that I didn't have access to, and which happened to be Don's obsession at the time. For a number of weeks, Don would spend the majority of the 30-minute car ride describing to me every twist and turn of the plot, not forgetting to include every possible detail that he could remember.

Those car journeys became great fun and the two of us were really starting to bond as friends. Throughout the time that I worked at Barclays, we would spend plenty of time together on and off the workplace, we introduced each other to our wives and went out socially on a few occasions. One day there was a friendly football match between Greece and South Korea, held at the Craven Cottage stadium in Fulham. What a treat – our two countries playing literally down the road from both our houses. We bought four tickets and each dressed up in our country colours, complete with football shirts and scarves. It was a great night out and even though Greece lost, I thoroughly enjoyed it.

Chapter Six
Change of Leadership

In the spring of 2005, things had started going wrong for Fred and Alex. They had been trading aggressively for a few months and had built up considerable risk in the newly-formed Short End USD Swaps book. They were both known for their aggressiveness in the market and were certainly keeping up with their reputation.

There was one position in particular, which had been growing particularly large in the book: the 3s1s Basis position. Without going into unnecessary detail, the 3s1s Basis position can be simply described as the difference (or '*spread*', or '*basis*') between the one-month LIBOR and three-month LIBOR rates.

Fred and Alex had been building a monstrous three-year 3s1s Basis position, where they had bet that the spread would widen from current levels. This was theoretically a good position, as the spread had been at historically very narrow levels and could well widen in the future. However, they probably didn't account for one little detail, which often catches out aggressive traders:

If you hold the market's biggest position in a particular instrument, you must make sure that none of the other participants ever find out.

If the competition finds out, they will know that you are very vulnerable to even small market moves, and they will do their best to 'stop you out', i.e. to force you to exit the position once your losses exceed your tolerance limits.

Unsurprisingly, this is exactly what happened with the book's 3s1s Basis position (along with some other similar basis positions), where Fred and Alex eventually accumulated over two million dollars per basis point risk. This meant that for each basis point that the basis moved, the book stood to gain or lose more than two million dollars. Once the market had discovered this fact, it started a relentless push lower.

That particular basis typically traded between 0 and +3 basis points, hence being long at around +1 basis point didn't seem like a bad idea when they initiated the trade. However, things didn't turn out as planned. One basis point became zero basis points and then, completely contrary to logic, it went negative. *Very* negative. Fred, being the owner of the book, was in deep trouble.

Each derivatives book within the bank (such as the USD Short-Term Swaps book), had its Profit & Loss (or '*P&L*') marked on a daily basis against the prevailing market levels. This was called mark-to-market, and it was the standard procedure among all major banks. At the time, the Barclays systems which were used for mark-to-market, were driven off a specific set of yield curves. The important detail to note here is that these yield curves had some *automatic* inputs (taken from various sources, such as electronic exchanges), and some *manual* inputs which were maintained by certain individuals.

The 3s1s basis levels were in fact *manual* inputs, maintained by none other than Mr Gourtay himself. So, once this basis started moving against him, Fred had two options – of which one was highly improper. He could move the 3s1s basis manual inputs and instantly realise a big negative mark-to-market loss. Or, he could take the easy-but-wrong route and simply not move them at all. This was called 'mismarking' and an absolutely wrong thing to do. From my days on the Sterling group, I had been told by the senior traders that one should *never* mismark a book. Any potential losses due to market movements should be instantly identified and realised – it was a golden rule and senior management were adamant about it.

I knew exactly how the bank's curve-building model worked and all the inputs involved in generating it. After all, I had helped develop it and knew all its ins-and-outs. Upon noticing that the manual inputs for the 3s1s basis started to diverge from reality, I naturally became concerned.

Over a period of a few weeks, I reached out to Fred and expressed my thoughts. Fred's response to my concerns was dismissive, claiming that the markets were somehow 'wrong' and expressing confidence that they would eventually come back. That was very frustrating for me, as I could clearly see that there was a problem. Every time I had to make a price in certain swaps, I was having to mentally adjust the price for the discrepancy. It was hard work and also introduced the possibility of errors; and I didn't like that at all. However, that all paled into insignificance compared to the fact that I was witnessing my boss do something improper. I had to do something *now*.

Having flagged the problem with Fred and got nowhere, I knew I needed to do something more drastic. I felt very nervous – I was still very junior after all – but I pulled myself together and realised there was only one thing I could do: tell Harry Harrison. I would be breaking hierarchy and effectively putting my direct boss in danger. It was a perilous move even for myself, as I had no idea who was aware of Fred's mismarking. Maybe Harry was also aware and complicit; if this was the case, my job and potentially my career could be over. Nevertheless, I didn't hesitate. It needed to be done, because it was the right thing to do.

***

London, August 2005

Harry was normally based in New York, but one particular week in the summer of 2005 he spent a few days in the London office. I didn't waste any time and on the first day I sent him a message:

'Harry, we need to talk. Do you have five minutes sometime today?' Not long after, Harry walked by my desk, looked at me and simply said: 'Let's go.'

We walked a few metres further down the trading floor, where the glass-walled meeting rooms and senior managers' offices were. We entered an empty room and sat down on the round conference table. Harry sat with his back towards the trading floor, while I sat opposite him. I wanted to look Harry in the eyes when I told him what I knew.

'Harry, I think we have a problem,' I began slowly.

'What is it?' Harry replied, leaning in and looking clearly intrigued.

'I think that Fred has been mismarking the book in some places, with one particular instrument being very worrying,' I continued as I gained some more courage. 'The 3s1s basis is way off.'

'What's the damage?' was Harry's instant response, in true senior management style. Banks were in business to make money, so profit and loss was always first and foremost.

'Fifteen million, I think. Maybe twenty,' I said.

In the grand scheme of things, fifteen or twenty million dollars wasn't a huge deal. When certain other trading books made a hundred million or more, twenty million would be a negative hit for the group, but a mere flesh wound compared to the whole investment bank's performance. It wasn't the amount lost that was the problem – it was the fact that Fred had tried to hide it.

Harry sat there quietly for a few seconds, in his typical calm and collected demeanour. Finally, he looked at me and responded.

'Go out on the floor and get back to your desk. Move all the 3s1s Basis inputs to where you think the right levels are. I'll take care of the rest.'

What an immense relief for me, as it was exactly what I wanted to hear. I quickly got back to my desk and started preparing for this daunting task. I wanted to make absolutely sure that the numbers I supplied were 100% correct, so I took a great deal of time speaking to brokers and getting markets for all the related instruments. Approximately half an hour later, I was ready. I corrected all the inputs one-by-one and in the end, I slowly moved my eyes towards the book's Total P&L figure. I almost couldn't bear to see what the number was.

It showed negative seventeen million Dollars. *Ouch.*

As soon as I moved all the inputs and the negative figure showed, that would have been instantly reflected in the systems that Fred and Alex were using in New York. I was certain that they would start shouting at me down the line; but that never happened. It seems that Harry had already spoken to them just like he promised me half an hour earlier.

I leaned back in my chair, trying to take in all that transpired that morning. I had done the right thing – the honest thing – and it had clearly been the right decision. Shortly after, news broke out that Fred had unexpectedly gone on holidays. This was the typical banking description when someone was under investigation for serious wrong-doing. A few weeks later, Fred was terminated.

***

Only a couple of weeks earlier, the bank had held its mid-year appraisals round. Appraisals were a big deal, as each employee was extensively evaluated and ultimately graded in various business aspects, with grades ranging from A to E (A being the best grade and E being the worst). Fred had completed my appraisal and it turned out to be a huge disappointment for me.

While I was on the Sterling desk all my appraisals had been outstanding, consisting exclusively of A's and B's and coupled with great comments. This time round, I couldn't believe my eyes when I read the appraisal.

During the first six months of 2005, I had worked extremely hard to make a positive contribution to the desk. I traded the book successfully without making any glaring errors. I serviced the bank's clients and the broker market and provided salespeople with commentary and market insight. I worked on the desk's spreadsheets and systems, lending my IT expertise when needed. I got along very well with Don and the other people who sat around me. All that, while I was constantly learning and educating myself on markets and products. I had hardly put a foot wrong.

I glanced at the front page of the assessment. '*Overall Grade: C*'. I stopped and just stared at that for a minute.

C grade?? What the hell are they expecting me to do? Make a hundred million dollars for the book? Become the best trader on the street? Cure cancer? What the hell?' I thought, clearly angry at what I was seeing.

'Stelios needs to become more proactive and take more risk,' read some of the comments. 'He needs to stop being the junior trader and start making some major decisions of his own.'

I tried to take in all these comments but still failed to see how I could have taken more risk as a first-time trader. I had spent the first six months of the year getting comfortable with my new position and building up my confidence.

No way can a junior trader step into a trading role and take big risk straight away, was my first reaction. *This would be a recipe for disaster. If something went wrong, the junior trader wouldn't be able to react and adapt, and that would be a disaster for the book. This kind of mentality can only lead to a big P&L loss,* I thought. Then I remembered the huge problems that the Short-Term book was facing under Fred's leadership. Maybe the way things turn out in real life are not by accident after all.

***

At this point, the Short-Term Swaps book was headless, so to speak. Alex was still based in New York and did the bulk of the trading, but he was a Vice President and not senior enough to run it. I was an Associate, which was the second most junior level in the bank, and I was clearly not eligible either. Harry had to find someone to take over, and fast.

Being the great manager, he quickly identified the perfect individual for the role: Jay Merchant. Jay had been successfully trading the Euro Short-Term Swaps book and this would be a deserved promotion. Jay had been trying to move up from the Short-Term Swaps book to the Medium-Term Swaps book, and that move made perfect sense. The Medium-Term book had much more business and was vastly more profitable. Jay had played his cards right, negotiating this move right when the group was in distress. Finally, Harry agreed to make him the head of the Medium-Term Swaps book, but also wanted him to oversee the Short-End book's recovery until someone else was taken on board to manage it. A few weeks later Jay had already packed his bags and moved to New York, where he was put in charge.

At the time, I thought that Jay was also the owner and manager of the Short-Term Swaps book, as he was my new line manager. It turned out that he wasn't, a fact that I would find out much later during the 2016 trial. This information was on a need-to-know basis, and I was clearly too junior to know.

Alex continued to trade the book from New York, and I babysat it during London hours, just like before. I welcomed this change in leadership, as I liked Jay much more than I had ever liked Fred, and I got along much better with him. I also thought that Jay was a much better trader than Fred, and that could only be a good thing for the swaps book. A profitable swaps book reflected well on everyone associated with it – there was no doubt about that.

***

It was a well-known fact that compensation in many banking jobs consisted of a fixed annual salary and a discretionary year-end bonus. Being very junior at the time, I was paid the standard bank-wide Associate level annual salary and a small bonus at year end. My bonus was in no way linked to the Short-Term Swaps book's performance; I knew that, and it would become evident in my 2005 year-end compensation.

Even though my pay had no direct link to the book's P&L, I still tried my best to make money on it and welcomed any change that would make it more profitable. For me, it was simply a matter of pride. I wanted the Short-Term USD Swaps book to become one of the big revenue-generating books of the bank.

Jay seemed to really get along well with me and ensured that my contribution was appreciated and valued. That made me feel a lot better than under Fred's leadership, and in return I worked even harder than before. I wanted to show Jay that I was worthy of my seat. In return, Jay gradually started giving me further responsibilities and let me take more initiative. I was particularly happy about that, although I was fully aware that we were in total 'damage control' mode. Fred's basis positions had driven the book to the ground P&L-wise, but the positions actually still remained. Jay's main job now was to take those positions off with the minimum possible damage.

Only a few days after Jay had taken over the book from New York, a familiar message landed on my inbox, coming from Jay himself.

'Stelios, the book has a big one-month fixing tomorrow. Please tell PJ that we need a low fixing. Thanks, Jay.'

Business as usual, it seemed.

From that point on, Jay kept the requests coming on a regular basis. The book remained in damage control mode and was still in danger of losing more money, so Jay would take any help he could. For the following months, the requests were continuous and frequent. Sometimes they came every single day for weeks.

They would sometimes be soft ('*could you please ask PJ for a high fixing*') and occasionally they would be very aggressive and in huge bold font ('*WE NEED A 4.47% three-month FIXING. NOTHING LESS!!!*'). The end result was the same: try to nudge the LIBOR fixing in such a way that would benefit the Swaps book's position. I was aware and fully understood why those requests were being made, and what their ultimate goal was.

***

As mentioned previously, I was aware that LIBOR had to do with where banks lend money to each other. By definition, on any given day, there was not just one single '*correct*' or '*true*' LIBOR rate that a bank could submit.

Let me explain, suppose that Barclays Bank needed to submit its three-month LIBOR rate for a specific day. In order to do that, the submitter would need to know where Barclays could borrow three-month unsecured funds in the market, in normal market size. If Barclays went to the market asking for three-month cash in, say, $500 million, they would most likely get three different rates. This is because individual banks like Citibank, JP Morgan, BNP or Banca Intesa would have very different risk appetites and liquidity positions. For example, it's very likely that having asked for offers in $500 million of three-month cash, Barclays could get 4.10%, 4.11% and 4.12% in return. All three would be levels at which the bank could borrow the required cash, and all three would probably be perfectly acceptable rates to submit for the bank's three-month LIBOR rate.

It really was as simple as that.

Now, which rate out of the possible alternatives would the LIBOR submitter choose? That's his or her decision. Is there a specific rule that dictates which rate to use? Do you pick the lowest rate? Do you pick the average? Do you pick the rate offered by the bank with the highest credit rating? As far as I knew, there was no rule or guidance. And frankly, it wasn't my job to know. The whole process and mechanics of submitting LIBOR rates was totally alien and irrelevant to my job, or to any other interest rate swaps trader, for that matter.

***

Returning to the current situation with the USD Short-Term Swaps book, I knew exactly what had to be done in order to get rid of the toxic positions that Fred & Alex had amassed that year. I worked hard towards that goal every single day, for a considerable period of time. Jay, Alex and I together eventually removed most of the troublesome positions at little cost and brought back the book to near normality. That was no mean feat, given the circumstances and the magnitude of the task.

The next few months went by in a flash, as I remained buried deep within my work. I had got married to Paulina in June that year – just before the trouble with Fred started – but I didn't get to spend much time with my new wife. I would devote some weekends working too, much to her dismay. It was a difficult period in my life, and she tried hard to be patient and understand the situation. However, she wasn't a terribly easy-going person. She enjoyed the highs and lows in a relationship, and in fact I was eventually convinced that she even manufactured them when things were too calm for too long. Paulina could see that I was being overworked and constantly stressed, and she thoroughly disliked that. In late 2005, her distaste for the situation grew so large that she suggested I find a job elsewhere.

I started looking for another trading job but in this line of business people didn't exactly send out CVs when they were already working somewhere. It was a small market and news circulated fast. Unless you were one of the star traders, if your bosses found out that you were unhappy and wanted to leave, they would most often start proactively looking for your replacement and let you go once they had found someone suitable. One of management's primary goals was to achieve stability within the trading ranks; someone who was looking to leave would disrupt that stability and was often pre-emptively cast off.

Due to the nature of trading, I had to be very discreet when looking for another job. I could have gone to a random head-hunter but even though they are supposed to never divulge information to third parties, it's common knowledge that some of them do. Some senior managers had strong links with many of the big head-hunting firms and were always the first to know when their own people were out on the market.

There was another way to find out about potential job openings, and that was via the swaps brokers. This was even riskier than going through head-hunters because – let's face it – most brokers were driven purely by money. Their job was very different to that of a trader, as brokers didn't take any market risk or execute their own trades.

Thankfully, not all brokers were alike; some were in fact educated, intelligent and trustworthy. They were a rare breed, and Chris was one of them. He worked at Prebon and had been consistently my best-performing swaps broker. He was sharp, quick to react to market moves and an all-round nice guy. I often went to him whenever I needed to check a price, or to get a second opinion on a particular instrument. Likewise, when Chris needed to check a market level, or he required an expert view on something, I would be his first port of call. There was mutual trust between us, which eventually came in very handy and became the Launchpad for my move away from Barclays.

Chapter Seven
The Big Step Forward

November, 2005

I was at work, sitting on my trading station, when my cell phone started ringing. I glanced at the screen and was surprised to see Chris calling me. It was odd, since Chris had a direct line to me on my desk and we spoke dozens of times during the day – why call me on my cell phone? The answer was evident shortly thereafter.

'Hey Stelios, can you speak?' asked Chris excitedly.

'Sure mate, what's up? Is everything OK?' I replied, showing some concern.

'Yes, yes, all good. Listen, you know Andrea at Merrill Lynch?'

'Sure,' I said. 'I've met him on a couple of occasions during social drinks between USD swaps traders from various banks. Nice guy, much laid back, typical Italian bloke,' I chuckled.

'Indeed. Well, Andrea has had a few successful years and he's made some decent money. However, he has decided that he's had enough for now, and wants to take some time off. He's bought a sailing boat and will spend the next couple of years sailing around the Mediterranean.'

'Wow, that sounds nice. I wish I could do that!' I exclaimed.

'Yeah, you and me both mate,' laughed Chris. But let's get to the meat of the issue, shall we? His job is up for grabs and his boss is already looking for a replacement. He asked me if I knew any good swaps traders and your name was the first one I mentioned.'

In trading, brokers usually had a very good idea of the market and all the individuals involved. They were aware who was active, who made money and who the real stars were. This was the main reason why managers often consulted brokers whenever they were looking to hire someone for a highly specialised position. I felt honoured and grateful that Chris suggested me to the Merrill Lynch trading head. I had wanted to trade my own swaps book for some time, and I could now see the opportunity to make this a reality.

'Thank you, Chris. I really appreciate it,' I said enthusiastically. 'It would be a great move for me, if it happens. Fingers crossed!' I said and hung up the call. I sat back on my chair and put my hands around the back of my head, as I let out a deep breath. Suddenly, I felt quite nervous.

***

Warwick Palmer was the head of the STIRT (*Short Term Interest Rate Trading*) group at Merrill Lynch back in 2005. The group consisted of Interest Rate Swaps traders and Repo traders for the three major currencies: US Dollar, Pound Sterling and Euro. Warwick was a slim, bald man in his late thirties. He was extremely intelligent, strong-minded and never afraid to speak his mind. He never really bothered with politics or subtlety. Warwick would speak out his thoughts without any prior filtering or processing; a habit which often caused him to be disliked by some of his colleagues. He was the epitome of someone who was either loved or hated, and for most people there was no middle ground as far as he was concerned.

Warwick had spent a number of years successfully trading Euro Short-Term swaps, and he had naturally got promoted to group head. However, he was worried, as he was about to lose Andrea, a valuable member of his team. He was desperate to find a good replacement. In his mind, I was a good replacement; yet, a slightly inexperienced choice. But I came well-recommended, so he decided to give me a shot.

The first meeting was scheduled just between Warwick and me, and it went smoothly. I think I made a good first impression, showing confidence in my technical abilities but also being humble enough to indicate my willingness and eagerness to learn and grow. There were many traders around who thought they were Gods – and not minor Gods either, proper Zeus-like figures. Warwick had absolutely no time for such people, and he was pleasantly surprised by my character and demeanour.

When the end of 2005 came, I was anxious to see what my superiors at Barclays thought of my performance. Fortunately for me, Jay's year-end review was entirely favourable. He had given me excellent grades and praised my overall performance. I finally felt appreciated and that gave me a definite moral boost, given that the book had performed very badly that year due to the terrible Basis trades. Interestingly, come bonus time, I got direct confirmation that my pay was in fact *not* linked at all to the book's performance.

Traders associated with a successful book are likely to get paid a handsome year-end bonus. Traders associated with an underperforming book usually get paid a big fat zero. Traders who, god forbid, are associated with a book which has lost a lot of money are often terminated.

As it turns out, I received a decent 2005 year-end bonus, in fact my best bonus up to that point, which was a clear message that my efforts were appreciated by the management. That was a relief for me, although I was well aware that my compensation was still sub-par compared to my peers. This was frustrating because I knew that I was paid less due to factors which were beyond my control, and through no fault of my own. The Short-Term Swaps book was in much better shape now, but it would still be an uphill struggle to make it profitable the following year. That precise fact turned out to be one of the main reasons why I finally made the important decision to go after the Merrill Lynch job.

***

The second interview with Warwick took place at the Merrill Lynch headquarters, in the City. It was a beautiful early 1900s building which used to be the general post office headquarters for years, before it was converted into the bank's headquarters. It had a beautiful spire at the front and a green garden that got completely covered in snow during the winter. During spring, bright and colourful flowers would grow alongside the main pathway, making it a truly spectacular scene.

I entered the building feeling slightly nervous and went up to the large trading floor on the first level. Warwick was waiting for me in one of the meeting rooms at the side of the building, together with two other traders from the STIRT group. This time round the gloves were off, and the interview turned more aggressive. The traders grilled me on yield curves, specific instruments and trading strategies. I tried hard not to sweat or show signs of stress, as one question relentlessly followed another.

Around half an hour later the interview was over, and Warwick took me to meet all the other traders in his group. We chatted for a little while and then it was time to go. The whole process lasted just over an hour and I had little indication as to how well I had done. One thing was certain: I really wanted the job and was anxious to see what the final verdict was.

***

April, 2006

Thankfully, I didn't have to wait very long. A few days later I got a call from Nick, the head-hunter who had been mediating the whole process.

'Hi Stelios, it's Nick.'

'Nick! My favourite head hunter! Also, my only head hunter,' I teased him. 'What's the news?'

'I have good news and bad news.'

'OK, what's the good news?' I asked, trying to hide my excitement.

'The good news,' said Nick joyfully, 'is that the guys at Merrill all liked you and they want you to take Andrea's place.'

'Great!' I said and felt relieved, 'What's the bad news?'

'The bad news,' replied Nick, 'is that we now have the tricky task of agreeing on a financial package.'

'Trust me Nick,' I said cheerfully, 'that's going to be the easy part.'

I was delighted, as I was finally on the cusp of making a major step forward in my career. I was happy to be leaving the troubled USD Short-Term Swaps book at Barclays and looked forward to starting fresh with my very own book. I also realised that I was going to miss some good colleagues, but that was part of the whole game.

When I met up with Nick to go over the details, I knew that if the offer was half-decent, I would take it with both hands. The terms turned out to be just as I

57

expected, in terms of job description and responsibilities. I would be the sole owner and primary market-maker for the bank's USD Short-Term Swaps book. The financial aspect of the contract was also very good: a base salary and a generous 'guaranteed' year-end bonus. That meant that no matter what my performance was like, I would still get paid that guaranteed bonus at the end of the year. This was all very good, but the icing on the cake was something totally unexpected: I would join the bank on a Director level.

It was April, 2006, and just a couple of months back I had been finally promoted at Barclays from Associate to Vice President. This was a natural and expected development, having had such an outstanding year-end review. Joining Merrill Lynch as a Director had double significance: I would effectively be receiving two promotions within the space of only a few months (from Associate to Vice President to Director), and I would be paid the standard Director-level base salary, which was a near 100% pay rise. *What a result.*

I had no trouble signing the Merrill Lynch contract – that was certainly the easy part. What was now left was the not-so-easy task of informing my employer. Nick had warned me that the people at Barclays would probably do whatever they could to make me stay, and I should be well prepared for that. They could promise me more money and promotions, or they could even scare me into thinking that I wouldn't be successful if I left the bank. As it turned out, Nick was right on both counts.

On a quiet Monday morning, I went to the office as I always did. I arrived slightly later than usual, and I skipped my morning routine for the first time in over a year. I didn't poll the brokers for their LIBOR estimates. I didn't read any research pieces. I didn't scan the online platforms for important news items. My mind was set on one thing and one thing only: get a hold of Harry and resign.

Harry was spending that week in the London office and on that particular day he arrived at the desk just prior to 8 a.m. I saw him sit down and gave him a few minutes to get settled in.

OK, you can do this, I thought, psyching myself up, and then got up and walked up to Harry's desk.

'Harry, we need to talk.'

'It's usually serious when you say those words,' replied Harry. 'Off we go.'

We entered one of the offices and sat down at the round wooden table. I silently took out a piece of paper from my pocket and handed it to Harry, who took a minute to read it. It was a resignation letter, short and simple. In it, I was informing Harry that I had decided to resign and join another bank. I thanked Harry personally and the other members of the team and asked them to respect my decision. Harry slowly folded the piece of paper and laid it back on the table. He wasn't going to let me go that easily.

'What are they offering you? We will match it,' was the first effort.

'I cannot say. It's an excellent opportunity and it's too good to miss,' was the well-rehearsed answer.

'Come on Stelios, give me something to work with. What guaranteed bonus will they pay you? What position will you have?'

'It's an excellent opportunity which is too good to miss,' I repeated.

'What seniority level will you be at? We can promote you, if that's what you want.'

'It's an excellent opportunity and I simply cannot let it go,' was the stubborn answer.

Harry was getting visibly annoyed with my prepared answers and general inflexibility. He had always been very calm no matter what the situation, but he was now starting to show some frustration.

'You will go to a new bank with totally new systems in place. They will not be nearly as good as ours and you will struggle. You will lose money and then possibly your job too. Stay here and we will find a way to make it work.'

'I'm sorry Harry, but my mind is made up and nothing you or anyone else says will change it.'

Harry continued to pressure me into staying, coming up with all sorts of reasons and excuses to back up his view – just as Nick had predicted.

Finally, Harry gave up and got up from his chair.

'That's disappointing,' he sighed. 'You have five minutes to collect your things from your desk and leave the building.'

Just like that, my time at Barclays was over. It had been a turbulent time, but I had absolutely no idea what seeds of misfortune had already been planted during my stay there. I barely had any time to say goodbye to a few colleagues, empty my drawers and rush to the exit. My face was totally devoid of sentiment but inside, I was ecstatic.

***

It's common practice for certain banking jobs – including jobs in trading – that when people resign from a bank, they are sometimes contractually bound for an extra period of time. During that time, they can't start employment elsewhere as they remain a paid employee of their former employer (often referred to as 'garden leave'). In my case, this period was a full three months. I didn't complain; I had just been effectively given three months of paid holidays and I was going to take full advantage. I hadn't taken any proper holidays since my two-week honeymoon back in June 2005, and I couldn't wait to get some well-deserved rest and relaxation. Paulina and I spent the next couple of months travelling around the world, making up for the previous four years of near-zero time off. We were both happy to be able to finally relax for a while and, as it turns out, it was our first proper opportunity to really get to know each other.

The timing of the garden leave was perfect, as it spanned late spring and early summer. We went on a road trip to Germany and Belgium. Straight after, we visited the Caribbean for the first time in our lives, spending two weeks in Jamaica. Finally, we went back home to Greece for some quality time with friends and loved ones. It was a great way for me to recharge and mentally prepare for the new job ahead.

London, July 2006

On Monday the seventeenth of July, I woke up early in the morning feeling edgy. I had managed to manoeuvre myself in a highly sought-after trading position – a position which had significant responsibilities and potentially big rewards. I was fully aware that I was relatively inexperienced for a job of this calibre, and that there would be big expectations of me. My annual budget would be ten million dollars, a number that would have seemed crazy to me only a few months before.

I was having all these thoughts while shaving in the bathroom and suddenly I felt very light-headed. I quickly sat down, fearing that I might faint.

Today is not the day for this, I thought, and gave myself a couple of slaps on the face. *Get your act together man. This is your big opportunity. You will rise to the occasion and show Warwick what a great choice he made. Now GET UP and go to work.*

I entered the beautiful building in St. Paul's and headed straight for the STIRT group on the first floor. All the other traders were there, waiting to greet me and welcome me to the team. Straight away, I was surprised by the very different atmosphere compared to Barclays. There was a lot of banter and fun at Barclays, but when it came to business it was all extremely serious. You could even say that your worst enemy was the guy sitting next to you. It was every man for himself and one trader wouldn't hesitate to make money at the expense of another.

However, at Merrill, things were different. Warwick was the head of the STIRT group, and he was always serious and professional. Yet, he was there to look out for every single one of his traders. His goal was to constantly improve the group as a business unit, but he also wanted to keep it tight like a family. He supported all his traders, no matter what the seniority or performance, and he was genuinely there to give help and advice. I found that out first hand when, just a few months after joining, my marriage started faltering.

As time went by, Paulina and I both realised that we were incompatible in many ways. It was clear to both of us that we had rushed into marriage, not really having lived with each other long enough beforehand. It was a typical mistake that many men make when they turn thirty and are still single – they panic and rush into an incompatible relationship. Paulina was a very strong-minded woman, and at times she was quite pushy. She was often hard to please and would become aggressive against me, and that caused me to get detached emotionally and physically. Having said that, I was certainly not blameless – my long hours at work drained me, and when I returned home all I wanted to do was rest and sleep.

My personal situation would no doubt have a big effect on my work, so I took Warwick aside one day and explained things to him. Psychologically I was a mess, and I knew that my trading performance was going to inevitably suffer. I asked Warwick if it would be OK for me to take my trading volume down to the bare minimum. This way I would at least protect the book and avoid doing something rash that could create a big hole in the group's performance. To his credit, Warwick didn't even blink.

'Take as much time as you need, Stelios,' he said reassuringly. 'The desk needs you to be at 100% and we will be here to support you until you get there.'

The rest of the year was a blur to me as I tried to save my marriage, but it was all in vain. We separated shortly after and got officially divorced two years later. Something ends in order for something new and better to begin, as I would later find out.

***

The year 2007, began with a clean slate for me: a new trading book and a new personal life. I had got to know my team members quite well by then and appreciated each person's character. Among them, one stood out.

Richard was a junior trader who used to work in middle office. He took care of the STIRT group's middle office needs, which included trade entry and checking, confirmations, settlements, daily reporting and other related tasks. He actually looked a lot like me visually, a fact that the team subsequently joked a lot about. He had very little hair on his head, a round face, and he disliked shaving just like I did. He also used to be heavily into sports, but the banking job had put some extra kilos on him which stubbornly refused to go away. Richard had frequent interaction with Warwick and the rest of the team, and eventually became well known among them, with Warwick in particular taking a liking to him from the start. Richard was diligent, smart and disciplined, and he rarely ever made mistakes.

Following Andrea's resignation and before I came on board, Richard was hastily put in his place as a stop-gap solution. He was going to slowly learn how to trade, while generally helping out on the desk. By the time I took over, Richard had a good knowledge of the various products and trading strategies, but he still had some way to go. He was assigned to sit and work closely with me, learning as much as he could from me in order to eventually have his own trading book as well. Richard and I would go on to become good friends, looking out for each other like brothers.

***

While at my new job at Merrill, I still kept in touch with a few of my old colleagues. One of those was Don, with whom I still carpooled in the mornings. We no longer worked at the same place, but I would pick him up every day and drop him off at Westminster tube station; those ten minutes were a good opportunity to chat and catch up.

One day as we were in my car, I remembered the LIBOR requests that Fred, Alex and Jay used to ask me to pass on to the submitters.

'Mate, do you still speak to PJ?' I asked.

'Sure,' said Don.

'OK great, perhaps on occasion I will tell you what positions and biases I have in terms of LIBOR fixings, and if it doesn't conflict with your positions – or PJ's positions. Maybe you can tell him for me?' I continued nonchalantly.

In my mind, there was nothing wrong with making such requests, even though I was now based at another bank. I had no idea what the mechanics behind selecting specific LIBOR rates were, and as far as I was concerned the submitter properly and honestly followed the rules when picking a number from the available range each day.

In the following few months, I made a dozen or so requests from Don, who would pass them onto PJ. It was done totally in the open, using email or Bloomberg messages, which we both knew were recorded and stored for years. I could easily have told Don my preference verbally during the morning ride to work, and there would have been no evidence or trace of it. But I did not, as I never tried to hide it in any way; I never thought that there was anything wrong with them. These requests ended once and for all when I moved to another area of London and Don's house was no longer in my path. The carpooling stopped and as our interaction was gradually reduced to a minimum, the requests stopped altogether.

The rest of the year flew by and I felt like a man reborn. After a few months of psychological distress due to my split with Paulina, I had got to a much better mental state. I started going out with friends and enjoying London life. I had a new girlfriend, feeling like an 18-year old kid and having fun. My trading became highly disciplined and effective, and I was on course to actually beat my ten-million-dollar target.

'Bonus Day' is the day that traders find out what their annual bonuses are, and it finally arrived in December. Warwick took all his traders into an office, one by one, and communicated to them what their bonuses would be for that year. The group had performed very well as a whole, so spirits were running high. When my turn came, I was obviously anxious to see what I was going to get paid. I knocked on the door and waited patiently outside.

'Come in,' said Warwick, as he sat on one side of the dark oval table. I sat right across from him, so that I could face him directly. I always liked looking people in the eye whenever there was an important conversation to be had. I knew that it had been a good year for me, but naturally I was slightly nervous.

'Stelios, I am proud of you,' were Warwick's first words. 'You overcame a difficult personal situation and came out of it like a true fighter. You managed to surpass your annual budget. You helped out within the team and you have taken Richard under your wing. As a manager, I can't really ask for more than that. Your performance has been excellent, and your bonus will reflect that.'

Warwick was a well-established and influential manager in the City, so those words of praise officially recognised me as one of the market's outstanding traders. That personal acknowledgement and gratification were immensely satisfying for me; the money in the bank was also welcome, of course.

Chapter Eight
The Global Financial Crisis

London, July 2008

The year had finished on a high for me and the STIRT team. However, being a trader always had one big drawback: your 'score' (i.e. the annual P&L figure) would reset to zero on the first of January of every year. It was quite depressing sometimes to start from scratch, especially following a successful year. Nevertheless, 2007 had been an absolute dream, so I was particularly happy and optimistic about 2008. Little did I know that it would prove to be one of the most difficult years in history for the banking industry.

The warm-up for the hectic times of 2008 actually came from elsewhere for me and the STIRT group. Oliver, the Short-Term GBP Swaps trader, was in trouble. He was a typical Englishman, very well-spoken and with impeccable manners. He had ginger hair, a slight beer belly, white skin and red cheeks. One day, I noticed that his cheeks were actually looking particularly bright. Oliver was flustered. He knew that Warwick always took care of his traders, but he also knew that what he had done was unacceptable. He asked Warwick for a meeting and explained the situation to him.

Oliver's book had some big positions which had been going wrong over the previous weeks. This was actually quite normal, as traders will often have big winning streaks but also big losing streaks. However, Oliver had not been realising the losses in his daily marks. Rather, it seemed that he fiddled with the yield curve inputs and hid the losses, in the hope that the markets would eventually turn in his favour.

What was the damage? Roughly ten million dollars.

I had already seen this happen before, of course, in the case of Fred at Barclays. Oliver had been up five million dollars before he ran into trouble, and the losses had amounted to ten million dollars thus far. He could have easily gradually showed the loss and take his year-to-date P&L to negative five million. It would have been bad, but not a total disaster. There are many traders who go to negative P&L territory – as long as they fight hard to get it back, that can be tolerated. What Oliver did was inexcusable.

Oliver confessed everything to Warwick and unsurprisingly he was dismissed shortly after. Warwick had no choice. He was there to help and support his traders in any way he could, but he could never tolerate lies and improper behaviour.

The aftermath of this episode was very straightforward: someone had to trade the Short-Term GBP Swaps book and I was the glaringly obvious candidate for the job. After all, I had been involved with GBP Swaps at Barclays and had some limited trading experience in that currency. Warwick approached me and asked if I could trade both the USD and GBP Swaps books, at least until some other solution was found. I reassured Warwick right away.

'Of course, I'll help,' I said. 'It will be a lot of hard work and I may not be able to efficiently trade both books simultaneously, but I'll do everything I can to help the group. You can count on me.'

All these events took place just before the summer of 2008 and the disastrous Global Financial Crisis. My workload had become very heavy due to trading both swaps books, and being the responsible person, I tried hard to do the best I could. However, I eventually started to struggle. As the crisis hit hard, my stress levels went through the roof. Actively trading and managing those two important swaps books was becoming a near to impossible task.

***

As the crisis started escalating further, I had the good sense to position both books in such a way that they would make money, if things worsened globally. I placed trades which would become very profitable if LIBOR started rising, something that theoretically wouldn't make much sense to most people given the prevailing conditions.

Let me explain.

There is a direct link between LIBOR rates and the main Central Bank interest rate (for example, the Fed Funds Effective Rate for USD or the Bank of England Base Rate for GBP), and central banks were broadly expected to cut rates going forward. So, theoretically if the global economic situation worsened, central banks would have to cut interest rates. If there is a direct link between LIBOR rates and the Central Bank interest rates, shouldn't my positions lose money, if I wanted LIBOR rates to increase? Why did I think that my positions would make money?

Remember, LIBOR broadly reflected the rates at which banks borrowed unsecured funds from each other. After the summer of 2008, with banks, such as Bear Stearns and Lehman Brothers failing, banks simply no longer wanted to lend out money. They were too scared of lending money to a bank which could fail before paying the money back. The main consideration of interbank lending was no longer the return *on* capital, it was rather the return *of* capital. The end result of this sentiment shift was equally spectacular and surprising: banks simply refused to lend money to each other, and LIBOR rates skyrocketed, even as Central Bank interest rates were slashed.

My trading decision turned out to be spot-on and my books performed very well, producing my best year ever with a total profit of nearly twenty million dollars. Not only did I successfully manage both books and made excellent profits, but also, I helped out within the STIRT group as much as I could with my short-term swaps knowledge. One particular example was when the medium-term GBP swaps trader ran into big trouble with his short-term positions. He had very little knowledge on how to handle such extreme events and got caught in some terrible LIBOR positions. His book started draining money and eventually his whole year's P&L evaporated. At that point, Luke – Warwick's boss and the head of all derivatives trading – stepped in. He politely asked me if I could take on some of those losing LIBOR positions on my book, as the medium-term trader was clearly out of his depth.

Once again, I showed that I was a team player. I realised that these positions could easily cost me over one million dollars to unwind, but I didn't hesitate.

'I'll take them all, Luke.'

The second half of 2008 was particularly stressful for traders, as they invariably held positions with many other banks as counterparties. Now that there was a real chance of more banks failing, traders needed to be adequately prepared for such an event. At the peak of the crisis, I spent several weekends working with the team, evaluating scenarios which involved other banks failing. We needed to be ready with a specific course of action for each scenario, and we also needed to know exactly how the various trading books would be affected. It was a challenging and mentally draining period, but it had to be done. Little did Warwick and I know that the next bank to be in serious trouble would in fact be Merrill Lynch.

There had been whispers in the markets that Merrill had a large amount of toxic sub-prime mortgages on its books, and that they had been imploding since the start of the Global Financial Crisis. I had heard these whispers but had always tried to reassure myself that the bank was going to be fine. Reality, however, was a million miles from being 'fine'. Merrill reported catastrophic results and revealed that its balance sheet was in dire straits. If the bank was unable to find either a cash injection or a willing buyer, it was going to implode spectacularly *a-la* Lehman Brothers. In September 2008, Bank of America came to the rescue and bought Merrill Lynch for fifty billion dollars.

As is common in such takeovers, every single job was under threat and thousands could become unemployed. After all, the two banks had duplicate divisions, particularly in trading, there could only be one person per role. When senior management had to decide on the fate of the two competing Interest Rate Derivatives desks (the larger group that I belonged to), the decision was practically a no-brainer. The rumour was that during the previous twelve months, the Merrill Lynch group had made nearly four times the revenues that the Bank of America group had managed. The senior management's eventual decision was to keep the Merrill group intact, while the Bank of America group was decimated. Such is the cruel world of banking and finance; an acquisition often spells the end of many of the acquirer's employees. My job was safe for now.

By this time, we were squarely in the middle of the dreadful Global Financial Crisis, and in the second half of 2008 something extraordinary happened in the LIBOR markets.

Let's recall that LIBOR rates had exploded higher as banks refused to lend cash to each other, fearing that they would never get the money paid back. This was a natural market reaction and something that persisted for a number of months.

However, one day seemingly totally out of the blue – and with nothing else having changed in the underlying credit conditions – things changed dramatically.

***

On a random Wednesday just after 11 a.m. UK time, the LIBOR rates were published. Seeing them, swaps traders around the world couldn't believe their eyes. They thought that there had been some kind of error. Some even joked that the junior person who made that mistake would soon be out of a job.

But it was no mistake; LIBOR rates had collapsed across most maturities. This inexplicable behaviour was subsequently called 'Lowballing', and it would play a crucial role in the events that followed.

Seeing this bizarre market behaviour, swaps traders and anyone who had meaningful exposure to LIBOR scrambled to find a plausible explanation. *Was this a one-off event? Would rates continue to move lower?* Some traders found themselves – by accident – making a lot of money. Others were furious, seeing their annual profits collapse for no apparent reason.

Hedge funds mostly fell in the latter category, and they were probably mad as hell. Hedge funds are investment funds that engage in speculation using credit or borrowed capital, and being only loosely regulated, they can invest in a wider range of products than mutual funds can. As such, they are often preferred by sophisticated investors. Hedge funds usually employ exceptionally intelligent and experienced individuals, many of them former bank employees and star traders themselves.

One thing hedge funds absolutely hate is losing money, so when this LIBOR collapse happened, they were probably not going to just accept it and move on. It appears that they began asking questions and officially requested of regulators to investigate. They likely suspected foul play and couldn't believe that it had simply been regular market movement. The wheels had been set in motion for what was later described as the *biggest financial scandal in history*.

Chapter Nine
The Investigation

The last quarter of 2008 passed, and I had somehow managed to escape unscathed. Not only that, but I had yet another great year at the bank and rightfully expected to get paid for my efforts. In the previous six months many experienced traders had made losses, and some were at risk of being terminated. Based on my performance, I belonged to an elite group of traders who outperformed their peers.

However, reaching the bonus time, my hopes were dashed. The bank had been in deep trouble just before it was acquired by Bank of America and David, the head of Global Markets, told his subordinates that there was very little money to distribute. My personal bonus figure was around half of what I expected, and it was a big disappointment for me, but it actually made some sense. I decided to take it on the chin and set my sights on the new year that was about to begin, watching the P&L counter reset to zero once again on January, first.

The newly-formed Bank of America/Merrill Lynch bank itself ran into trouble in late 2008 and needed a cash injection from the government TARP (Troubled Asset Relief Program) scheme, which was designed to support the financial services industry. This cash injection worked very well and was probably one of the main reasons why the Global Financial Crisis eventually receded, and stability was restored.

One interesting parameter of the TARP scheme was that any banks that used it had to fully disclose their senior management compensation for the past year. As it turned out, David was one of the designated senior managers and his compensation was finally made public. When I saw the figures, I was outraged.

TWENTY MILLION DOLLARS.

David's pay had doubled from the previous year, which meant that on the face of it, he had effectively taken a big chunk of his employees' bonuses in order to pay himself. So much for the 'no money to distribute' line.

At that precise moment, something broke deep within me, realising just how unfair and unethical the banking sector was. I had always believed in working hard and helping others, no matter what the situation, but here was an example of the exact opposite. From that point on, my trading performance slowly drifted lower until the day it was violently stopped in its tracks.

Following the scandalous compensation revelations, my motivation dropped significantly. I no longer had the energy and drive to give everything to my work. My reduced efforts were reflected in my trading performance, although by normal standards I still performed well. I made a little over ten million dollars in 2009 and maintained my consistent track record. The following year continued in much the same way, with my results remaining steady but my motivation and work satisfaction constantly declining to a bare minimum.

***

London, 10th October 2010

This brings us squarely to the point where I received the letter from Ron the lawyer, informing me that I was required to meet with him in the context of the broad Barclays LIBOR investigation. I was startled and scared, as I genuinely had no clue what this could be about.

I nervously called the number on the letter and arranged a meeting in the following days. During the next few hours, I couldn't help but constantly think about that letter. I undoubtedly wanted to assist with the investigation, but there was no way in hell I was going to hide it from my employer. I remembered reading in one of the bank's new joiner documents that if I was ever involved in any regulatory or criminal investigation, I was contractually required to inform the bank. Having considered the issue, I realised that it was in fact a dead simple decision to make.

I emailed the lawyers and made it crystal clear to them: if they wanted to speak to me, I was going to first inform the bank.

Ron quickly emailed back, reluctantly accepting my proposal, specifying that I could inform my line manager but no one else. I was forbidden from discussing it with anyone else or divulging any specifics.

The following morning, I was ready to perform my duty. I remembered Ron's warning about risking criminal charges if I told anyone about the investigation, so I didn't message Luke to ask for a meeting with him. Instead, I waited until Luke came into the office and grabbed him straight away. We went in one of the small meeting rooms on the trading floor and I anxiously told him what was on my mind.

'Luke, I got a letter from a lawyer, yesterday,' I said. 'Apparently there's a big investigation about some events that happened while I was working at Barclays. I'm not exactly sure what it's about, but I have arranged to meet with him within the next few days, if you have no objections. I told him that I had to inform my manager first, before I attended the interview.'

'I see,' said Luke hesitantly. 'First of all, thanks for informing me. Do you know what it's about?' he enquired.

'No, I don't.'

'Are we OK? he asked in a concerned manner.

'I think we're fine,' I reassured him.

'OK, thanks telling me Stelios. You did the right thing.'

The following day, I arrived at the law firm's offices and was greeted by Ron himself. Being the naïve and trusting person I always had been, I didn't even think to have my lawyer present at the meeting. I hadn't asked for any legal help, because I simply wanted to help out with whatever the investigation focus was.

As we entered the meeting room, I noticed that there was another lawyer present. Helen was a middle-aged American woman, dressed in a bland grey suit, her long blonde hair neatly flowing down the back of her neck. She was gorgeous, her body putting to shame most women half her age. Ron was also American, but he was visibly younger. He had wavy black hair, wore a pinstriped suit and his black shoes were shiny like mirrors. They were both very polite as they started briefing me and asking some basic questions.

It became soon clear that the investigation was solely about LIBOR, as all of the questions involved that particular instrument. My initial thought was that they were looking at the inexplicable lowballing period during the Global Financial Crisis, but I was shocked to discover that they were in fact investigating the LIBOR trader request practice from over a decade ago. They asked extensive questions about Fred, Alex, Jay and the cash traders. They wanted to know as much as possible about them, about their roles in the bank and their relationships with me. They made it very clear that the practice of making LIBOR requests had somehow been wrong, and I struggled to understand why that was. There had been no training, no rule or regulation that stated it was prohibited. My superiors and everyone involved in the requests always behaved as if it was standard market practice. If it was forbidden, I certainly wasn't aware of it.

The initial shock was soon overcome, once I had some time to process exactly what was happening. I reminded myself that I was extremely junior at the time, in what was effectively my first trading job. I had been following orders from my managers, which for the vast majority were in written form.

They probably want to understand what the process was, before they speak to Fred, Alex and Jay, I thought to myself, trying to calm my nerves.

The meeting with the lawyers lasted for around an hour and there was one more similar meeting a few days later. I never heard from Ron and Helen, or from anyone else regarding this matter, for several months. I guessed that it was over, but unfortunately for me it was just the beginning.

***

Athens, December 2013

I turned my Volkswagen Golf into the garage, taking care not to run over the flower bed on the left side of the pathway. I turned off the ignition and took my seatbelt off. I turned around and looked at my one-year old daughter, Kallirroi, who was still fast asleep in her baby car seat. From a life of dramatic and vastly impractical supercars, I had turned into a fully-fledged family man. I smiled and reached over, briefly caressing her dangling foot.

We had just spent the best part of two hours in the playground nearby, and she was well and truly spent from all the playing. It was a Monday, so the playground wasn't as busy as it usually was on weekends, and she was able to enjoy every bit of it. I unclipped the baby car seat and clipped it onto the pram.

I just love this technology, I thought, and wondered how my parents managed to get things done when I was a kid myself.

I pushed the pram towards the entrance door but quickly stopped, noticing that the mailbox was full. I grabbed the pack of letters and quickly returned to my sleeping princess. I carefully guided her inside the house and eventually made it to the sofa, exhaling loudly as I sat down.

Within the bunch of envelopes, one of them was different. It was sent by my UK lawyers.

Why the hell are they mailing me something when we speak over the phone all the time? I thought.

No... surely it can't be?

I slumped in the sofa as I continued reading. The SFO had decided to charge me with '*Conspiracy to defraud*'.

I felt like my life was ending.

***

Athens, January 2000

During my time at Accenture in Athens more than ten years back, I worked alongside a consultant called Maria. The two of us spent a couple of years working together and got to know each other very well. One day in early 2000, she announced something that sounded quite amusing to me at the time.

'Stelios, I have a friend who I think would be a perfect match for you. Let's go out one day and arrange for you to meet her.'

I was never a fan of blind dates, but I trusted Maria's instincts, so I grudgingly agreed. A few days later we arranged to go ice skating, and I finally met Semiramis. She was a Greek woman, one year my junior, petite with dark hair and a captivating smile. Her body was distinctly athletic, sculpted from countless hours of yoga, gym training and competitive sailing. She was intelligent, educated and most importantly she was full of positive energy.

As soon as I laid eyes on her, it became a clear case of instant attraction. I thought she was one of the prettiest women I had ever seen and was determined to get to know her better. Initially, we really hit it off and met up on several occasions in the following few weeks, thoroughly enjoying our time together. I was having the time of my life and found myself gradually falling in love with her. However, I soon brought myself back to reality: my goal was to pursue an MBA abroad and then work outside my home country. She had her friends and family in Athens and her career in shipping was flourishing. There was no way I could get involved with someone at this stage in my life, especially not in a long-distance relationship.

We continued seeing each other socially for a few months but nothing romantic happened between the two of us. I eventually left Greece in September 2000 in order to start my MBA, and our interaction became more infrequent. We remained friends, meeting up whenever I returned to Athens and catching up over our favourite milkshake and pancakes.

As chance would have it, Semiramis and I got married within a week of each other in 2005, excitedly exchanging wedding ideas and discussing details in the run-up to our wedding days. We genuinely felt happy for each other and doubtless deep down we both wondered what it would have been like if our relationship had taken a different path. For the next five years our interaction decreased to a minimum, consisting of only a few emails and the occasional phone call.

In late 2010, the story between the two of us was about to take a new twist. She had recently got divorced and was looking for a way out of her life in Greece. Wanting to make a new beginning in her life, the obvious choice was to move to another country and gain new experiences.

She had always worked in the shipping industry and had managed to secure an interview with a major London-based company. She was genuinely excited about the prospect, especially since it looked like it could give her the opportunity to live and work in one of her favourite cities in the whole world. She arranged a four-day trip for the interview and, not having a place to stay, she asked me if I could help her out. She actually only wanted me to help find a place to stay for those few days, but I pleasantly surprised her.

'You'll stay at my flat, no way am I letting you stay anywhere else,' I said. 'You're going to ace the interview and we'll go out to celebrate!' I excitedly told her.

The interview was scheduled for Thursday morning and Semiramis was feeling confident. She wore her favourite black suit and a pair of stylish but comfortable shoes. The last thing she wanted was to get to the office and have uncomfortably aching feet. She left the bedroom and headed for the kitchen to make some breakfast. I was already there, having made pancakes and orange juice, and waited with a big smile. When she appeared, I was knocked down by her beauty.

'Wow!' I exclaimed. 'You're hired!'

We both laughed and enjoyed a quick breakfast before heading off.

I went to work as normal that day, but I just couldn't concentrate on anything. My mind was with Semiramis as I secretly wished she would land the job. Having her close to me once again after all those years brought back a multitude of feelings. Feelings that I had tried so hard to suppress in the past, but which were now galloping back.

My phone rang later that morning. I glanced at my screen and I saw 'Semiramis calling' on the screen. I answered faster than I had ever answered a phone in my life.

'Tell me the good news!' I exclaimed.

'It went really well,' Semiramis said excitedly. 'I got some excellent feedback and they will tell me the decision by tomorrow. Fingers crossed!'

The news came the following day and it was exactly what we both wanted to hear. She had been hired and was due to start a week later; barely enough time to go back home and pack her belongings. I had promised to take her out to dinner and celebrate, so we went to my favourite restaurant in Wandsworth.

'Chez Bruce' is a small, quiet French restaurant and even though it 'only' had one Michelin star, I always felt that it had the best cuisine in the whole of London. I wanted to make a good impression, so I wore my favourite Canali suit and my lucky pink Hermes tie. I ordered some champagne as a pre-dinner drink and we both toasted to her bright future.

The food was at its usual high quality and after four courses and a generous amount of Bordeaux, we were both in a state of euphoria. I moved my seat a bit closer to hers and raised my glass.

'I want to make yet another toast – how many has it been already tonight?'

We both laughed merrily.

'I wish you a successful career, health, happiness, and –' I stopped for a second and composed myself, all while looking straight in her eyes.

'… and may you find the love that you deserve,' I added.

She understood exactly what I meant, and her heartbeat accelerated. I leaned closer to her and we kissed for the first time in the twelve years that we had known each other. It was a kiss that had had been a long time coming, but now the circumstances were just right.

Semiramis and I spent the weekend together, thoroughly enjoying each other's company. *Why had it taken us that long to finally be together?* I took her to the airport on Sunday and just as she was about to pass through security, I grabbed her in my arms. I kissed her and spoke softly in her ear.

'Please don't look for a place to rent when you come back next week. Let's live together. I know that it may sound crazy or rushed to you, but I've never been more certain of anything in my life.'

She looked at me with a warm smile and nodded.

The following week, Semiramis arrived at the airport with her suitcases and I was there once again to pick her up and take her to her new home – my flat in Sloane Square.

***

At first, our life together was taken straight out of a romantic Hollywood movie. I had to get to work early as usual, but Semiramis didn't start until 8:30 in the morning. That didn't matter to her though, as she wanted to spend as much time as she could with me. She was making up for lost time, and she absolutely loved every minute of it.

We would wake up and have breakfast together, and then climb in the Audi at seven o'clock every morning. I would drop her off at work by 7:15, giving her a full hour to spend at the gym getting energised for the day ahead, while I would continue and reach my office ten minutes later. We both finished work roughly at the same time in the afternoon, so I would pick her up on the way back and we'd talk about our day in the car ride home.

We were making an excellent combined income, so we lived a happy and stress-free life. We went on holidays to exotic places such as Barbados, to picturesque European cities like Bruges, and to the English countryside. Having one failed marriage apiece, we were reborn. We felt like teenagers, constantly looking for opportunities to fool around and have fun.

It was a time of pure happiness, as it was becoming clear to us that we were totally made for each other. I knew exactly what I wanted from our future, as I lovingly told her one day.

'I want to have two gorgeous girls with you, who will have beautiful eyes just like yours.'

***

As is usually the case, the care-free period for Semiramis and me didn't last long. In early 2011, I received a call from my lawyer. The US authorities wanted to have an interview with me, as the investigation had now extended to both sides of the Atlantic. I needed to get set-up with specialist US lawyers, as it seemed that this case was now growing in size and importance.

The bank put me in touch with Guy Petrillo and Dan Goldman from Petrillo Klein LLP, a leading US law firm, who would take care of the US side of the investigation going forward. I felt happy that at least the bank still supported me in the legal aspect of this investigation, given that such legal fees can often rise to exorbitant amounts.

Up to that point, I had been hoping that this investigation would end as far as I was concerned, so I hadn't yet felt the need to tell Semiramis about it. There had been no reason to cause her any unnecessary stress or sadness before the situation became clearer. But the investigation hadn't gone away. It was now getting serious, and I felt that I couldn't keep it from her any longer.

I decided to approach her early in the morning, as I knew that this is the time of day when the human brain has the most clarity. She was a classic morning person, always joyous and happy no matter how early she had got out of the bed. We were sitting at the kitchen table over a warm cup of coffee when I decided to take the plunge. I gave her every single detail and I explained to her all the various possible scenarios, making sure that I was calm and covered every aspect of the issue.

She listened carefully and asked a few questions every now and then. She kept complete focus in what I was telling her, as it was a lot of information to process in a very short period of time. When I was done, she took a few moments to consider everything she had been told, and then put her elbows on the table and slightly leaned into them. She let go of a short breath and put my hands in hers.

73

'My dear, I don't care what others say or think about you,' she said. 'I know exactly what kind of a person you are, and no investigation or lawyer can tell me otherwise. However, as far as this story goes, I'll be standing next to you every step of the way. It took so many years for us to finally be together and nothing will ever tear us apart.'

I teared up as I took her hands and held them tightly, feeling extremely lucky to have a woman like her by my side during that difficult time.

***

New York, April 2011

It was the spring of 2011 and I prepared myself for the trip to the United States. My sole goal was to go there and tell the truth. The truth, the whole truth and nothing but the truth. Throughout my life I had found that honesty was *always* the answer.

I flew into New York and settled in at a trendy Manhattan hotel, realising that it had been over five years since my last visit. I hadn't been to New York since the days when I would switch places with Alex and sit alongside Fred, and those trips felt like a lifetime ago. For some reason, as much as I loved London, I really disliked New York. I found it too busy, the people were too aggressive, and I was quite uncomfortable being around so many skyscrapers. I couldn't wait for this interview to be over and return to London which felt to me much more like a quiet village in comparison.

I arrived at my lawyers' office in the morning, finally meeting them in person. Guy was a man in his late fifties, tall and slim with short grey hair. He was one of the partners of the law firm and very well established in the legal arena. Dan was his young apprentice, in his late twenties and sharp as a knife. Their job was to successfully navigate the US side of the investigation, and the first big hurdle was the interview with the Department of Justice.

The two lawyers had spoken to me extensively over the phone and were fully clued-up on all the details of the case. They were both smart and methodical, and they kept reassuring me that as long as we stuck to the plan – and the truth – I was going to get through it just fine. I was instantly at ease with them both and I trusted them, contrary to my UK legal team, with whom I never really got comfortable.

The three of us spent a couple of hours discussing the case and preparing, and then it was time to get to the airport, as the meeting was going to take place at the Department of Justice headquarters in Washington DC. I had flown into New York on Saturday and it was now Sunday morning. We were going to spend the whole day in DC, and I would then fly to London on the red-eye and go straight to work on Monday morning. I knew it was going to be an exhausting weekend, but it had to be done.

As we arrived outside the DOJ building in Pennsylvania Avenue, I took a deep breath. It was an imposing rectangular white building, built in 1935 and dwarfing the neighbouring structures. As we entered the building and stepped through the metal detector, I gazed at the high ceilings and striking interior which was dominated by large paintings on the walls.

What the hell am I doing here? I thought to myself.

Just past the guards we were greeted by Rob, the head of the investigation. Rob was a proper DOJ old-timer; he'd been in service for two decades and you could tell just by looking at his face that he had seen it all. He had led countless cases and investigations, but it soon became clear that this particular one intrigued him. The sheer breadth and alleged impact of the actions in question already had insiders calling it the 'biggest financial fraud in history'. Rob was enormously interested but he undoubtedly wanted first to get all the facts before jumping into conclusions. He could see that this case was going to attract immense global publicity.

Rob politely introduced himself to the three of us and shook our hands in turn. He had a slow, soft voice which inspired confidence. We entered one of the ground floor lifts and made our way upstairs to one of the vast conference rooms. When the door opened, I felt like I had just been thrust in a Hollywood movie. It was a big rectangular room with dark brown wood all around the walls. In the middle was a massive black oval table with microphones and speakers in front of every seat. On the wall across them was a big DOJ emblem with the familiar bald eagle in the middle. It all felt extremely serious to me, and the dark colours of the room certainly accentuated that feeling. Sat around the oval table were a number of men and women, all staring at the men who had just entered. Rob broke the silence.

'Please, do sit down,' he said to us and pointed to the three empty seats on the near side of the table.

I instinctively sat in the middle, with Guy on my left and Dan on my right. Once everyone was comfortable, Rob took the initiative and started introducing everyone in the room. There were people from the Department of Justice (DOJ), the Federal Bureau of Investigation (FBI) and the US Commodity Futures Trading Commission (CFTC). *Holy crap*, I thought to myself, *this is serious*.

Rob took a few minutes to explain the situation to me and my lawyers, and to outline what the investigation entailed. He described where I fit within the investigation and what was required of me at that point. As he spoke, I felt calmer; it was becoming obvious that what they were mostly after was information. They had been called to investigate something that they had very little idea about, having collected hundreds of thousands of documents and urgently needing someone to help understand them. My goal had always been to assist in whatever way I could, so that's precisely what I did.

For the next six hours or so, I was faced with a barrage of questions on LIBOR, derivatives and trading. I was asked to explain simple terminology and lingo that was not naturally understood by outsiders, but I also gave insight on some more technical aspects. I often had to answer similar – or even identical – questions, because some of the individuals in the room found it hard to get their heads round the principles and concepts involved.

What really impressed me was the quality of two FBI agents. They were two men dressed as if they were from the movie 'Men in Black': black suit, white shirt, narrow black tie and they looked immaculate. They always had a deadly serious expression on their faces and didn't speak much, but when they did, their observations were spot on. They quickly understood and assimilated what was effectively brand-new information for them, and they asked all the right questions. They were clearly the smartest people on the other side of the table, and definitely not the ones to be taken lightly.

After several hours of questioning, I began to feel totally drained. I started having trouble concentrating and often mumbled and repeated myself. This eventually became visible to everyone and Rob decided to step in.

'Thank you, Mr Contogoulas,' he said. 'We are all very thankful that you took the time to come to the US and answered our questions. You have been extremely helpful and have greatly aided us in this investigation. We appreciate that you agreed to fly over and speak to us, and for that we are grateful. We will be in touch with you if we need anything further in the future. Thank you and have a good trip back to London.'

Guy, Dan and I thanked everyone in the room, we got up and quietly left the building. We spent the next fifteen minutes at a nearby coffee shop, getting some much-needed food and going over the day's events and assessing the situation. Guy was quietly confident; he thought that I had tackled every question as well as he could have hoped for.

'You can always tell when someone is telling the truth, if you spend enough time with them,' he said. 'Today's interview lasted several hours, and I'm sure everyone in the room appreciated that you were being truthful throughout,' he said smiling, coffee cup in hand.

I thanked Guy and Dan for their invaluable help preparing me for the interview. I was fully aware that they were probably one of the main reasons why it had been successful. We all agreed to stay in touch in case there were any further developments, and a few minutes later I was in a taxi on my way to the airport.

***

London, July 2011

It was now the middle of 2011. Following the Global Financial Crisis, customer orders at the bank had decreased significantly and accounted for only a small fraction of my annual profits. The vast majority of my profits was down to my own proprietary trading – *me versus the market* – as I often said. The bank didn't actually have a dedicated proprietary trading desk at the time, and senior management had long considered building one. My proprietary trading skills hadn't gone unnoticed and I had become one of the prime candidates for the job. I had been a Director at the bank for nearly five years and was now eligible for consideration to be promoted to Managing Director (or 'MD').

It was common knowledge that being promoted to MD was the holy grail of the banking industry. MDs had managerial roles with important responsibilities, but they were also compensated extremely well. The base salary for MDs at the time was around half a million dollars per year, but that paled into insignificance compared to the average MD year-end bonus. The figure would vary depending on the individual, but it was very common for MDs to receive multi-million bonuses. There even were some MDs who were paid eight-figure sums. Those were numbers that I could only dream of, and yet I found myself slowly getting ever closer to them.

I think that I was actually quite different to most of the other bankers at the time. My goal wasn't to work fifteen-hour per day, until I reached retirement, making as much money as possible in the process. Rather, it was to start a family and to be able to spend quality time with them. I wanted to accumulate enough money in the bank to be able to have a quiet life with my wife and kids. I wanted to have enough wealth so that I could make a comfortable living primarily from the returns of my investments.

Apart from my clear love for cars, I didn't actually live an extravagant life at all. I personally had a target in mind: five million dollars. Once I reached that number, I was going to quit my job and just enjoy the rest of my life with my family. Being an MD meant that I could even potentially make that amount within a single year.

I once had an interesting conversation with one of the senior managers on that subject:

'What's your number, James?' I asked.

'What do you mean?' James responded with a puzzled look on his face.

'How much money do you need to have in the bank, in order to retire and just enjoy life?'

'There is no number,' replied James without batting an eyelid. 'A car, a boat, a plane, a house, it's never enough. You always have to want more.'

I was actually not surprised to hear that reply, as practically everyone in the Square Mile was driven by money and greed. 'Greed is good', as Gordon Gekko famously said in the movie, *Wall Street*.

***

It had been a few weeks since the DOJ interview and although it had gone well, I couldn't get the whole LIBOR story from my mind. I was hoping that my trip to the US signified the end of it, as far as I was concerned personally.

Not much later that same day, I received an email that got my hopes dashed yet again. It was from my lawyers who had been dealing with the UK side of the investigation, informing me that the Financial Services Authority (FSA) wanted to interview me. At the time, the FSA was a quasi-judicial body responsible for the regulation of the financial services industry in the UK, and they had been themselves getting interested in the LIBOR case. Just like with the DOJ interview, I was eager to speak to the FSA and help to the best of my abilities. My UK-based lawyer Adam, however, had other ideas.

'I strongly suggest that you should decline to attend this voluntary interview,' he said firmly.

'But I want to help. I have nothing to hide!' I replied in frustration.

'I understand, but there's a very important detail that we need to consider,' continued Adam. 'If you attend a voluntary interview, anything you say can be used in trial, if you are ever charged in the future.'

'Charged? For *what*? Following my bosses' orders? Passing on direct orders from my superiors? That's insane!' I grunted.

'We have to prepare for every possible eventuality,' Adam said calmly, attempting to diffuse the situation.

'So, what do we do?' I said, trying to tame my anger.

'We wait for the FSA to compel you to attend the interview. Once they do that, you will attend the interview and they won't be able to use any of it against you in the future.'

'That's honestly your best advice?'

'Yes sir, it is.'

I reluctantly agreed, and Adam subsequently informed the FSA that their voluntary interview request had been declined. The next logical step from there would be to compel me for an interview, but there was always an outside chance that the FSA might just drop it.

Once again, I didn't get the luck I was hoping for. Sure enough, the FSA compelled me to attend the interview, and this time if I declined it could mean charges being pressed against me.

The interview was scheduled for the end of October, so I had over a month to get adequately prepared. I thought I had enough worries on my mind, but what hit me next was a real sledgehammer.

Chapter Ten
Terminated

It was 7:15 a.m. on a cold Monday morning and I had just taken the first sip of my morning coffee. I was sitting at my desk, getting all my systems up-and-running, and reading up on some research. My screens were busy flashing various prices and headlines, while there were already several voices being heard from the complex dealer board system in front of me. I was a seasoned veteran by now, a far cry from the nervous and overwhelmed young man who first stepped foot in a trading floor a decade earlier.

My immediate boss for the past few months had been Chris, a former USD swaps trader and now manager of the whole group following Luke's resignation earlier that year. Chris stood next to my desk and tapped on my shoulder.

'Stelios, I got a call from Human Resources and they want to have a meeting with us straight away. Come with me,' he said, and we both quickly made our way to the designated meeting room.

It was a tiny room around the back of the trading floor, at the edge of the general area where all the IT staff usually sat. Chris opened the door and we took a seat at the two empty seats available directly in front of us.

In the room, there was two women and it turned out they were from the Legal and Human Resources departments. I couldn't help noticing that they both had a deadly serious look on their faces. The HR woman silently reached over to me and gave me a piece of paper to read. I took a minute to study it and as I read on, my face turned white from terror. I was being terminated for gross misconduct, because I hadn't informed my employer that I was the subject of a regulatory investigation.

I was gobsmacked. I was so shocked in fact, that I just sat there, unable to utter a single word. The HR woman started speaking, outlining the next steps for me. For as long as the she was talking, I tried to muster the energy to speak up. I tried to tell her that I had, in fact, informed Luke at the time. I wanted desperately to tell her that informing my employer was something I would never compromise on.

But the words just wouldn't come out.

The only thing I managed to mutter was an 'OK,' after she was done. I mechanically got up and left the room and Chris followed me down the corridor, accompanying me back to my desk. Chris had been instructed to watch me pack my things and escort me out of the building.

As we were both walking, my voice suddenly returned.

'Chris, I told Luke!' I shouted. 'I told him before attending the very first interview with the Barclays lawyers!'

My voice was trembling and my speech was shaking, as I felt the injustice gripping me all over.

'And what did Luke do?' asked Chris.

'*I HAVE NO FUCKING IDEA WHAT HE DID!*' I snapped back angrily, my voice finally gaining a thunderous tone. I would very rarely curse, but at that moment I just couldn't control myself.

'He's the bloody manager, he's supposed to know what to do and how to direct his employees, *right?*'

I was furious. I had turned bright red and my eyes were tearing up. Once more, I had done nothing wrong and yet I found myself on the wrong end of the stick again.

'This is not bloody fair!' I shouted.

'What can I say, Stelios,' Chris muttered. 'I'm afraid there's nothing I can do, you have to pack your stuff and go.'

Five minutes later, I was out on the street holding a cardboard box with my belongings. I felt lost and disorientated. I stood there for a couple of minutes, looking around, anxiously trying to think about what to do next. I put the box down and took my phone out from my pocket. I called Semiramis and hastily explained what had happened.

'Wait right there, I'll be over in five minutes,' she said and hung up.

***

Semiramis's response to the events was everything you would have expected from a person like her. She had always been extremely loyal to her friends and family. No matter what happened, her allegiance and blind trust was always there for her loved ones.

When she found me outside the Merrill Lynch building, I was visibly shaken. I had always been a strong and resourceful man, but right there and then, I was really struggling. She took me in her arms and calmed me down with some soft, soothing words.

'Remember what we always say, baby? Everything happens for a reason. For a *good* reason. One step at a time, baby,' she whispered in my ear. From the corner of her eye she saw a black cab approaching.

'*Taxi!*' she shouted, and moments later we were on our way home.

The following day, the shock of the whole experience finally started to recede, and I no longer felt numb. I started considering my immediate options. One of my first thoughts was to contest his termination, citing grounds of unfair dismissal. I believed that the reason for my dismissal was simply untrue, as I had informed Luke about the investigation from the outset.

I recalled that when I was fired, I was given an email contact from the bank and seven days to contest the dismissal. I switched on my laptop and started typing frantically.

'I'm going to contest this, Semiramis!' I said to her in a hopeful but unmistakeably sad voice.

'I did everything I was supposed to do. They just can't do this!' I added, as I continued typing. A few moments later, I lifted my hands from the keyboard and paused.

'Maybe I should speak to a lawyer before I do anything hasty.'

***

I arranged a meeting with an employment lawyer and my hopes were once again shot down. The lawyer summarily explained that it would be practically impossible to successfully contest my dismissal. The rulebook for most banks at the time (including Merrill Lynch) explicitly stated that if an employee was ever the subject of a regulatory investigation, he or she had to immediately inform management *and* the compliance and legal departments.

I had informed the former but not the latter.

'Who the hell actually reads all two hundred pages of the company rulebook when they join?' I snapped. 'I told my boss – the bloody group head. He should have known what to do. He should have told me that I needed to also inform legal and compliance. Or maybe, he should have informed them himself. This is absurd!' I said, slouching in my chair and putting my hands on the top of my head. My lawyer agreed and reminded me that legally I didn't have many chances to succeed.

'So, the banks win every time, do they?' I moaned. 'They have mountains of money and armies of lawyers behind them, so if it ever comes to a legal fight, they always have an unfair advantage. There's no way an Average Joe can ever take them on and win. No wonder people hate bankers, they seem to have rigged the whole system in their favour!'

I spent the next couple of days considering what I'd just been told. I was a broken man, conquered by disappointment and frustration, reluctantly deciding in the end not to contest the dismissal.

At this point, I was unemployed and had zero chances of securing another trading job before the investigation was over. No bank or other financial institution would ever consider hiring someone who was the subject of regulatory – and potentially criminal – investigation. I spoke to a few people I knew in the business and, predictably, they were all resolute about it. I had saved a good amount of money in the bank, but without my income it could get depleted relatively quickly. Semiramis still had her job and it was a well-paid one, but we were now at a crossroads and needed to make a major life decision.

'*Everything happens for a reason,*' we both always said, and once again we were about to get proof positive of our mantra.

***

Semiramis's employer had for months been looking to expand the company's operations to other countries. One of the potential locations was Greece, given the nature and interests of the business. Shipping was huge in Greece and the company owned or controlled many Greek-flagged vessels. The fact that Greece had recently been thrown in economic crisis, with wages and rents dropping dramatically, was an added bonus for the company. Senior management had decided to establish an office in Athens, as it made good business sense.

Only a few days after I was sacked, Semiramis's boss, Agis, called her in for a meeting. He was a Greek-Cypriot man in his early thirties, and the person who had interviewed and hired Semiramis into the company. She always felt very fortunate to have him as her boss; in fact, he was probably the best boss she had ever had, and they had even become good friends. Agis wasted no time, in his typical no-nonsense attitude.

'Semiramis, the company has decided to open an office in Athens. The wheels have already been set in motion and we should be able to have it up-and-running by the start of the new year. I'll be moving there to head the office and I want you to come with me. Together we will need to hire at least five or six more people to start, and we'll need to move fast. What do you think?'

Semiramis paused, as she started to appreciate just how incredible the timing was.

'You know, I've been in London for only a year and I already hate the weather,' she joked. 'I'm in.'

Just like that, within the space of a few days our life had been turned upside down. We summarily agreed to move back to Athens by year end and that unexpectedly filled us with renewed hope and positivity for the future.

***

At this point, there was still the small matter of the FSA interview for me to tackle. My preparation with the lawyers had been comprehensive and with the experience of the DOJ interview behind me, I was naturally feeling more confident. The interview was scheduled for late October 2011 and I was eager to get it over with and start a new life in Greece.

When the day of the interview arrived, I made it to the FSA offices in Canary Wharf, feeling full of energy and positivity. Adam noticed this and tried to calm me down.

'It's good that you're optimistic Stelios, but let's not get too cocky. We have a job to do, let's go in there and get it done right.'

'You're right Adam,' I agreed. 'I just want to get this over with, pack my things and move back to Greece. This industry has destroyed my life, and I never want to be a part of it again.'

The FSA building was quite different to the other buildings on the street. With its plain design and no distinguishing features, it almost faded into the background next to the newly-built skyscrapers and modern glass creations. It was as if it was purposely made in a way to mirror the FSA's mundane task of regulating the all-powerful banking industry.

The interview room was particularly small, with a cheap-looking table in the middle and a few random chairs scattered round it. There was one small window in the back wall, but it looked on an empty back street that was had a row of trash cans arranged along its side. The carpet was worn and stained, and a distinct plastic smell filled the room.

As I sat down on one of the flimsy chairs, I couldn't help comparing it to the building in Washington. They were two completely different worlds – could it be a sign that reflected the difference in enforcement mentality between the two countries?

There were four FSA employees present, alongside Adam and me. They started the recording device and introduced themselves. Then, within the space of a few seconds, the questions started coming thick and fast. They didn't appear to have any logical order, as the interviewers seemed to jump from one subject to another. They sometimes failed to understand the basic concepts that I explained to them, or to piece together simple continuity items. I felt like I was teaching a bunch of ten-year olds advanced mathematics; it was an uphill struggle. The difference between the Americans and the English was monumental. After several hours of grinding through the list of prepared questions, the ordeal was finally over.

The debriefing with Adam was quick. I had answered all the questions I was asked, sticking to the truth and being as helpful as possible. I had tried to make the FSA people understand how things worked, even though some of it may have been lost on them.

Adam told me that this could be the end of the investigation as far as I was concerned, just like my US lawyers had told me a few months back. However, there was always a chance that I might be charged by either side and I should be fully aware of that. Then Adam said something that frightened me deeply: *I could be charged in the UK and not be allowed to leave the country until the trial.*

I panicked. I went home and told Semiramis everything that had happened, placing particular emphasis on Adam's last words.

'There's no way I'm staying here in the UK any longer,' I said nervously. 'I want to go back to Athens, and you can come as soon as your job allows you. What do you think?'

'Well, I would hate being away from you, but if this is what it takes to put your mind at ease, that's what we'll do,' she answered.

'I'm scared, Semiramis,' I said. 'I want to go home. Once I'm there, I'll check the extradition treaty between Greece and England, and see what the legal framework is. If they can't extradite me, maybe the solution is for me to never visit the UK or the USA again.'

'Don't you think that's going a bit far?' she said, trying to calm me down.

'Is it?' I snapped back. 'I don't like running like a fugitive, but there's someone big pulling the strings here. I can *feel* it. Either that, or these people are crazy!'

'OK, honey,' she said calmly. 'One step at a time, baby.'

Two days later I was on a plane to Athens, leaving the UK for good.

Chapter Eleven
A New Life

I moved back to my hometown Athens in late 2011. My parents had mixed feelings for the events that had brought me back. Happiness was evident on their faces, because they finally got their son back in their home. There was obvious sadness too, because of the circumstances of my return. The turmoil with the investigation had calmed down by now, but I had no prospects of getting a job. I soon realised that the timing was perfect for something I had always wanted – start a family.

A few weeks later, Semiramis joined me in Athens and we were united once again for the start of our new life. It was a very different life to what we were used to in London; no more Caribbean holidays, no more Michelin-starred restaurants or luxuries. We depended solely on her income now, and we had to adjust our lifestyle accordingly.

Thankfully, neither of us really cared about that. All we wanted was to be together and live a happy and healthy life. Then, in early 2012 Semiramis announced that she was pregnant. I was ecstatic. When she told me the news, I ran up and down the house for several minutes, screaming with joy. We were no spring chickens – I was forty-one and she was forty years old at the time – so we were delighted that we had managed to conceive with very little effort.

Only a few weeks earlier, we had adopted a stray dog. We both loved dogs and had always talked about getting one when the time was right. Milly was a three-month old mixed-race white dog, medium sized with dark brown eyes. She was a quiet creature, but never wasted an opportunity to cuddle. She quickly became what we jokingly called 'our first child', and we spent countless joyous hours in her company.

One morning, while both Semiramis and Milly were asleep, I was silently making preparations. I carefully fastened a small red box on Milly's collar and took her in my arms. I then quietly walked to the bedroom, laid Milly next to Semiramis, and gently woke her up.

'Good morning, my love,' I said softly.

'Mm... good morning,' said Semiramis, as she turned and slowly sat up in the bed. 'What's up at this early hour?'

'Oh, nothing really,' I replied, but the huge grin in my face suggested otherwise. 'I think Milly wanted to cuddle with you, so I brought her to bed,' I continued and placed a clearly still very sleepy puppy next to her.

Semiramis looked at Milly and stroked her head for a few seconds, but then she suddenly stopped. She stared at Milly for a brief moment and then turned her eyes to me. Her eyes started to well up.

'What have you done?' she asked me playfully.

I didn't reply, letting my smile do all the talking. She unclipped the box from Milly's collar and opened it, revealing a sparkling diamond ring inside. It wasn't a particularly large or expensive ring, being just what we could afford at the time. For Semiramis, however, it was the most beautiful engagement ring she had ever seen. For her, it was the whole world.

***

The wedding was planned for late August of that year, which meant that Semiramis would be well into her pregnancy on the day. Greek weddings were typically large, with hundreds of guests and extravagant set-ups. Luckily, since we'd already had one previous wedding each, we were able to keep it small the second time round. Just forty guests, including family and very close friends.

Semiramis wore a lovely plain white dress, her bulging belly distinctly revealing that she was now six months pregnant. It was a small ceremony in the south suburbs of Athens, under a full moon and a stone's throw from the sea, followed by an unforgettable night of dancing and celebration.

For a few hours, I was totally happy and carefree. I was marrying the love of my life and had a baby daughter on the way – my 'little treasure', as I playfully called her while she was still in her mother's womb. I was surrounded by people who loved me, and who were there to share the happiest day of my life.

Inevitably, in a random moment of that wonderful night, the LIBOR affair came to my mind and suddenly everything went dark. I recalled all the events of the past year – lawyers, interviews, and the lot. Without realising it, I spent several minutes just standing there, staring into the void in a trance-like state. I felt like I was shaking.

'Stelios are you OK?!?' Semiramis asked, holding me by the shoulders and looking clearly worried. 'You've been standing there for some time and you look like you're lost in space.'

'I'm… I'm fine,' I mumbled, and hastily re-joined the party.

It was supposed to be the happiest day of my life, but it had just been utterly ruined.

***

Shortly after our wedding, Semiramis and I went on a mini-honeymoon to Santorini, an incredibly romantic island set in the middle of the Aegean Sea. It was our chance to spend a few precious days solely in each other's company, and to take a much-deserved break. We stayed in her favourite hotel overlooking the Caldera, with extraordinary views of the legendary Santorini sunsets. Whenever we weren't swimming or enjoying the exquisite local cuisine, we were out taking long, slow strolls along the Cliffside. The winding pathways provided the perfect route among the bright white houses, neatly tucked into the side of the volcanic rock. It was an idyllic setting, providing the perfect backdrop for our brief honeymoon.

One afternoon, I switched on my laptop and browsed through the day's news. One headline instantly grabbed my attention:

'Barclays agrees to pay $453 million to settle LIBOR probe.'

I read on, anxiously trying to establish what implications this move would have on me personally. The article cited trader requests, but it also mentioned lowballing during the crisis. I was shocked to see one my emails being mentioned in the article, although thankfully I had not been named. I finished reading the piece and then I immediately re-read it for good measure.

My first reaction was that the bank had successfully wiggled its way out of a bad situation. Sure, it was going to pay a big fine, but that was effectively just money taken from its shareholders. Nothing was coming out of senior managers' pockets and, crucially, the bank would have the opportunity to choose which individuals to serve up as scapegoats to the regulators.

By that point, the LIBOR story had become a global news story and a huge deal. People had always been aware that bankers were compensated extremely well, and that had already given them a bad reputation. This, however, would be the straw that broke the camel's back. It would most likely destroy the reputation and public image of bankers as a whole.

Suddenly, I felt cold sweat running down my face.

When push comes to shove, who will the bank choose to sacrifice to the people who are demanding blood? The senior managers who were the main decision-makers behind lowballing and trader requests, or the juniors who were just following orders? Who would get the axe, the generals or the lowly soldiers?

In the article, the Barclays CEO was quoted as saying that he was sorry that some people acted in a manner not consistent with the bank's culture and values. I realised that *'some people'* should refer to managers like Fred and others higher in the hierarchy, but in all likelihood, it meant juniors like myself. I felt disgusted, and in imminent danger.

As I searched the internet for related articles and more information, I stumbled upon another very interesting piece, which was reported by several UK news outlets. Bob Diamond, the Barclays CEO, together with Jerry Del Missier, the bank's COO, had both quit in early July 2012. They went on to give testimony to the Treasury Select Committee later that month, as did Paul Tucker of the BoE and Marcus Agius, the bank's chairman. They answered a series of burning questions involving LIBOR and the Lowballing practice, and in particular, the following was reported:

'Jerry Del Missier, The Barclays executive at the centre of the Libor interest rate-fixing scandal, said last night that he had only passed on "instructions" from a conversation he had with his then boss Bob Diamond.

In potentially explosive testimony to the Treasury Select Committee, Jerry Del Missier, who quit last week as chief operating officer along with the Barclays chief executive Mr Diamond, said: "He (Mr Diamond) said he had had a conversation with Mr (Paul) Tucker at the Bank of England. (He said) the Bank of England was getting pressure from Whitehall about the health of Barclays and that we should get our Libor rates down. That we shouldn't be outliers. "

The 50-year-old Canadian's testimony appears to contradict Mr Diamond, who told MPs there was no instruction from the Bank and that he did not intend to relay one.

Mr Del Missier said: "I passed the instruction as I had received it on to the money markets desk. I relayed the contents of the conversation I had had with Mr Diamond and expected the Bank of England's views would be incorporated into Libor submissions".

Challenged on the point he said: "It was an instruction, yes. "

Del Missier's questioning revealed a very nonchalant attitude towards moving LIBOR submissions to levels which would satisfy the bank's preference. More importantly, a few specific questions from Mr Ruffley of the TSC actually got an explicit answer from Del Missier on this issue:

*'**Ruffley**: My final question is: when did you first realise – I am looking for a date here – that you had authorised, knowingly or unknowingly, illegal activity, found to be illegal by the Us Department of Justice? When did you find out that you had a problem on your hands?*

***Del Missier**: The investigation was –*

***Ruffley**: No, on what date did you discover that?*

***Del Missier**: In the early months of 2010. I can give a timeline around the investigation, which commenced in December 2008 – the CFTC through the FSA.*

***Ruffley**: And you knew it was illegal at that point, did you?*

***Del Missier**: Then, as we went through the –*

***Ruffley**: You were notified that it was a potentially illegal activity.*

***Del Missier**: No.*

***TSC Chair**: Just to be clear, in response to questions there you said, or at least you tried to avoid saying, that it was illegal. Do you consider it to have been improper?*

***Del Missier**: No, I don't.'*

Del Missier said he did not see anything wrong with what he was doing. He said:

'I passed the instruction on to the head of the money market desk. I relayed the content of the conversation I had with Mr Diamond and fully expected the

Bank of England views would be fully incorporated in the Libor submission. I expected that they would take those views into account,' Del Missier said.

So, here was Jerry Del Missier, an extremely senior member of the bank and a former derivatives trader himself, clearly stating that trying to influence LIBOR submissions was not something he considered to have been improper. If this was the case, wouldn't it be normal that this attitude would have been passed down the ranks, all the way to junior people like me? Wouldn't this information be crucial in my defence? As it turned out, this evidence was one of many supporting pieces for junior traders which were not allowed to be introduced in court.

Bob Diamond, in his own testimony to the Treasury Select Committee, apologised for the 'reprehensible' behaviour of his traders who fixed interest rates, referring to the 'Trader Request' practice that I was caught up in. He added:

'When I read the e-mails from those traders, I got physically ill. That behaviour was reprehensible, it was wrong. I am sorry, I am disappointed, and I am also angry. Those involved in rigging interest rates should be subject to criminal investigation and dealt with harshly.'

In essence, the bank's CEO considered trying to influence LIBOR submissions to be 'reprehensible' and wrong, and the same bank's COO considered it to have normal and proper. I wonder, did Diamond only want junior traders like myself to be 'dealt with harshly', or did that include people like Del Missier?

***

A few months later, another piece of the puzzle was revealed. Tom Hayes, an English Swaps trader who had worked at UBS and Citigroup, was arrested by British authorities for his involvement for allegedly manipulating Japanese Yen LIBOR. He had effectively been doing exactly what Fred Gourtay and Jay Merchant had done, but on a bigger scale.

Tom was an extremely successful trader, making millions for the bank and taking home an excellent pay check for him. Interestingly, he had actually been coordinating with LIBOR submitters in his own bank and a number of others, which meant that the probability of his requests having significant effect on the final published numbers was greatly elevated. Remember, the final published LIBOR number was calculated by first discarding the four highest and four lowest numbers, and then averaging the remaining eight. If you were making a request to one LIBOR submitter, that submission would end up being discarded practically every single time. However, if you were cooperating with several other submitters, the effect of your request could potentially be more pronounced.

Tom was a very special kind of trader. I had never met him personally, but people who knew him and worked with him described him as extremely intelligent, quiet and introvert. He always kept a low profile, avoiding showing off or being extravagant. He was known for not drinking alcohol and particularly disliking office parties and social events. He was a man whose single focus was to be the best trader he possibly could.

He also suffered from Asperger's syndrome, a fact that was discovered some years later, and which explained some of his personality traits. Tom was married to a lovely English lawyer, Sarah, and they had a baby boy called Joshua.

The prosecuting authority overseeing the LIBOR case on the UK side was the Serious Fraud Office (SFO). The SFO was an organisation that had recently been in the line of fire (as made quite public by several newspapers and publications in the UK) for some questionable tactics and alleged internal corruption. It had been accused of utilising scare tactics to threaten businesses, and individuals had even been caught using private email addresses to exchange internal messages that could otherwise cause enormous damage if made public.

The SFO head, David Green, had decided to make the LIBOR cases the cornerstone of the organisation's future. There had been doubts over its future funding and independence, so he needed to produce results – *fast*. Green was in dire need of a confession and guilty plea from Tom, and he would likely do everything within his power to make it happen.

The SFO had an ace up its sleeve, which was the possibility of Hayes's extradition to the US, to face charges for the same events. It seems that the DOJ had also been eager to get their hands on Tom, but the SFO had beaten them to it.

The US justice system was notorious for its draconian sentencing, and that scared the hell out of Tom. In light of that, the SFO proceeded to play their cards perfectly; they made Tom think that if he didn't confess, they would extradite him to the US, where he would face the prospect of spending endless years in an American prison. And the prison was, of course, thousands of miles from his family and home country.

Their plan worked to perfection and Tom initially cooperated with the SFO, providing nearly eighty hours of interviews, ensuring that he would be charged in the UK. During those interviews, and under severe strain, he confessed to being part of a fraudulent and dishonest scheme involving the 'rigging' of LIBOR rates.

It was probably an extremely difficult decision by Tom, under a mountain of pressure and stress, because it was actually not the truth. He never believed that what he had done was fraudulent or dishonest, but he had to confess in order to avoid extradition (he would subsequently explain all his actions in detail during his trial). His confession naturally brought charges against him – in particular he was charged with eight counts of '*Conspiracy to defraud*', a charge that carried a maximum of ten years imprisonment for each count.

Hayes was supposed to cooperate with the prosecution and plead guilty, but something changed materially along the way. As his legal team started receiving disclosure documents, he realised that LIBOR requests were happening in practically every single bank and in most currencies. It was a market-wide practice, which had been going on for decades. Tom had been doing it with his superiors' full knowledge and support, but they had now all turned against him. According to him, there was even a UBS 'handbook' which described this practice among others. To his dismay, every senior person involved was now denying all knowledge and condemning the practice.

Tom felt crushed, as it had become evident to him that he had been served up as the perfect scapegoat for a long-established and industry-wide practice. They set him up to take the fall for hundreds of other people, but he wasn't about to let that happen without a fight.

Prior to the start of his trial, Tom withdrew his cooperation and chose to fight the charges levied by the SFO. The SFO, in a vindictive way, proceeded to narrow the scope of the charges and thus leave less overlap between the American and British prosecutors. By doing so, the SFO created the possibility of another trial in the United States, in case they lost the UK trial – ensuring that Tom could suffer over a second trial in the US. The UK trial was scheduled to take place in 2015, just over two years down the road.

Chapter Twelve
Charged

The following year was relatively uneventful for me and my wife. Our daughter Kallirroi was born in late 2012 and we found ourselves in a constant state of bliss. After her twelve-week maternity leave, Semiramis went back to work and I assumed my role as a stay-at-home dad, taking care of our baby and our dog Milly.

Within the space of two years, my life had been turned upside-down. My savings had taken a big hit due to the mounting legal fees and the costs of raising a family. Semiramis's income was not enough to cover our monthly costs, so the money I had accumulated over the years was quickly depleting. Our wealth was nearly non-existent compared to my London days, but I felt like the richest person on the planet. I had a caring and loving wife whom I adored, and I got to spend all day with my little treasure.

It had been over a year since my last interaction with lawyers regarding the LIBOR investigation, and I was secretly hopeful that I would never hear from them again. I even started thinking about how I was going to get back in the professional arena, getting in contact with friends and acquaintances who were in the financial services industry. I wasn't having much luck to start with; the minute I mentioned the investigation the doors would get slammed shut. Being an honest and a truthful person, I never even for a second considered hiding it from prospective employers.

***

November 2013

It was as if a curse had fallen on me, because once again the period of peace and happiness was brutally disrupted. The first event happened in late 2013, where the UK Court of Appeals declared that making trader requests in the LIBOR submission process was illegal and improper.

When I read about that decision, I actually had a glimmer of hope inside me. If a UK court is declaring that something is illegal *now* that means that there was no such directive or law *in the past*. Surely if judges make up a new law, they can't subsequently go back over a decade and enforce it in what seems like a retrospective manner?

The answer lied within the envelope I was holding in my hands, just a few weeks later. It was awful news. I was going to be charged by the SFO, under the

'Conspiracy to defraud' charge. The SFO eventually charged five other people alongside me: Jay Merchant, Alex Pabon, Peter Johnson, Jonathan Matthew and Ryan Reich – a US-based Barclays' trader whom I had never actually met because I had left the bank before Ryan joined.

Semiramis and I simply couldn't believe what was happening. It felt like we were in a movie or a particularly bad dream, waiting to wake up from it at any moment. Unfortunately for us, we were wide awake.

Neither of us got much sleep during the next 48 hours – we just lay in bed silently, staring at the ceiling and trying to make sense of it all. We wouldn't eat, we roamed around the house like zombies, and we could barely take care of our child. To complicate matters further, Semiramis was already five months pregnant to our second daughter and she simply couldn't afford to collapse psychologically.

The shocking development was that Fred had in fact not been charged. Fred Gourtay and Don Lee had been named as co-conspirators in the indictment but were actually not charged by the SFO. I was absolutely outraged by the SFO's stance towards Fred. *How could he not have been charged, when he was seemingly the one who initiated the practice?* The evidence was right there, what could have possibly been the reason he was spared?

I racked my brains and eventually I came up with one very plausible answer. Harry Harrison's boss, Eric Bommensath, was a French national and an extremely senior Managing Director within the bank. One day when Fred was in London, I witnessed Eric coming over to Fred's desk which was situated next to mine. The two of them started chatting and probably didn't realise that I was actually fluent in French and could understand everything they said. I distinctly remembered hearing their conversation, during which I appreciated that although in public they showed a strictly professional relationship, they seemed in fact to be close friends. My view was suddenly made clear: *the big boys always take care of their own people.*

***

London, April 2017

I nervously sat in my designated seat within the dock of the British court of justice. I was all alone and suddenly realised that within the following minutes I would discover whether I would be spending a considerable time in a cold jail cell, or if I would be on the next flight home.

The jury had announced that they had reached a verdict, and although I was quietly confident, I couldn't help feeling totally helpless. The envelope had been passed from the jury foreman to the court clerk, and onto the judge.

For me, every second felt like a year now. I was trembling with fear.

***

Athens, December 2013

After a few days of deep stress and frustration, something clicked within Semiramis and me. I was being charged by the SFO with '*Conspiracy to defraud*', a charge that we both found incomprehensible and vastly unfair. We were both in shock. However, we suddenly found the inner strength to think rationally and tackle the problem head-on. We decided that we weren't just going to lie down and face defeat; we were going to fight every step of the way.

One person who took the news much worse was my father, Dimitri. He was visibly shaken and deeply upset. He couldn't believe that his son was being put through this injustice. He had raised his sons to be decent, law-abiding citizens, and he was disgusted at the charges against me.

A few days after my world had been turned upside down, I received some more bad news. My father had suffered a minor stroke and had been admitted to the hospital. Following several medical tests, the diagnosis was that he needed to undergo quadruple heart bypass surgery. He was in his early seventies, but he had been in excellent health, often making me to joke about his triceps being bigger than my own. Happily, the operation was successful, and my father returned home a few days later, feeling and looking like nothing had ever happened.

One afternoon, I was sitting on the garden lawn, watching my daughter play with her beloved grandfather. I cherished those moments and realised that the picture I was seeing would not have been possible if my father's operation had not gone well. I was convinced that the timing of the charges against me, and my father's stroke were no coincidence. I didn't mind suffering personally from this story, but I could never forgive the prosecutors for the pain they caused to my father. That precise moment, I vowed to fight with all my strength in order to clear my name and expose the true story behind the events that were now unfolding. I was a man on a mission.

Chapter Thirteen
Trial Preparations

By this time, I had practically run out of cash. The cost of the upcoming trial was estimated to be well into seven figures, so there was no way I could fund it personally. I was going to have to get help from Legal Aid, a UK government scheme that was designed to help people like myself fund expensive litigation proceedings. I needed to find a good lead barrister, a person who would be the cornerstone of my defence. I eventually selected David, a slim Englishman who had a long and successful career behind him in the British courts.

I first met David during our initial preparatory meeting in London. Being physically located in different countries meant that we could get a lot of work done remotely, but these face-to-face meetings became essential. We went on to have a few meetings where I would visit London for a few days. We spent the entire day with David and the rest of the legal team, and deciding on the plan of action. The team would then spend countless hours going over the vast array of documents and putting them under the microscope. I eventually got to know the five people of his legal team very well:

- David Stern, the lead barrister.
- James Fletcher, the supporting barrister.
- Karl Masi, the junior barrister.
- Steve Sharp and Roland Ellis of Bivonas LLP, the lawyers doing most of the behind-the-scenes work and helping out the barristers with preparation.

Tom Hayes's trial soon started, and it instantly grabbed the attention of the world media. I followed it closely, feeling particularly saddened about the way Tom's life was being paraded on the TV screens and newspapers.

The prosecution painted a particularly nasty picture of him, and the media duly took its side and regurgitated it on the front pages. I often thought that the way Tom was being treated was horrendous. They were calling him a 'ringmaster' and made him appear like some hideous criminal. However, I knew that the reality of what Tom had done was probably exactly the same as in my case. Was this standard practice, condoned by senior management? Most likely.

Tom certainly seemed to have stretched the limits of what could be done while keeping within the boundaries of legality, but as far as everyone was concerned, there was nothing wrong with it at the time – that was probably the reason why he was allowed to do it while at UBS. His wife and son were thrust in the spotlight, having never asked or approved to be treated that way. It was total violation of a person's private life and chances were that I was going to get the exact same treatment.

During Tom's trial, it soon became evident that it was going to be a one-sided fight. The prosecution was throwing one punch after another, knowing full well that Tom's Asperger's syndrome would give him a mountain of trouble. At the same time, a number of crucial pieces of evidence were not allowed to be used in court, severely damaging Tom's defence arguments.

In the summer of 2015 and following many days of deliberations by the twelve-person jury, Tom was finally found guilty. In an inexplicable turn of events, upon delivering their verdict, some jurors burst into tears. They seemed conflicted and helpless.

Judge Cooke sentenced Hayes to fourteen years in prison, a sentence which many people found absurdly harsh for such a non-violent crime. The judge explicitly stated that he *wanted to send a signal* to traders involved in illegal trading. Tom had maintained his innocence throughout the trial, but he was now heading to prison.

I was crushed, as I knew very well that an acquittal for Tom would have practically guaranteed my own freedom. As Tom was taken to jail, the world was divided. On one side there were the banker-bashers, who considered Tom to have been a privileged person who abused his position of power, and who should be punished accordingly. On the other hand, there were the people who simply couldn't understand why the prosecution was on such a mission to punish one person for what was evidently industry-wide standard practice. There must have been a deeper story behind it all.

***

During my preparation for the trial, there was an incident which would turn out to be absolutely crucial for my defence. My lawyers had naturally asked me to inform them of anything that I thought would be relevant for our defence case. As we went through the timeline of events, I told them about Fred's book mismarking and my actions once I realised that something improper was being done.

'This is the perfect example of your character,' said David. 'It shows what you're made of. It clearly demonstrates your tolerance, or rather intolerance, towards dishonesty. This is pure gold for us!' he exclaimed.

The only problem was that there was no recorded evidence of my meeting with Harry back in 2005. For now, it was simply something that I had claimed to be true. The good news was that the SFO was scheduled to interview Harry in the upcoming weeks, so the team had an easy way to address that problem.

'We're going to write a letter to the SFO, explicitly requesting them to ask Harry Harrison about the specific event,' said David. 'Harry needs to answer a simple question: *Did Stelios go to Harry when he realised that Fred was mismarking the book*? It's a simple Yes/No answer,' he concluded and sat back on his chair.

David knew full well that this could potentially be their strongest weapon in the upcoming trial, and he was going to do everything in his power to make sure they utilised it fully.

The letter was duly sent to the SFO and a few weeks later Harry was interviewed by them. My team were astounded to see that the particular question we had requested had not in fact been mentioned at all. We were stunned actually, given the directness of our request to the SFO on this particular matter. We decided to give the prosecution the benefit of the doubt and offered them another chance to correct their mistake. Once more, we requested that the SFO ask Harry that specific question, thus getting his official response in writing.

The SFO's subsequent response was astonishing. They had refused to ask Harry the question, citing a seemingly outrageous reason for not doing so: *It was not relevant to the investigation.*

'Not relevant!' shouted David, nervously pacing up and down the meeting room. 'It's the perfect example of Stelios's inner rulebook, so to speak. It's totally relevant evidence of his attitude towards dishonesty. He's being accused of being dishonest, how is this not relevant??!' he howled.

It was a terribly disappointing turn of events for me and my defence. The SFO was supposed to be completely impartial when collecting the relevant material for the trial, but in this case, I felt that their bias was unquestionable.

'It's a joke!' I shouted. 'You simply cannot have the SFO being the investigator *and* the prosecutor on a case. I think that there will always exist a deep conflict of interest, no matter what they say or how they claim to be truly impartial.'

It was now becoming obvious to me that the SFO was going to use every trick in the book in order to win the trial. I simply couldn't see a quest for the truth or justice here. They needed to secure convictions, and they would probably do everything in their power to achieve that. Without Harrison's response to the specific question, my team and I would have to fly blind. Harry would certainly be asked the question during cross-examination, but there was no way of knowing what his response would be.

'David, you're going to ask Harry whether I went to him when I realised that Fred was mismarking the book, right?' I asked. I knew the answer to that question, but I wanted to find out all the available options.

'You bet,' said David. 'We're going to build up the questioning in a very calm and friendly way. Harrison needs to be our ally or as close to our ally as possible, given that he is a prosecution witness,' he continued.

'That makes sense,' I replied. 'Guys, I really like Harry, and I think that he likes me too. I know deep inside that if he had a free hand, he would help us greatly.'

'That's possible, Stelios,' acknowledged David. 'Now, I'll do my very best to get him nicely prepared for that big question. However, we have no idea what he's going to reply.'

'Understood. What do you think the possible answers could be?' I enquired.

'Well, the first – and unfortunately the least likely – alternative is that he goes on to confirm your story. If he does that then he will personally be in trouble. You see, Gourtay was dismissed for making losses, which is quite a benign reason for terminating someone. He was not dismissed for mismarking the book, which is a serious offense and is classified as gross misconduct. If they had dismissed him for mismarking, there would have been a proper enquiry to find out who else was involved, and it would also have very negative repercussions on Gourtay's career. They chose not to go down that route because they probably wanted to keep things simple. Also, Gourtay must have had some powerful friends, for sure,' continued David with his on-the-fly analysis.

'Yeah, no surprise there,' I said, with a disgusted look on my face.

'We can safely assume that Harrison will not answer this way,' continued David after taking a sip of water.

'The second alternative is that he completely denies the incident took place. He can easily claim that you never went to him, and that will be the end of it. This is the most likely outcome, and unfortunately the worst one for us.'

'I can see how this avenue would keep things really simple for him,' I reflected. 'You know, I'm usually a pretty good judge of character, and I think that Harry will have some trouble doing that. He knows I'm a good person and I believe that he wouldn't stab me in the back like that.'

'Right,' said David. 'That brings us to the third alternative, which is that he gives a half-way answer. He could very well say that he doesn't remember, or something similar. This way he wouldn't actually answer with a simple 'Yes' or 'No,' and he wouldn't feel like he's a back-stabbing snake.'

'Well, let's hope Harry has at least *some* dignity and self-respect left,' I grumbled.

***

During the pre-trial preparations, I noticed something peculiar. The events in question had taken place many years back, so it was often difficult to remember much of the material that had been disclosed. I would often look at some of the emails and not recognise them at all, while others were particularly characteristic and memorable. There were also some communications that I distinctly remembered having taken place, but which were not included in the material provided by the SFO. There were several communications between myself and Fred which were simply not there, and I was quick to point this out.

'I'm pretty sure there are a number of missing emails and recorded conversations, especially between myself and Fred. How can they not be here?' I enquired.

'This folder contains every single piece of evidence that was given to us by the SFO,' Roland confirmed without hesitating.

One of Roland's duties in this case was to collect the evidence, and he was extremely diligent. He didn't make mistakes – that was definitely the whole bunch of documents.

'Well, I am convinced that some items are missing,' I continued as I started getting visibly annoyed. 'How does the evidence collection and disclosure process work exactly, Roland?'

'It's actually quite simple,' said Roland in his steady and reassuring voice. 'The SFO asks Barclays to perform a search using certain criteria such as dates, senders, recipients and keywords. The bank then does the required search and collects every single piece of digital, audio and other material that matches the specified parameters. Once all the data is collected, the bank delivers the information bundle to the SFO. Finally, given that this may involve literally millions of documents, the SFO goes through them and discards items which are judged to be irrelevant for this trial. The resulting bundle is what the SFO give us and this is what we have right here.'

As Roland finished talking, he glanced at me and saw an unmistakeable change in my demeanour. I looked like I was a volcano ready to erupt. My face turned red and my eyes opened wide, as I stood there processing what Roland had just said.

'Wait, wait, let me get this straight…' I mumbled and put my hand up, clearly getting agitated. 'So, you mean that the bank has control over what information gets given to the SFO? The *same bank* that has a vested interest to ensure that its senior managers escape unharmed from this mess? The *same bank* that can easily select which material to provide – or even worse, to hypothetically tamper with material and no one would ever know – in order to serve up a few people like myself as convenient scapegoats? *Are you bloody kidding me?*' I screamed at the top of my voice.

I was standing up and in a state of rage.

'Not only that,' I continued furiously, 'but following that step, the SFO can then move in and discard whatever items they deem to be irrelevant? That's an absolute travesty! They might as well skip the trial and lock me up already!'

I was absolutely fuming. I could clearly see that I was in dire straits. All along I had maintained my faith in the UK judicial system, hoping that the system would actually be my ally in this adventure. I always believed that I would have a fair trial and a realistic chance of success. *Innocent until proven guilty, remember?*

At that moment though, I realised that the system could be easily rigged against myself and my co-defendants. I was accused of being in a conspiracy, but the real conspiracy was now becoming crystal clear to me.

***

The months went by and I continued preparing myself for the upcoming trial in early 2016. I had been working hard with David and the rest of the legal team, and things had been progressing smoothly. We had gone through all the disclosure documents and had settled on a robust defence strategy. Thankfully for me, the strategy was effectively to tell the truth and not deviate at all from it.

Many barristers have at some point in their career worked with defendants who have things to hide, or who are in trouble due to certain pieces of evidence. In my case there were no such problems, only a few 'colourful' communications that could be simply attributed to my Mediterranean temperament. One of the toughest aspects of a court trial is when a defendant gives evidence; simply telling the truth would make that task a lot easier for me.

While preparations on the legal side were progressing well, things on a personal side were sluggish. I couldn't bear the thought of being away from Semiramis and the girls, who by the time of the trial would be three and two years old respectively. Semiramis dreaded having to spend so many weeks away from her husband, and this remained a frequent source of worry and sadness for her. The two of us made plans for how we would tackle the situation, hoping that I would be able to travel back home perhaps every other weekend during the trial. We both were strong mentally and although we had decided to fight, we were fully aware of all possible outcomes.

'What's the maximum sentence for this charge?' Semiramis asked one day.

'The theoretical maximum is ten years in prison,' I replied. 'However, my lawyers are telling me that in my case, given my position and seniority at the time, it would most likely be considerably less. They think four or five years, tops. It's so frustrating because if Tom had received a shorter sentence we would already be starting off from a lower number. But it is what it is, I guess.'

'OK, four or five years. How much of that would you have to serve, if convicted?' continued Semiramis, trying to quantify the risk further.

'Typically, if convicts show good behaviour during their time, they get released after serving half the sentence.'

'Good. That's already much better – two, maybe two and a half years. If that's the worst-case scenario, we'll get through it. One step at a time, my love.'

Semiramis did her best to sound optimistic, trying to appease me but also herself. It was actually working.

'Absolutely,' I said, carrying on from her thoughts. 'If I have to spend two years in prison, I'll just read a bunch of books and work out every day. When I get out, I'll be really intelligent and totally ripped, you won't recognise me!' I said to her jokingly, and we both had a good laugh about it.

We were both determined to stay focused on the job at hand, and to keep our spirits high.

***

January 2016

The dreaded year of 2016 had finally arrived, and I was now fully ready for the trial. I had arranged for my parents to help Semiramis with the kids while I was away. Dimitri and Kallirroi were both anxious about the whole prospect, but they tried hard not to show it. They were determined to be as much help as they could until their boy came back home for good.

The final piece of the puzzle before the April trial was the trial of the six brokers who were accused of conspiring with Tom Hayes to manipulate LIBOR. They were all money brokers and were being tried separately from him. The SFO had previously managed to secure Tom's conviction, but this case was going to be several orders of magnitude tougher for David Green and his people.

The six men were very likeable people and far removed from the stereotypical banker type. Most of them were of humble origins and had quite a pleasant demeanour. It was going to be an expensive twelve-week trial for the UK taxpayers, as many of the defendants were on Legal Aid and their legal costs were fully covered by the government.

As the trial progressed, it became obvious that the defendants firmly had the upper hand in the proceedings. The prosecution's case was unclear at best, and their arguments were weak. The SFO's main line of attack was that these brokers had been part of a dishonest criminal conspiracy, but the facts failed to match the allegations.

The final nail in the coffin was when the men all gave evidence, one by one delivering excellent and convincing all-round performances. When someone is telling the truth it's usually crystal clear in their eyes, their body language and their general demeanour. There was very little doubt in the jurors' minds; these men were all telling the truth.

The jury began deliberating in late February 2016 and merely a day later they acquitted five of the six defendants. Upon hearing the verdicts, the defendants were understandably emotional, cheering in relief and hugging each other. The following day the jury reached the sixth and final 'not guilty' verdict, sealing a slam dunk result for the defence. The verdicts – and the sheer speed of reaching them – dealt a devastating blow to the British authorities. I had a glimmer of hope that this result would cause the SFO to reconsider the subsequent LIBOR trials.

Upon their exit from the court building, many of the brokers spoke to the press and expressed their utter frustration at how the whole case was handled by the SFO. Their lawyers argued that the men were being made scapegoats for a flawed system. One of the brokers said about the case:

'...it has turned our lives upside down. Realistically, we should never have been here. We feel we've been scapegoated. There are things to be answered but we are not the ones who should be answering them.'

Another one of the brokers said:

'...the case has been a sham. The SFO didn't investigate it properly and didn't listen.'

David Green's response to these comments was:

'...nobody could sensibly suggest that these charges should not have been brought and considered by a jury.'

A predictable response, but a very subjective one, and one which didn't really answer any of the burning questions.

The verdicts also showed that something had gone very wrong with Tom Hayes's trial. The six brokers were supposed to have been party to a dishonest agreement with Tom, but the jury decided that this was in fact not the case. Consequently, the big question had become: *Whom did Tom Hayes conspire with? How can he be guilty of 'conspiracy to defraud' if he hadn't actually conspired with anyone?* The February verdicts posed all sorts of questions that the SFO needed to steer well clear of.

***

In October 2014, news broke out that Peter Johnson had pleaded guilty to the charge. My lawyers were mystified when they heard of Johnson's guilty plea, but they didn't waste much time trying to figure out why he had done that. Maybe he had negotiated a good deal with the SFO, or perhaps the stress had got to him – they had no way of knowing. The issue now was to determine what effect it would have on my defence. After some thought and debate, the team inevitably concluded that it was a definite negative development which could certainly harm all the defendants' chances.

During the trial, the SFO's main task would be to actually prove that a conspiracy took place; PJ's guilty plea had just given them this task on a silver platter. Interestingly, for someone as junior as myself, there was a remote possibility that PJ's plea could be used to my advantage. David noted that the jury usually want to see someone who is guilty in fraud cases, just so that they are satisfied that at least one person will take the fall for the alleged crime. I secretly hoped that for this trial, PJ would turn out to be the only guilty person.

I was now ready for the trial and I felt relief that the date had nearly arrived. Two years of preparations had really taken their toll on me. I wanted to just get it over with, but there was meant to be yet another unexpected turn of events. Twelve days before the trial was due to start, I was in Athens when I received an unexpected phone call from Steve.

'Stelios, it's Steve. I have some very important news to tell you,' he said very seriously.

'Good news or bad news?' was my concerned reply, sensing Steve's troubled tone.

'It's bad news, I'm afraid. David was diagnosed with acute Crohn's syndrome yesterday and he's been instructed by his doctor to take the next six months off work. He needs to fully rest, which means that he will not be able to represent you at the trial.'

I was obviously very sad to hear about David's health problem, but yet again, I couldn't believe my rotten luck. From the beginning of the investigation, I had felt that whenever there was a crossroad – a point where things could go in a good way or a bad way for me – I always got the short end of the stick. I was enormously disappointed, but as always, I composed myself and tried to assess the damage.

'What are my options now, Steve? The trial is only twelve days away,' I asked, realising that getting upset wouldn't help anyone at this point.

'There are two scenarios now. *One,* we find someone else who can represent you, but this is only a remote possibility. This person must not only be able to represent you, but they should also be willing to do so,' explained Steve.

'I understand,' I said, clearly disappointed with the first option presented to me.

'*Two,*' continued Steve, 'they proceed with the trial of the other five defendants and try you on your own later this year. This would be a particularly bad scenario for us, because it's usually an uphill struggle when defendants are tried on their own. You always need to have perspective in a trial and being tried alongside the other five defendants is extremely important for you,' concluded Steve.

'I see. To sum it up, I'm stuck between a rock and a hard place, right?' I half-joked.

I had tried to be positive throughout the previous two years, but I was now getting desperate. Little did I know, what had just transpired with David was probably one of the biggest strokes of luck I'd ever had.

***

Two days after the shocking news about David's health, my phone rang once again. I looked at my phone's screen and saw the familiar UK phone number of my lawyers. I sighed and picked up, expecting the usual barrage of bad news to continue.

However, as soon as Steve started talking, I instantly noticed a tone of positivity in his voice. I had actually forgotten what good news sounded like. There had been a totally unexpected turn of events, which had resulted in finding a barrister who could represent me after all.

John Ryder was a leading defence barrister and greatly respected in the British legal community. He was a Queen's Counsel – the highest honour in the profession – often referred to as a '*QC*' or a '*Silk*' due to the silk gown that these barristers wore in court. He was considered by many to be the very best in the field, consistently being ranked by the relevant directory as a leading silk. He was in his fifties with white hair, impeccable dress sense and a perfect British accent. He was extremely eloquent and well-spoken. So much so, that I would subsequently often joke about John being the '*James Bond of barristers.*'

John had originally been unavailable to represent me because he was already involved in the UBS broker trial. However, that trial was now over, and John had no other obligations over the following months. Crucially, he was deeply familiar with the LIBOR case and was one of only a handful of people who would be in a position to replace David as my lead counsel. I soon realised the magnitude of my lucky strike; due to David's inability to continue (no offence to his own legal skills) I was actually going to be represented by possibly the most well-suited and skilled person on the planet.

Chapter Fourteen
The Start-Up Project

By 2016, I had already been involved in the creation of a start-up company with big aspirations. The sequence of events that had led to that point was quite unexpected, but I always thought that nothing happens by accident. I believed that people can achieve anything they want, as long as they desire it enough and work hard for it. I characteristically often said that the universe would always conspire to make wishes come true, as long as they are clearly defined and vividly pursued.

Here's how the events unfolded, leading to the start of this project. In early 2012, I had been back in Greece for a few months and was looking for ways to restart my career. Due to the ongoing investigation, going back to a job within a financial institution was impossible, so I had to find alternative avenues. Semiramis was pregnant at the time, so I was preparing for a life being a stay-at-home dad, and the prospect filled me with happiness. Nevertheless, I wanted to do more. I had considerable energy inside me and was eager to get back to work.

One day, I did what I always had done whenever I wanted to make a considerable change in my life – I made my order to the universe. I sat down in front of a mirror and explicitly stated what I wanted: '*I want to be able to take care of my children at home, but I also want to have a flexible, rewarding occupation. This occupation will complement my family's income and it will bring me the satisfaction of being a part of an exciting project.*'

Having made my declaration, I started thinking about how I would actually make it come true. The obvious answer came to me almost instantly, and it was through social media. I created an account on Twitter, the most popular social media platform for finance professionals at the time, and started sharing information. I spent the next few months contributing market views and trading ideas, eventually building a considerable network of contacts. I was always willing to voice my thoughts and engage in discussions and debates, something that I think made me likeable and popular within a relatively short period of time. I actually found the whole process very stimulating and satisfying, so my pace continued unabated.

Among the contacts I had made, there was one individual, Steve, whom I really got along well with. Our views, characters and general attitudes matched extremely well, and we very much enjoyed engaging in conversation. Steve was also Greek and lived in Athens, so it made perfect sense that at some point we finally met up in person.

We started socialising with our wives and acquaintances, and eventually bonded as friends. From a certain point onwards, we communicated on a daily basis and helped each other with markets, personal issues and anything else that came along. I had only known Steve for a few months, but I felt confident that he was going to be a friend for life.

I had also met an American man called Blake, via the Twitter platform. Blake had been the chief currency strategist at a major online brokerage, and he was extremely well known in the markets. He had over twenty years of experience and a very impressive track record. Blake and I interacted a few dozen times on social media, but apart from that we really didn't know each other in great depth. We did, however, have mutual admiration in terms of market knowledge and trading skills.

One day in 2015, Steve rang me up asking to meet up and discuss something important. When we sat down, Steve got straight to the point.

'OK, there's something really exciting I want to talk to you about,' he said.

'Sure Steve, what's it about?' I asked curiously.

'Blake has had enough with his employer and wants to start his own company.'

'Wow, I had no idea that he wasn't happy there. What are his plans?'

'He wants to create a start-up company which will provide analysis for a number of financial instruments. He wants to cover all major analysis types – something that isn't being done by anyone at the moment,' continued Steve, speaking practically without taking a breath.

'That makes sense, it would fill a pretty clear gap in the market.'

'That's the idea. But most importantly, Blake wants this service to help people. He's sick and tired of seeing the markets become so one-sided. Big banks and all these new algorithmic trading companies, which of course are owned by the banks, have massively skewed the odds in their favour. They are using superfast speeds and expensive infrastructure, coupled to some questionable ethical tactics, to slowly push the average retail trader to extinction. Blake is sick of this – and frankly I'm with him on this 100% – and he wants to try and redress the balance.'

'I agree, man!' I said excitedly. 'Algos were already a big problem when I was still a market-maker in London. I still remember what a huge difference it made when the first algo came into the Short Sterling futures market; it was manic! Wouldn't it be great if there was such a company, which could help the little guy in this unjust battle? So, tell me, how can I help in all this?'

'Well, Blake has asked for you specifically, actually. He's been very impressed by your knowledge and most importantly your positive attitude. He's seen you on social media sharing your views and helping others with opinion and analysis, and he thoroughly liked it. He wants you to be a partner in the company, along with him and myself, and he wants you to be our Macro analysis expert.'

I nodded slowly, taking in all the information, and feeling honoured to be approached by a seasoned veteran like Blake. The fact that my good friend,

Steve, would also be a partner made the decision an instant no-brainer. That very moment marked the inception of the project, which the three of us would work on with great excitement and motivation going forward.

Chapter Fifteen
The Trial

April 2016

I arrived at Heathrow airport on Saturday 2nd April 2016, just two days before the trial was due to start. I grabbed my two black suitcases and started walking briskly down the winding airport corridors, my long grey coat flowing behind me as I took big strides forward. I had my favourite AC/DC playlist playing full blast on my powerful wireless headphones, with every beat wholly in sync with my footsteps. As I carried on walking, I started to feel confident. My sole focus was to get through the twelve weeks, get the acquittal, and go back home to my family. I was going to stay at my brother Constantine's flat, so at least I would be in a familiar environment with great company for the duration of the trial.

***

LIBOR Trial: Week One

Roland had warned me about the first day of court. There would undoubtedly be a number of reporters from television channels, newspapers and other publications. The cameras and flashlights would all be pointed on me, so I would have to be mentally prepared for the experience.

I initially met up with Roland and Steve a block away, before we all headed towards the building together for the very first time. It was a move that would make it slightly easier for my first encounter with the paparazzi, and it was in fact pretty standard practice.

The three of us started walking towards the building side by side, at a steady pace. As soon as the reporters spotted me, they flocked around me trying to take the best possible shot. Some were calling out my name and asking questions, but I kept looking straight ahead and refused to interact with them. At some point they nearly made physical contact with me, pushing and shoving each other in the process.

I was nervous inside, but I tried not to show it at all. I had seen video clips of famous people entering courtrooms, and they invariably had very serious expressions in their faces. I had noticed that such expressions sometimes belied a sense of guilt, and I wanted to avoid that at all costs. I had decided to always keep a regular, straight-faced expression, no matter what was happening around me. I wanted to send out a message that I wasn't afraid – I was confident, and I had absolutely nothing to hide.

Southwark Crown Court was a 1980s building with fifteen courtrooms and the place where most of the UK's serious fraud cases were tried. It was a particularly ugly building, built with plain beige bricks and littered with many small windows across its sides. It was as if it was purposely built to look unpleasant and gloomy, to reflect the psychology of the accused people who walked through its doors. This is where my legal team and I would be spending the majority of our time during the following twelve weeks.

As the three of us finally entered the big revolving doors, I breathed a sigh of relief. Those final thirty steps had been particularly difficult, and thankfully that experience would actually not be repeated again. The next day there were only a couple of reporters present, and by the third day there were none.

Courtroom number two was on the second floor of the building and I soon found myself standing right outside its entrance. To the left of the door, there was a TV monitor which showed the trial currently in session. The name 'Contogoulas' was displayed on that monitor, alongside the other four defendants' names. I glanced at it and let out a short sigh. I had sometimes imagined being famous when I was younger, but my newly-found fame was unfortunately for all the wrong reasons.

I entered the double doors and for the first time in my life, I was standing inside a British court of justice. It was larger than I had imagined. There was dark brown wood everywhere in the room, as all desks and filing cabinets were made out of it. Not only that, but the walls were also covered in wooden panels from the floor level until mid-height. At the far end of the room, there was the row that housed the judge and some support staff, as well as the desk used when people gave evidence. This judge's seat was on an elevated level and towered commandingly above everyone else.

The middle of the room was taken up by three rows of desks where the prosecution and defence barristers sat, along with all the supporting lawyers. There were five defence teams on this trial – one per defendant – and there would be typically at least two or three representatives of each defendant present in court at any point in time. On the left-hand side of the courtroom was the public gallery, where members of the public could sit and observe the proceedings. In high-profile cases such as this one, those twenty or thirty seats would often be jam-packed with people.

Finally, in the back of the room was the 'dock', where the defendants sat. This was a completely closed area with walls made of thick wood and glass on the top half. It had to be able to hold violent or potentially dangerous criminals, so it was made to be secure. The dock had a door which could be locked, but during trials involving non-violent crime – such as the LIBOR trials – this door remained open for the duration.

I slowly made my way towards the dock and saw the other defendants already sitting there. I realised that I hadn't seen them since I had left Barclays in 2006, except Ryan whom I had actually never met before. There were a few available seats and I purposely picked one in the front row. I wasn't going to sit in the background or try to hide. I wanted the jury to be able to clearly see my face, as I strongly believed that a person's face always reveals his true self. We were told that we would sit in the same seat for the duration of the trial – to help jurors – and I immediately selected the one at the front and centre of the dock.

I greeted my co-defendants one by one, and when it came to Jay I leaned over and shook his hand. I still felt a lot of respect for him, as he had been one of the people who always supported me at Barclays. Jay looked at me and nodded, without saying a word. We both knew that we had a long and perilous road ahead of us.

I had something in common with the other men in the dock: we had young families to take care of, and in Jay's case, he had another baby on the way. Just like in Tom Hayes's case and his young son, yet more toddlers were at risk of spending the next few years without their fathers.

What cruel injustice, I thought to myself, as I looked at the men sitting beside me. *I'm not going to let these wicked people separate me from my family*, I thought and psyched myself up. *If it's war they want, that's exactly what they're going to get.*

A few minutes later, the court clerk stood up and knocked on the door at the far side of the room. That was the cue for everyone present to stand up. '*All rise!*' she said, as Judge Leonard entered the room and headed to his chair. He was the stereotypical judge; a slightly chubby man in his sixties with white hair and thick eyebrows. He wore glasses on his wrinkly round face, and he had a near-permanent serious look. Judge Leonard was a well-respected judge, and an apparently good choice for a case of such high importance. Being the judge, he wore a distinctive white wig and a black and purple robe. He placed his laptop and folders on the desk and sat down, and the rest of the room followed suit. The trial had officially begun.

***

The prosecution consisted of three barristers, which were all required given the size and importance of the trial. James Hines was the lead QC and a particularly well known and competent barrister. Emma Deacon was the supporting QC and one of the up-and-coming stars in the profession. Dominic Lewis was their surprisingly likeable junior whose main responsibility was to support the two leading barristers.

James and Emma were both exclusively prosecuting barristers and had a great deal of experience in such cases. The SFO had selected two of their most highly ranked individuals for this case, a fact that highlighted just how desperately they wanted to win. Hines was a man in his fifties who was characterised by a steady and methodical manner. Everything he did – walking, reading, talking – was slow and meticulous. He was a man who wouldn't miss a single detail or overlook even the tiniest of clues. The defence teams had a great deal of respect for him and knew full well that he was going to be a formidable opponent.

I found Emma Deacon to be quite unlike Hines in many ways. She might have been more junior than him, but as some of the defence barristers had distinctly said about her, '*she is no slouch.*' She had a quite particular style, being very articulate and speaking every single word slowly but clearly. She often smiled and tried to connect with the jury, in contrast to Hines who was clearly there to get a job done in a sequence of well-defined steps. Hines would read from his notes in a steady and monotonous manner, but Deacon was a lot more colourful. She would frequently raise her voice considerably in order to emphasise certain points, and she would also clearly show emotion.

On many occasions she would smile and laugh at defendants' answers that she found to be lacking, hoping to influence the jury to her direction. She would also visibly get annoyed when the defendants wouldn't give the answer she was hoping for. She was a tall, slim woman with black hair and a white skin complexion. Her face matched her character well, with angular features and regularly frowned eyebrows. John was familiar with Emma's work and he knew from the start that she could be unpredictable – she could turn out to be a dangerous opponent but was also susceptible to hot-blooded mistakes.

***

The first two days of the trial were taken up by jury selection, an extremely dull and purely procedural stage. A sample of around eighty people had been summoned for jury duty and were called out in random, one after the other. When a person's name was called out, they were directed to take a seat at the jury section. If there was a particular reason why they could not be a juror in that particular case, they were required to walk up to the judge and explain to him the precise reasons why that was the case. It was going to be a very long trial by regular standards and many of the potential jurors were clearly unwilling to be a part of it.

Jury selection was concluded by the second day, having ended up with the required twelve jurors and two reserves. If any of the jurors needed to be replaced during the first two weeks, the reserve jurors would step in as replacements.

As the jurors took their seats, I noticed something slightly worrying – they didn't actually look like a representative sample of the local English population. They were overwhelmingly of a young age and, as I subsequently understood, a good number of them were unemployed or on benefits. During the following twelve weeks, they were going to be told by the prosecution about the highly paid defendants' alleged conspiracy. Our annual compensation would be shown and emphasised, with the prosecution constantly reminding the jurors that they were amounts most people would never see in their whole lifetime. The other defendants and I would undoubtedly be painted as privileged individuals who were greedy, corrupt and who broke the law in order to get even richer. Suddenly, I realised that we already had a mountain to climb with this particular jury.

Within the first couple of weeks, I noticed another surprising and disappointing development. Judge Leonard was a well-respected and established judge, with a long and distinguished career behind him. My team had repeatedly told me that Leonard was a good judge who would ensure that both sides got a fair chance to put forward their arguments. However, as the first weeks came to a close, I wasn't so sure about that. There had already been a number of legal arguments addressed by the judge, and he distinctly favoured the prosecution on nearly every occasion. Whenever there were contested items – especially, if they were important – the prosecution would get their way. In my view, Judge Leonard's stance was consistently harsh against the defence, throughout the trial. *Was there a hidden agenda? Was it just my impression?* Those were questions that unfortunately I could not answer.

***

Our team had been given a designated meeting room where we could spend out-of-court time to work on the case, or to just hang around during short breaks. It was a tiny dark rectangular room which could only fit three chairs, so if the whole team was to meet, two of us would have to be standing up. It was not ideal, but it would have to do.

There was a coffee shop on the ground floor of the building, but its coffee quality was universally considered to be mediocre at best. On the very first day, John expressed his utter dislike for it and suggested we find another solution. In fact, he had a Nespresso machine in his office which he volunteered to bring in for our everyday use in court. The team unanimously applauded the idea, clearly agreeing on the atrocious quality of the in-house offering.

I immediately took the initiative and bought a wide array of coffee flavours, as well as stacks of paper espresso cups. From that day on, the team could enjoy a tasty hot cup of coffee whenever they fancied. I even offered coffee to members of the other defence teams, eventually turning the meeting room into what they all jokingly called '*Café Stelios*'.

***

During the trial, I was destined to meet two reporters who would influence my life in very different ways.

Anne was a reporter from a leading publication who was assigned to cover the LIBOR trials. She was a young professional in her late twenties, with long blond hair and blue eyes. She tried to approach me from the very early stages of the trial, exchanging a few words with me every now and then. She was always polite, courteous and wore a pretty smile, so it was easy for her to make a good first impression.

Andy Verity was a distinguished television reporter, with a long and distinguished track record, and the BBC economics correspondent at the time. He was a man in his early forties with a great deal of experience, and he had been closely following the preceding Hayes and UBS broker trials. Andy was keenly interested in the LIBOR trial, often attending court from the public gallery and constantly taking notes. From the outset it became clear that he was quite frustrated with the LIBOR trial, and he was particularly upset with the prosecution's apparent desire to scapegoat a handful of juniors making innocuous and standard-practice requests. He probably saw no logical explanation why they had taken this course rather than going after the 'Lowballing' incidents. It seemed to me that the intention to keep senior management away from harm was obvious to him as well, and he wanted to ensure that the world was also fully aware of it. Andy was conscious that I was not allowed by law to discuss the trial with him while it was still in progress, so we kept the conversation very casual. His ongoing support and frequent presence in court quickly earned my respect, forming a solid base for our relationship going forward.

***

LIBOR Trial: Week Two

Following the lengthy jury selection process, the first stage of the trial was the opening speeches. John had warned me that this would be one of the toughest parts of the trial for me. During the next few days, the prosecution would present their arguments continuously and uninterrupted. It would be a barrage of accusations against the defendants, many of which could be inaccurate or border on being untrue. The defence would simply have to sit there and wait for the prosecution to finish, before they could fight back.

As expected, the prosecution followed an intensely aggressive strategy. They were extremely attacking and hostile towards the defendants, in an effort to make a substantial first impression with the jury. They repeatedly called us dishonest and greedy, while they spoke about 'billions of dollars' and 'eye-watering sums' being involved. They claimed that the traders put money before honesty and that they essentially cheated, in a relentless personal attack.

The prosecution tried to hit all the right notes and make the jury engage and agree with them, with Hines even hinting that this practice of LIBOR requests may have been one of the causes of the 2008 financial crisis. That was not the case of course, but in the heat of the moment even such subtle hints could stick in the jurors' minds. Hines knew exactly what he was doing and didn't seem to hesitate to stretch the boundaries of allowed practice. Such a strategy can sometimes be a double-edged sword, as it can only really work when the prosecution's case is absolutely rock solid.

At the end of the three days, the prosecution had tried to demolish the defendants' characters in a relentless barrage of attacking statements. No one could know for sure if it had worked at that point, apart from the jurors themselves. After three days of punishment, it was finally time for the defendants to counter attack. The defence barristers took turns, each one putting forward their clients' case.

When John took centre stage, I thought that he was on a completely different level from the other barristers. Maybe I was biased, but his approach and delivery seemed to be several notches higher than anyone else's. He started out in a smooth fashion, describing my background, my education and career progression up to the point where I was employed at Barclays. He went through my responsibilities and evolution at the bank, step by step, until he got to the part where I was moved to the USD Short Term Swaps book.

John paused and placed extra focus on the meeting between Gourtay, Johnson and me – this was a pivotal part of the defence and he was going to take his time making it crystal clear to the jury. He reiterated that the meeting had been done openly, casually, with no intent of concealment and in front of several other people. John stressed that both Gourtay's and Johnson's attitude towards LIBOR requests was completely normal and totally relaxed. He then proceeded to make it absolutely clear that there had been no training, directive, rule or regulation which could possibly have alerted me to the potential impropriety of such requests.

'Ladies and gentlemen of the jury,' said John, 'how was a junior supposed to know that this was wrong, in the context of all the relevant information, training and procedures? Would he somehow learn this, perhaps by *osmosis*?' he joked, although that word was probably totally foreign for the majority of the jurors.

Throughout his opening speech, John had been clear, steady and easy to understand. With the help of James and Karl, his opening arguments had been carefully laid out, laying down the foundations for the all-important examination-in-chief a few weeks down the road.

Note: 'examination-in-chief' is the first part of giving evidence, where the defendant is being questioned by his or her own barrister.

John had kept a serious and authoritative tone, mixing it up with just the right amount of humour to keep the jury interested. The jurors seemed to follow him well, engaging with his arguments, taking notes, and often laughing at his impeccably-timed jokes. The nature of the trial was very technical and specialised, and John's worry was always the possibility of the jury failing to follow and 'switching off' due to tiredness. The general feeling was that John had struck the balance very well, much to my personal satisfaction.

***

LIBOR Trial: Week Three

With the opening speeches completed, the next part was the really tedious one. All the evidence had to be introduced, which effectively meant that each and every document was read in court, out loud. There were hundreds of often repetitive items, read by a person with arguably the most monotonous and mind-numbing voice on the planet. It was a few days of torture for the jurors, who were visibly tired and eager to see the end of it.

Salvation came soon after, but what came next wasn't a great deal better either. It was the turn of a Barclays compliance officer to give evidence, outlining exactly how the data collection process was structured and took place. He actually confirmed my fears, indicating that the filtering, collection and delivery of relevant material were all controlled by the bank. He described how the whole process was secure and complete, but I just shook my head in amazement.

The next person to give evidence was Professor Anderson. He was an economics professor at a leading UK university, with extensive theoretical knowledge on LIBOR. He was a man in his sixties with grey hair and glasses, clearly displaying knowledge and authority. He spoke in a calm and steady voice, gesticulating with his hands whenever he needed to make a particular point. He explained how trillions of dollars of instruments were indexed to LIBOR and just how important the index was – and of course he was right about that. He spent just under a day outlining the theory and mechanics behind LIBOR and interest-rate swaps, doing an excellent job putting all these concepts in front of the jury in a simple and effective way.

After a weekend break, the following person to testify was Saul Rowe, and he struck a stark contrast to Professor Anderson in many ways. The difference was crystal clear from the minute he started walking to the stand. He walked nervously, with a hunched back and frequently looking down at his feet. He stood to take the oath and most people in the room could sense that something wasn't right. He sat down and I thought he never really looked comfortable. He adjusted his seat and fiddled with the microphone, clearing his throat a couple of times.

Rowe was the 'market expert', responsible for explaining all the relevant documents to the jury, along with their contents. He had been a trader for a few years in the 1990s and was now working for a specialist company whose job was to provide expert witness services for cases just like the LIBOR case. He was effectively going to be translating many of the lingo-heavy documents into regular English, for the jury's benefit. His job was supposed to be akin to a dictionary – concise, accurate and completely neutral towards either side of the trial.

Rowe was examined in-chief by James Hines, initially going over some of the easier basic concepts. His demeanour did not inspire confidence and he was already starting to show signs of weakness when it came to his knowledge. Hines, being the experienced barrister, would steer him away from dangerous situations or any paths which might uncover serious problems.

When the time came for cross-examination, however, Rowe soon discovered that he had nowhere to hide. Adrian Darbishire, Ryan Reich's barrister, led the charge for the defendants. He relentlessly attacked Rowe, exposing his weaknesses and clearly demonstrating to the jury that he was actually not an expert at all. When Rowe revealed that he didn't fully understand what a simple trading term, such as 'Delta' actually meant, Adrian piled on the pressure.

(Note: 'Delta' is the total risk that a trading book carries, in terms of $ per basis point move. For example, if a book's delta is +$10,000, it means that if the market moves higher by one basis point, the book will make $10,000. Conversely, if the market moves lower by one basis point, the book will lose $10,000).

Saul Rowe's evidence was a nightmare for the prosecution, and they probably couldn't wait for him to be finished. Finally, after a sequence of Adrian's piercing questions, the ordeal was over. At the end of it, the reality was that more questions had been raised than answered. *Could this man seriously be the best available 'expert' witness for the prosecution?* There were undoubtedly dozens of professionals who would have done a much better job than that. Why did the SFO pick this particular individual? What kind of background checks had been done prior to appointing him for this particular trial?

The following two prosecution witnesses were Sally Scutt and John Ewan, who worked at the British Bankers Association (BBA) during the time in question. They had both been called as witnesses on the Hayes trial and while Scutt's evidence had been quite straightforward, Ewan had struggled.

The defence teams were well aware of the Hayes trial and all its intricacies, and thus were well prepared for these two witnesses. Sally Scutt kicked off and immediately went into defence mode. She was a scruffy, middle-aged woman with a long history at the BBA behind her. I was soon convinced that she had been professionally prepared for the event, her answers being laconic and to the point. She was mindful to give the bare minimum amount of information required to answer each question. Her tone was stubbornly constant, never really giving away anything in terms of her psychology. All her answers revolved around a single apparent mantra:

Scutt or the BBA were never aware of trader LIBOR requests. She now considered them to have been improper and had she been made aware of them at the time, she would have taken the appropriate actions.

Put simply, she washed her hands clean of any knowledge or responsibility.

John Ewan was a totally different proposition to Scutt. From the moment he entered the room and started walking towards his seat, he was visibly uncomfortable, just like Rowe. Even during the examination-in-chief by the prosecuting barrister, he seemed nervous and tense. His answers were erratic, uncertain and sometimes inconsistent. The defence teams were busy making notes throughout the examination-in-chief, recognising that he would be one of their best attacking weapons.

Adrian Darbishire led the charge for the defendants once again, wasting no time with a number of penetrating questions. The ultimate target for Adrian was a specific email sent to Ewan by one of the panel banks, following one of the regular biannual FXMMC meetings.

The FXMMC (*Foreign Exchange and Money Markets Committee*) was a steering committee for LIBOR and other related market instruments, comprising of BBA employees, as well as senior people from many of the contributing banks.

The email in question was one where the treasurer of a major British bank told Ewan – in no uncertain terms – that there was always a natural bias for banks to skew their LIBOR submissions according to their commercial interest. Put simply, this email was strong evidence that Ewan was aware of the trader request practice for nearly a decade. This fact was communicated to Ewan in a direct and unambiguous way, and it would be a herculean task to convincingly deny it.

'Mr Ewan, can you please turn to exhibit item MW40015 please,' said Adrian authoritatively.

'OK,' said Ewan, almost whispering. He slowly turned the pages in his folder, but he was merely delaying the inevitable.

'Have you found it?' asked Adrian with a purposeful and impatient tone. He was now really piling on the pressure.

'Yes.'

'The sender of this email, Mr Ewan, is the treasurer of Lloyds Bank in London. He is an extremely senior person, wouldn't you agree?'

'Yes.'

'You are the recipient of this email, aren't you Mr Ewan?'

'Yes.'

'You *do* read your emails, don't you Mr Ewan?' Adrian was now interrogating Ewan as if he was a ten-year-old.

'Yes.'

'When you read your emails, you understand their meaning, don't you Mr Ewan?'

'Yes.' Ewan was giving single-word answers, terrified of what was coming next.

'Can you please read out the third and fourth sentences of this email, starting with *Such high rates...*?' commanded Adrian. He could have read it out himself, but he wanted Ewan to do it for the jury's benefit. He wanted the jury to hear the words coming from Ewan's own mouth.

'Err... right...' mumbled Ewan. '*Such high rates simply reflect the banks' commercial preference. It's just how markets operate, and the BBA shouldn't try to do anything to correct this phenomenon.*'

'Thank you, Mr Ewan,' said Adrian and took a long pause. He wanted those words to sink in with the jury before he continued. He was timing his delivery to perfection.

'Let's take the first part of that passage, shall we, Mr Ewan? *Such high rates simply reflect the banks' commercial preference.* What does that mean to you, Mr Ewan?'

'Well, err... it might mean that banks have an interest one way or another on where these rates are,' said Ewan sheepishly.

'Correct, Mr Ewan. Therefore, the treasurer of Lloyds bank is telling you that they make their LIBOR submissions according to where their commercial preference is. In other words, they look at their own positions and nudge their submissions higher or lower. Don't you agree?' Adrian continued on his relentless assault.

Ewan had been taking a particularly long time to answer most of the questions he was being asked. He would just stare straight ahead into the void, his face all red, and many seconds later he would slowly begin to answer.

'No, I don't think that's what he means with that sentence,' said Ewan to everyone's surprise.

'Well, what do you *think* he means, Mr Ewan?' snapped Adrian.

'I don't know. I mean, reading it here now, what you're suggesting makes sense. But back then, over ten years ago, I just didn't understand it that way,' said Ewan with a distinctly apologetic tone.

'You didn't understand it that way? It's *plain English*, Mr Ewan. You are a British national, aren't you?' came the next scorching question.

'Yes.'

'You do understand *English*, don't you Mr Ewan?'

'Yes.'

'Then how did you not understand those simple few words? These five words: *Reflect. The. Banks. Commercial. Preference.* Tell me which word you're having trouble with, and I'll help, Mr Ewan.'

Adrian was ripping into Ewan, showing absolutely no mercy. He could have made his point in a more benign way, but he had no such desire. He was intent on making his point crystal clear in front of the whole court. It was becoming clear to me that Ewan had probably known exactly what was happening with trader requests at the time, but he had done nothing to stop it. Now that things had got messy, it looked like he was trying to wiggle out of it and in the process, help incriminate a handful of unlucky and innocent traders.

For a minute, I felt sorry for Ewan, witnessing the battering that he was receiving. However, I then remembered that if Ewan had just told the truth, there would have been no case against me. He deserved everything he got.

A few minutes later, Adrian decided that Ewan had had enough. There was no point hammering the point anymore; the jury fully appreciated and understood the issue. Adrian looked at Ewan straight in the eyes and asked one final question.

'Mr Ewan, one last question if I may, and then you'll be happy to hear that you're free to go.'

You could see the relief in Ewan's face, as clear as day.

'Who is the primary stakeholder of the BBA?' Adrian asked.

'The banks.'

'*The banks!*' exclaimed Adrian. He already knew the answer of course, but he was making it purposely theatrical.

'So, let me get this straight, Mr Ewan. The BBA was supposed to be overseeing and coordinating the operation of LIBOR and other instruments. If a bank did something improper or wrong in any way, the BBA was supposed to flag it and take appropriate action, correct?'

'Yes.'

118

'But now you tell us that, effectively, the banks control the BBA.'

'Yes.'

'Don't you see the problem with this picture, Mr Ewan?'

'I understand what you're implying, but that's how things were setup at the time.'

'I suggest, Mr Ewan, that you understood exactly the contents of that email, you knew what the precise implications were, but you decided to do nothing about it.'

'N-No, that's not true,' stuttered Ewan.

'Thank you for your help, Mr Ewan,' said Adrian and sat back down in his seat.

LIBOR Trial: Week Four

Ewan had turned out to be exactly what the defence had hoped for. The judge released him and called the next prosecution witness to give evidence: Nick McLaughlin, the lead investigator on behalf of the SFO. He was the man mainly responsible for bringing the defendants to trial, and I must admit that I particularly disliked him.

He was an Irishman in his late thirties, tall and slim with a full beard and brushy eyebrows. His voice had an achingly monotonous drone which, added to his strong Irish accent, made him utterly dull to listen to. If anyone was suffering from insomnia, this was the perfect antidote.

McLaughlin was examined in-chief by Emma Deacon, who took him step-by-step through the whole investigative process. He explained exactly how things had progressed, outlining many of the relevant details and parameters. He continued giving evidence for over two days; such was the bulk of tedious information that he had to present to the court. At the end of it, the jury were visibly exhausted and had most likely completely lost focus. It was totally expected and understandable. However, they were about to get a real treat during his cross-examination by John Ryder.

John actually started off in a very soft tone, being polite and even slightly predictable. He took McLaughlin through the sequence of events, asking him simple and easy to answer questions. John seemed like a completely different person compared to his opening speech, and it was no accident. He had been lowering the tone of the cross-examination to a level where McLaughlin would feel comfortable. Then, he started pulling out the punches.

'Mr McLaughlin,' said John, 'there is a particular event which the court needs to hear. I am referring to the incident where Mr Contogoulas alerted Mr Harrison when he discovered that his boss at the time, Mr Gourtay, was mismarking the swaps book,' he continued, raising his voice level a couple of notches.

'OK,' was the sheepish reply.

'In your SFO interview with Mr Harrison, you did not in fact ask him whether that event took place or not. Correct?'

'We did not.'

'Why not?'

'Because Mr Gourtay was dismissed due to the large losses incurred to his trading book, not due to mismarking of the book or any other reason.'

'But, Mr McLaughlin, my client explicitly asked you to pose this specific question to Mr Harrison, in writing and on several occasions, did he not?' John enquired.

'Yes, he did.'

'Then, why didn't you ask him?' Ryder's voice was starting to become thunderous.

'We didn't think there was any reason to ask him that specific question,' said McLaughlin.

He knew exactly what was coming and his answers were half-hearted. His voice softened, he started fidgeting and his eyes were looking down on his desk for prolonged periods of time. You didn't have to be an expert in body language to detect that he was extremely uncomfortable. John had him right where he wanted, and he was going to keep pounding until the jury had no doubt about what had actually happened.

'*You didn't think there was any reason?*' said John loudly.

'Mr McLaughlin, I'm not sure if you are fully aware of the situation here,' he continued. 'My client, Mr Contogoulas, is sitting in the dock being accused of dishonesty. He is at risk of going to prison for a long time, he could be taken away from his wife and baby daughters. You, the SFO, are supposed to be an *independent* investigator, carefully considering both sides of the equation when deciding to charge someone of a crime. And yet here you are, with a perfect opportunity to find out what Mr Contogoulas actually did when he found out that something dishonest was occurring, and yet you did nothing. *Nothing*!'

John couldn't help himself, his voice coming out several notches louder than usual. He was outraged.

'We, we… we didn't ask Mr Harrison because Mr Gourtay was dismissed due to the large sums of money that he lost, not… – '

'*I'M NOT ASKING WHY GOURTAY WAS DISMISSED*!' snapped John in a thunderous voice.

He was waving his arms around, showing everyone exactly how he felt about McLaughlin's feeble responses. He was stressing every word, placing much more emphasis than normal.

'Why Mr Gourtay was dismissed has *nothing* to do with what the question is here! The question here is what my client did when he found out that Mr Gourtay was dishonestly mismarking his book. Agreed?'

'Mr Gourtay was dismissed because…'

'For god's sake, Mr McLaughlin, surely you can answer a simple question?'

John's attack had been brutal. He was giving McLaughlin no room to breathe, and quite rightly so. I glanced at the jury who were deeply immersed in the exchange. Some of them looked in disbelief at what was happening. A young lady from the jury looked over at me and smiled at me. Instantly, I felt a wave of optimism take over me. *Surely the jury would be able to see exactly what was going on here? Would they be able to appreciate that myself and the others were perfect scapegoats for the bank and the prosecutor?*

LIBOR Trial: Week Five

Up to this point, the prosecution witnesses had not caused any damage to the defendants, and in fact individuals like Saul Rowe and John Ewan had even helped. The next witnesses, however, could change all that – it was the turn of Barclays senior managers who made up the hierarchy above Fred Gourtay and Jay Merchant between 2005 and 2007.

The three individuals in question were Mike Bagguley, Harry Harrison and Eric Bommensath. Mike was a former Euro Interest Rate Swaps trader and he had been promoted to head the swaps desk after a few successful years. I had heard that he and Eric had worked together many years before at another bank – Bankers Trust – and they knew each other very well. During Mike's tenure as desk head, Jay was his subordinate and reported directly to him. Mike and Jay spent a lot of time sitting next to each other on the floor, and they eventually became very close friends. As Jay himself subsequently described in the trial, they socialised together, went on holidays together and even lived in the same apartment block when Jay moved to New York. They had become good friends and it was no secret within the bank.

Bagguley took the stand first, and he started by reading the words of the standard oath. Jay looked at his good friend from the dock and noticed that Mike wasn't making any eye contact at all. Jay had a good idea of what was coming but he simply refused to believe it. *Would his friend turn his back on him as if all those years meant nothing to him?* The answer was about to genuinely hurt.

Hines led Bagguley through a series of questions, taking the jury through his history and career progression. It was like a well-rehearsed tango session, with both men taking just the right steps, one after the other. Mike was clearly nervous and just like in Rowe's case, his body language showed that he was uncomfortable. His answers lacked spontaneity and the usual punchiness of a confident person. Then came the meat of the questioning by Hines:

'Mr Bagguley, these men at the dock are being charged for conspiracy to defraud, due to the LIBOR requests that were being made from traders to submitters. Did you ever participate in such requests?'

'No.'

'Were you ever aware that these requests took place?'

'No,' he replied, as the volume of his voice started to wane.

'Given your understanding of LIBOR at the time, would you have considered such actions to be improper?'

'I would have done.'

Jay was stunned. He had always maintained that most other EUR swaps traders had also been making requests for years. In fact, Jay said during his evidence later that when Bommensath promoted him to USD desk head, he explicitly told him to copy all those standard practices to the USD desk when he took over. And yet there was Mike, saying the exact opposite in court. *Mike*

121

couldn't possibly say that he knew of or condoned the requests. Doing so would jeopardise his position at the bank and worse, it would instantly make him a co-conspirator – he might as well have walked straight to the dock himself.

It all started to make sense to Jay, but he must have felt extremely hurt and betrayed. Mike was effectively trying to put him in jail to save his own skin – behaviour which had practically become standard practice within the senior banking ranks.

It's no wonder people hate bankers, I thought to myself. *The industry is filled with back-stabbing snakes who will stop at nothing in pursuit of money and power.*

Mike's examination-in-chief eventually finished, and by the end of it he had painted a particularly damning picture of the defendants. He had explicitly told the jury that LIBOR requests were improper and senior management would never had allowed or condoned them. As far as the jury were concerned, these five people in the dock were the 'black sheep' of the story, and everyone else within the bank was squeaky clean. *What utter nonsense.*

***

Hugh Davis, Jay's lead barrister, naturally led Mike's cross-examination. There wasn't much he could really do, given that he wasn't actually able to prove that Bagguley was lying about knowing of the LIBOR request practice. However, there was one particular piece of evidence that was strong, but he would have to explore it to the full if it was to have any weight with the jury.

Davis produced an email chain involving Bagguley and two other Barclays employees. One of the Barclays employees was discussing a particular structured product which had a LIBOR element in it, and casually said that the bank stood to gain if LIBOR moved lower on that particular trade. He then went on to enquire who set LIBOR within the bank and how he made his submission decisions. Bagguley then replied, ending with the phrase '...*so, we ask him to move it lower*?' In the defence's view, that phrase was in clear reference to the LIBOR submission, and it would constitute an action that Bagguley himself was adamantly rejecting as illegal and improper.

Hugh grilled Bagguley on that particular email and Mike's answers were less than impressive. It was a pretty unambiguous sentence with very little scope for misinterpretation – however, Bagguley went to great lengths to convince the room that in the phrase '*ask him to move it lower*', '*it*' referred to something else and not LIBOR. It was a very poor effort and he knew it. However, he had to stick with this plan because it would otherwise be self-incriminating. The jurors were certainly not convinced, and that was plain to see from their body language and facial expressions.

To close the cross-examination, Hugh had a hidden ace up his sleeve. It's common practice for prosecution witnesses to often try to distance themselves from defendants, when they have been close acquaintances or friends. Hugh knew that in Mike's case such an approach was likely, and he was going to give it his best shot.

'Mr Bagguley, how well did you know Jay Merchant?' Hugh asked nonchalantly.

He really wanted Mike to distance himself from Jay, and so he asked the question without making any eye contact. Eye contact would have put more pressure on Mike and would perhaps make him think deeper on the reasons why he was being asked the question.

'We were work acquaintances,' came back the answer from Mike, exactly as Hugh had hoped.

'Mere acquaintances?' Hugh continued, still avoiding eye contact. 'Wouldn't you call yourselves friends? Did you not socialise together?' came the follow-up question.

Mike had already said that they were 'work acquaintances', so he now had to go in that direction.

'No, I wouldn't call us friends. I obviously worked alongside him for some time, so we had got to know each other. But we weren't friends or socialised together. Sure, we would meet up for a few drinks during the generic bank events, but that was it.'

Hugh had teed Mike up and was about to take out the three-wood. This was his big weapon against him, and he was about to take a full swing.

'I understand, Mr Bagguley,' he said and paused deliberately for a few seconds. 'Let's now go back a few years, to your wedding day.'

Hugh was now looking Mike straight in the eyes. He didn't need to read his notes; he knew this part inside out. He continued to stare at Mike purposely, trying to instil fear and doubt into him. As soon as the wedding day was mentioned, Mike knew exactly what was coming. He swallowed hard and his face started to turn red. A few beads of perspiration appeared on his forehead.

'Was it a big wedding, Mr Bagguley?'

'No, there were a few dozen guests.'

'Family and friends, Mr Bagguley?'

'Yes,' said Mike, suddenly wishing he was anywhere but in that courtroom.

'Did you invite Mr Merchant to your wedding, Mr Bagguley?' came the sledgehammer question.

I sat in my chair and couldn't believe my ears. I was aware that Mike and Jay had been good friends, but I didn't know the extent of it. I had absolutely no idea about the wedding and all these details, so I was just as excited as the jury to see this information come to light. Hugh's gaze was still fixated on Mike and I looked at the QC's hands. He was holding something that looked like a big card – I couldn't quite make it out.

Bagguley mumbled something that was incomprehensible.

'Could you please speak up, Mr Bagguley?' continued Hugh in his impeccable English accent.

'Did you invite Mr Merchant to your wedding? Hopefully it's a simple yes or no answer – a person was either there or not there on the day!'

'Y-Yes…' came the virtually inaudible answer.

It was one of those moments like you see in the movies – a gasp came from the jury area, and for a moment the whole courtroom stood completely still. The jurors finally saw Bagguley's true colours, and what I thought was clearly a lie. No person in the world would invite a mere work acquaintance – a subordinate too – to his very intimate wedding. Bagguley was seemingly lying, but would the jury think that he lied during the rest of his evidence as well?

Mike was released by the judge, so he got up from the stand and slowly walked down the corridor towards the exit. As he passed next to the dock, he kept his eyes on the floor and made absolutely no eye contact with any of the defendants. I looked at him, and once again I felt sorry for the prosecution witness. I couldn't imagine ever falling that low as a human being. As I turned my eyes forward again, I saw Hugh walking towards the dock with a sly smile. He was holding that mysterious card in his hand, and when he reached the wall, he thrust it face-up onto the glass pane: it was Mike's wedding invitation that he had sent to Jay all those years ago. It had not just been a well-played poker bluff on Hugh's part – he had the royal flush to back it up.

***

The second prosecution witness and next up in the Barclays hierarchy was Harry Harrison. He was Bagguley's boss during the indictment period, and a man of huge importance as far as I was concerned. The examination-in-chief was uneventful, with Harry answering clearly and concisely, in his usual smooth and calm style. He was very composed and didn't put a foot wrong throughout.

When the time came to cross-examine him, the defence teams had already decided that they were not going to attack him. They had very little to go on, and frankly they thought that Harry would effortlessly rise to the occasion. The only point of interest was for my team, where John would finally get to ask him the burning question about the Gourtay incident.

Mr Harrison, I have a question to ask you on behalf of Mr Contogoulas, said John, composing himself and using all his charm.

'It's a question of particular importance to him, and one that you were not asked by the SFO during your interviews.'

John deliberately slowed down the pace, in order to give Harry some extra time and make him realise the gravity of the situation. I was sitting on the edge of my seat, waiting for the question and the all-important answer. This could be one of our strongest weapons and we needed it badly.

'Mr Harrison, my client alleges that sometime in 2005 Mr Gourtay incurred some heavy losses, but instead of realising them he started mismarking the swaps book in order to hide them. Mr Contogoulas, having discovered what he thought was the mismarking of the book, faced Mr Gourtay and expressed his concern and discomfort. Mr Gourtay summarily dismissed his concerns and told him not to worry about it. However, Mr Contogoulas alleges that he couldn't, and in fact didn't, stop there. He remembers taking you to a meeting room at the back of the

124

trading floor – he even remembers exactly how you sat in the room – and informing you of the situation. He remembers you telling him to put all the marks exactly where he thought the correct values were, and that you would take care of the rest.'

John paused and looked Harrison in the eyes, wearing his most serious face. He wanted to give Harry a few seconds to think before he said something that could ruin his former protégé's life. Finally, there came the big question:

'Mr Harrison did the events that I just described take place in the summer of 2005?'

Harry sat there for a few seconds and processed the question. His face was totally devoid of expression, his voice hadn't changed or faltered throughout the questioning. He was cool as ice. His response came shortly after.

'I'm sorry, but I don't actually remember. It was nearly eleven years ago and for a person of my seniority, such events are not actually of any major importance.'

That was not the answer that John and I wanted to hear. I was stunned, as I really thought that Harry would not abandon me. However, as I sat there filled with disappointment, Harry continued speaking.

'I don't remember this event,' he said, 'but it may have well happened. I mean, it's quite possible – it sounds a lot like something Stelios would do.'

Bingo.

My face lit up; it was as if I had just won the lottery. Realistically, Harry could have never admitted it, but this was unquestionably the next best thing. He may not have remembered the event happening, but he gave the jury exactly what the defence needed: solid approval of my character and ethical compass. John was clearly satisfied with Harry's last comment and he summarily completed his cross-examination, with this practically mandatory concluding statement:

'Mr Harrison, I suggest to the court that you knew exactly what the status quo was at the time, regarding LIBOR requests. It had been standard practice for years, known and condoned by management. You knew all this, but you clearly can't admit to it in this court, because that would implicate you.'

'That …that is false,' said Harry in a low voice.

What a disappointing way for Harry to end his evidence. I was very surprised by the tone of Harry's voice when answering that very last question. If you're being accused of something that's false, wouldn't you answer in a strong voice? Wouldn't you want everyone to know just how wrong and unfair that statement was?

John thanked Harry for his time and slowly sat down in his chair. At that point, the judge called for a much-needed break and left the courtroom. As Harry got up from the stand and started walking down the main corridor, he lifted his eyes towards the dock. He looked directly at me and gave me a slight nod. For me, it was a silent acknowledgement that he had done everything he could to help, given the circumstances. I nodded back and rushed off to meet with my team for the debrief.

***

After the short break, it was time for the third and final Barclays prosecution witness. Eric Bommensath was the most senior of the three, a man who reported directly to the bank CEO and who was immensely experienced. He was a dark-haired Frenchman in his early fifties, but he somehow looked much younger. He was impeccably dressed and had a strong French accent when he spoke.

Of all three Barclays witnesses, he was the most aggressive against the defendants. Whenever there was a question about LIBOR requests and the propriety of it all, he was adamant. He repeatedly stated that he found the practice highly improper and illegal. He dismissed the whole idea of there being a 'range' of possible valid LIBOR values that a submitter could submit on any particular day. He was direct, punchy, and he came across as a very authoritative individual. He condemned the traders' actions and categorically said that had he known such actions were taking place, he would have immediately ended them and commenced the appropriate legal and disciplinary actions. Bommensath continued on his onslaught of the defendants, fully aligning himself with the prosecution throughout the examination by Hines.

When the time came to cross-examine Bommensath, the defence teams knew that they would get no help at all from him. They also had no evidence whatsoever that could be used against him, so the cross-examination was going to be a quick affair.

Jay's lead barrister, Hugh, handled it and he only had one point to put across. It was Jay's claim about the LIBOR request origins and subsequent development within the bank. Jay had categorically stated in his FSA interview that making LIBOR requests had been established many years before he joined the bank. He described how the practice had already been prevalent when he worked at the Euro swaps desk, and how everyone was aware of it being standard industry practice. He proclaimed that when he was selected to replace Gourtay in New York, Bommensath explicitly ordered him to replicate all the successful practices that he was familiar with from his time at the Euro desk. Jay also claimed that Bommensath specifically told him to introduce the practice of LIBOR requests and ensure it was followed to the firm's advantage.

Hugh confronted Bommensath with all these statements, but Eric immediately dismissed them. He claimed that he had never said those things and that Jay was simply lying to save his own skin. With that argument being a dead end – having just been reduced to Jay's word versus Eric's – the cross-examination came to an end.

The Barclays senior managers had been consistent in their message against the defendants, but they also provided some very useful points for them. Now came possibly the most important part for the defendants. A part that could very well determine the final verdicts: it was their turn to give evidence.

LIBOR Trial: Week Seven

The first step for the defendants was actually to decide whether to give evidence or not, and it was certainly not an easy decision for me. John and James both believed that the trial had been going very well thus far. Their main goal had always been to ensure the jurors knew exactly how junior and inexperienced I was at the time, and how I was simply following orders. This way, they would successfully distance me from the other defendants. If I refuse to give evidence, I would deprive the prosecution from the opportunity of cross-examining me and scoring points. The flipside was that I would run the risk of "negative inference" which can often be a game changer.

When a defendant refuses to give evidence, the jurors will naturally wonder why that is. If the defendant is innocent, why pass up on his only opportunity to personally proclaim his innocence? What reasons could he have for refusing to give evidence? That's the negative scenario that could play out, and something that I wanted to avoid at all costs.

John's initial thought was that the trial had been going well enough to warrant not giving evidence. However, as he discussed the matter with the other defence teams, it became evident that all of the other defendants were going to give evidence. That piece of information turned the tables and it was now clear that I had to follow suit. A single defendant refusing to give evidence could look suspicious – all five defendants had to be united on that decision in order to make it work. I had no choice but to comply and do the best I could.

***

The defendants would give evidence in the order of the indictment, and this meant that Jonathan Matthew would be first. Jonathan was a tall and slim Englishman in his early thirties, with very pale skin and reddish-brown hair on his receding hairline. During the indictment period he was barely in his twenties and a very junior person within the bank. He was a shy person with a particularly soft voice and low-key demeanour. His wife Lorna was a lovely person and had been in court every single day, never leaving her husband's side in support. Jonathan was a LIBOR submitter and PJ's subordinate, with just a year's experience at the start of the period in question.

Jonathan's lead barrister, Bill, had decided to take a very specific approach for his client's defence. Contrary to the other four defendants, he was going at it alone. In fact, he was seemingly going to try to convince the jury that a conspiracy had indeed existed, but Jonathan had nothing to do with it. His opening speech had attempted to compare Jonathan's average education with the co-defendants' outstanding academic records. He compared the humble public school that Jonathan attended to Yale, Imperial and Oxford that the others did.

'There was a conspiracy here,' Bill said authoritatively, 'but Mr Matthew knew nothing about it. The traders might have had some kind of agreement with Mr Johnson, but my client wasn't a part of it. He was simply an entry-level junior who was taking orders from his experienced boss and trying to do his job.'

It was an interesting approach, which admittedly surprised me. When Bill finished with the examination-in-chief, it was clear that Jonathan's performance had been lukewarm. Furthermore, out of all the defendants, Jonathan was theoretically the one who should have known if taking commercial interest in consideration when submitting LIBOR rates was allowed or not. This fact added further pressure on him, as the jury would be made aware of it by the prosecution.

Hines started the cross-examination with a very simple line of questioning:

'Mr Matthew, did you agree to procure LIBOR submissions that sometimes reflected the USD swaps traders' preferences?'

'Yes.'

My eyebrows immediately jumped. The word 'agree' implies a discussion and premeditated actions, dangerously close to the description of a conspiracy. I listened on anxiously.

'Mr Matthew, did you agree to procure these LIBOR submissions with Mr Merchant?'

'Yes.'

'With Mr Pabon?'

'Yes.'

'With Mr Reich?'

'Yes.'

'With Mr Contogoulas?'

'Yes.'

Did we agree?! I thought. An agreement involves two parties planning a course of action and making a common decision to follow it. *There had been no agreement*! As far as I was concerned, I was simply doing what my job entailed, an entirely regular part of my daily routine. It's like saying that a junior employee *agrees* to bring his boss's coffee every morning, or that the employee *agrees* to make photocopies when asked. It's an implicit aspect of someone's job!

It had been a bad start by Jonathan, who was being directed down the very path that the prosecution had wanted. Throughout the remainder of the cross-examination, Jonathan maintained his strategy of purely blaming PJ and the other defendants. He managed to stagger to the end of the questioning without any major damage, but it had admittedly been a mediocre showing.

***

The following morning, I woke up half an hour before my usual 7 a.m. alarm. I was due to start giving evidence a few hours later and I just couldn't get much sleep. I was scared, because I understood that my performance could turn out to be the main deciding factor for the jury. I was also excited, because this would be my chance to tell my side of the story. I could finally proclaim my innocence and defend it with all my energy. I knew that in three days' time this ordeal would be over, and I couldn't wait to get cracking.

I had a good breakfast, wore my favourite dark grey suit and walked out of the building. I usually took the bus to Sloane Square tube station, but today I decided to walk. It was a beautiful spring morning and I wanted to take advantage of the fifteen-minute walk to clear my mind.

When I arrived at Southwark Crown Court, I was ready to rumble. Entering the meeting room, I found the whole team already waiting for me there. They greeted me and started to psych me up, but it soon became apparent that there was no need. They could tell that I was ready from the look on my face, to the sound of my voice, to my confident body language. John patted me on the back and said just three words:

'You are ready.'

Examination-in-chief was always going to be a comfortable experience for me. John was taking an extraordinarily smooth and relaxed path through the required points, easing me into the process. Remember, this was the first time I was ever put in such a position in my life, and it was a pretty shocking experience. I often subsequently joked on that even if a completely random person was asked to give evidence about LIBOR – a person with absolutely no idea or involvement in the whole case – they would also be scared and nervous, even though they would have practically nothing to lose. It's the whole court setting and environment which puts a natural sense of fear in people sitting on the examination desk.

John started off by describing my life as a child, growing up as a teenager and maturing into my thirties. It was a perfect build up to my time at Barclays and the events in question.

John's first major point of interest was my first few days on the USD swaps desk, and Fred in particular. He took me through that central first meeting between me, Gourtay and PJ.

'Fred Gourtay introduced you to Mr Johnson, is that correct?' asked John.

'Correct.'

'What did he say of any relevance to us?'

'He said to me that I will be asked on occasion to pass on requests for LIBOR on to Mr Johnson.'

'All right. What was the relationship between you and Mr Gourtay at this stage?' continued John on his well-rehearsed questioning.

'Well, I had known him for maybe a couple of weeks.'

'How well?'

'Not very well at all.'

'What was his position in the hierarchy, in relation to you?'

'He was my boss.'

'And how senior was Mr Johnson?'

'At the time I didn't know his exact rank, but I had been told that he was very senior.'

'Again, we'll doubtless think about this later, but what was Mr Gourtay's manner when he said this to you?'

'It was done very openly, and that gave me the impression that it was a regular everyday thing.'

John's voice was now starting to get punchier and more authoritative. His elegant accent together with his unparalleled vocabulary and command of the English language were truly a formidable combination. He was intent on hammering the point home, ensuring that the jurors heard it again and again, in order for it to get ingrained in their brains.

'Again, just one further detail. Was there anything in Gourtay's manner which caused you any suspicion?' insisted John.

'No.'

'Any suggestion of secrecy, anything of that sort?'

'None at all.'

'And Mr Johnson, how did he behave in response to this?'

'He seemed perfectly normal and was very receptive to it. Nothing out of the ordinary, really.'

'Did you have any impression that this was or might in any way be improper or wrong?'

'No.'

'Or any impression that it was or might be dishonest?'

'Absolutely not,' I said, raising my tone a notch.

'Did you pass on these requests?'

'I did.'

'Did you ever seek to conceal what you were doing?'

'I did not.'

'To your knowledge, were your communications monitored?'

'Yes,' I confirmed. 'I remember there was a training course we took early on, which described that they were kept for years and could be subject to scrutiny,' I elaborated.

'If your communications were scrutinised and were found to breach standards of one sort or another, whether it be regulation or criminal, what would you expect to happen?'

'Well, I would expect somebody to tap me on the shoulder and start asking questions about it.'

'Did anyone ever comment on your e-mailed requests to submitters or suggest to you that it was wrong?'

'No.'

'What was the advantage to you in passing on these requests, if any, Mr Contogoulas?'

'There was no monetary advantage for me, let's put it that way. As far as I was concerned, it was part of my job – a very small part of my job – but I still had to do it.'

It had been a carefully thought-out sequence of questions, designed to bring out the truth one small step at a time. John and I knew the truth, but the herculean task at hand was to make the jurors understand it as well. The prosecution was going to try hard to muddle the waters and use every dirty trick in the book against me, but John had to remain consistent and focused.

I never denied making the requests or knowing why the requests were originated by my superiors. Passing on the requests took a minute or two of my day – it was one of a thousand other things my job entailed – and I never even gave it a second thought. It was simply a case of the bank taking commercial interest into consideration, and that made perfect sense. Over the next few years, I would go on to play the brief Gourtay-PJ meeting over and over in my head, and I would always come to that same conclusion – there was nothing that even hinted at it being improper or wrong.

John finally went on to cover my time at Barclays and Merrill Lynch in some detail, carefully outlining all the salient points. He also went through my appraisals during that time, putting particular emphasis on the sections regarding ethics and compliance, which were spotless. Lastly, he covered my compensation figures and straight away it became evident that I was the worst-paid of all the defendants.

The examination-in-chief had been methodical, clear and complete. John had managed to masterfully paint a very representative picture of the events that had taken place. Most importantly, he had successfully brought out my – *likeable*, I thought – character.

That was the easy part, and now came the tricky bit: cross-examination by the prosecution. The two prosecution barristers had taken turns to cross-examine the defendants, in order to share their workload. James Hines handled the more important individuals, such as Jay Merchant and Jonathan Matthew. Emma Deacon, being the more junior out of the two barristers, handled the less important defendants like myself.

I had been told that in the UK, it's not permitted by law for barristers to 'coach' or 'train' defendants in giving evidence. They can give broad directives and tips, but that's as far as it goes. Apparently, this is not the case in the US, where such specific client preparation may be comprehensive and is a vital part of a lawyer's job. My team had prepared me for the cross-examination as well as they could have, given the prevailing legal constraints. I was fully aware that this would be a crucial part of the case.

The team sat in our small meeting room shortly before the cross-examination was due to start, and for one last time, John reminded me just how important this was going to be. He wanted me to be focused and prepared, but he also wanted to calm my nerves and lift my spirits.

'It's highly probable that being acquitted or convicted will ultimately be up to you Stelios, and we cannot do anything to help you while you're up there,' John said meaningfully.

'How so?' I replied.

'Well, in such cases, a barrister can only do so much in setting the scene and events. I can explain to the jury what had happened and what your mind set was at the time, but what they *really* want is to hear it coming from you.'

'OK, that makes sense. They want to see me in real life, hear my tone of voice, and see my body language… right?'

'Precisely. A big part of what leads a juror to decide on a verdict is how he or she connects with you as a person. They will take in every little detail – audio and visual – and form a picture of who you really are. You might be surprised by this, but juries actually get it right in the vast majority of the cases.'

'That makes me feel good actually, since I know that I'm telling the truth and hopefully the jury will see it too.'

'They will, Stelios,' said John with a smile and took a sip from his coffee. 'They most certainly will.'

***

The tannoy announced that Court 2 was about to resume proceedings. After all the preparation, it was now time to get the job done. Deacon eagerly started the cross-examination by asking a long list of questions which were very easy and straightforward, and which all had one thing in common: My answer would have to be '*yes*'. This was the classic approach of putting a defendant in a state of mind where all answers were affirmative, and then asking one important question to which the prosecution really *wanted* the answer to be '*yes*'.

'Do you accept, Mr Contogoulas that you worked at Barclays from April 2002 until July 2006?' Deacon asked calmly.

'Yes.'

'Do you accept that during that period you made over sixty requests to LIBOR submitters about the book's preference on various LIBOR rates?'

'Yes.'

'Do you accept that you made those requests of Peter Johnson and Jonathan Matthew?'

'Yes.'

'Do you accept that those requests were sometimes for a high LIBOR and other times for a low LIBOR?'

'Yes.'

It would be a sequence of a dozen such simple questions with obvious answers, but then she sneaked in the important one:

'Do you accept that such requests may have not been viewed as *proper* by someone within the bank?'

I was concentrating hard, as I knew that it was the prosecution barrister's job to catch me off guard. Deacon naturally had an excellent command of the English language, which in combination with the fact that English was not my mother tongue, made this one of her strongest weapons against me. She was going to use complex multi-part questions and convoluted wording to try and confuse me into giving a favourable answer for her. She would often ask the same question several times using different wording, aiming to get contradicting or confusing answers, hence making me look weak. If I answered a question wrong, she would take it and use it like a sledgehammer on me, exploring avenues that would have otherwise been inaccessible for her. An outsider may have considered this to be a dirty tactic, but apparently it was a popular and permissible strategy; in law the main goal was clearly to win at any cost.

I started well, pausing after every question for a few moments before answering. John had given me some very important advice, which I tried to remember after every question:

'Don't try to second guess what the prosecution barrister is trying to get at, when they ask a particular question. Listen to the words of the question and answer it truthfully and as simply as you can. Don't elaborate on something unless specifically asked.'

I listened to Deacon asking the question:

'Do you accept that such requests may have not been viewed as *proper* by someone within the bank?'

I thought about it for a second or two and replied emphatically:

'Absolutely, not.'

The day progressed, and the pace of the questions continued unabated. One of the prosecution's main weapons was a purely biological one – tiredness. After several hours of intense cross-examination, the human body starts to get tired and lose concentration. It's a natural phenomenon that only a few gifted people can successfully fight, and I wasn't one of them. I had been going on for hours and was really starting to feel the effect. Unsurprisingly, Deacon had purposely kept some of the crucial questions for the latter part of the day, in order to take advantage of precisely that human weakness.

On some occasions, I was visibly irritated with the questions and it showed. My answers were sometimes snappy, and I raised my voice in frustration. However, I didn't crack. I even managed to produce a few humorous responses which lightened up the mood and made me look pleasant to the jurors.

'Mr Contogoulas, your primary objective as a trader was to make money, isn't that correct?' Deacon asked menacingly, trying to make it look like all other traders and me were driven solely by greed.

'Yes, Miss Deacon. *I worked at a bank,*' came back the instant punchline.

It was just like asking a footballer if his primary objective was to win matches; a well-timed response to an apparently poorly thought-out question.

The first day of cross-examination finished with no major mishaps or problems. The rules stated that I couldn't discuss my evidence with anyone, and that obviously included my legal team. This meant that while I was giving evidence, I would be fighting all alone. During the breaks, I would grab a cup of coffee or some water and sit on my own. At lunchtime I would go to an empty part of the building and have a solitary meal.

When the day was over, I went home and usually spent an hour at the gym. I would then have a quick bite to eat and start working on my start-up project. The project had been a welcome change of environment for me throughout the trial, giving me a much-needed escape from the stress of the trial. I would be at court from 9 a.m. until 5pm every day, and then I would spend most of the evening working until midnight. The project was still in the early stages of development, so it was particularly complex and demanding. I didn't care – I used the gym to exercise my body and the start-up to exercise my mind.

***

The second day of cross-examination by Deacon continued with the same unrelenting pace. She took me over the actual LIBOR definition, a move that proved quite costly for the prosecution. It turned out that none of the people involved – including the traders and senior managers like Bagguley, Harrison and Bommensath – actually knew its precise wording. In fact, it was treated by everyone as a vague concept of no particular importance. Deacon was trying everything she could in order to push me to make a mistake, but she wasn't having much success. Frustrated, she started making mistakes herself, launching what I thought were poorly-thought attacks based on specific pieces of evidence.

There was one particular email where I said to PJ the following:

'My bosses would like a high three-month and a low one-month LIBOR. And if you could also tell me the winning lottery numbers for next week that would be great.'

Deacon attacked me on that particular communication, alleging that I was aware just how valuable PJ's help influencing LIBOR was. She apparently claimed that, akin to winning the lottery, making these requests was worth millions of dollars. It seemed to me that she had failed to understand that my expression was merely banter. That proved to be a clear error on her part, as it also opened the door for the defence to quantify just how small the actual theoretical gain was – Hugh Davis, Jay's QC, was about to exploit that mistake a few days later.

Another communication that Deacon attacked was one where I used my usual colourful language to express my appreciation towards PJ for helping out with the requests. Playfully, I said:

'When I retire, you will have an open invitation to my bar in the Greek islands.'

When this particular email had been read out loud during the early parts of the trial, the jury actually found it quite amusing. Several of the jurors smiled and a couple of them even laughed out loud. It was clearly a pleasantry, having nothing to do with reality. Maybe Deacon didn't see it that way, or perhaps she was running out of ammunition. It didn't matter – the end result was the same. She grilled me on this particular exchange, implying that the invitation to the bar would be PJ's 'reward' for his part in the alleged conspiracy. There was even a hint that the bar may have in fact existed, and that it could have been acquired using the proceeds of my alleged criminal activity. It was an easy attack for me to shoot down.

'Miss Deacon, there is no bar in the Greek islands,' I said. 'If you can't distinguish an innocent humorous exchange from something sinister and crooked, then I really think you may be in the wrong business.'

Deacon was an excellent barrister and that meant that such mistakes were few and far between. She scored some important points with other emails, some of which gave me a pretty tough time. In one particular exchange I had made a specific request of PJ, who happened to have the opposite preference himself on that day. He agreed to comply with the request, but he then said the following:

'I'm going 90 although 91 is what I should be posting.'

Deacon jumped on the opportunity; this was the best piece of evidence she had, hinting that PJ might in fact have been submitting false or untrue rates.

'Mr Contogoulas, Peter Johnson clearly says to you here *'I'm going 90, although 91 is what I should be posting*, correct?' Deacon asked firmly.

'Yes.'

'91 being a basis point higher than 90, do you agree?'

'Yes.'

'Did you understand, Mr Contogoulas, he was telling you that his LIBOR submission should be 91 but he was going to do 90 for you?'

'He says he should be posting 91. I don't actually know what *should* refers to, but he's saying that he's going to post 90.'

'You don't know what *should* refers to?' Deacon said with an ironic smile.

'That is correct. It could be that he has the opposite position and based on that, he should be posting 91. I have no way of knowing.'

'Well, wouldn't you have understood that he was saying that his submission should be 91?'

'That's what he's saying, but as I said before, I don't know what he refers to when he says *should*.'

'Wouldn't you have understood it in the way I've just suggested?'

'Not necessarily, no, because you have to put this in context again. You've been spending months and years scrutinising these emails, looking at every single word, every single punctuation mark. If you look at the timestamps of these emails, they are 7:48 a.m., 7:49 a.m., 7:50 a.m. You are examining these emails with a microscope, but I barely spent a few seconds thinking about these things. It was *bang-bang-bang*, done.'

I was feeling the pressure getting heavier. I knew that I was telling the truth, but it wasn't easy to get it through to the jury. Deacon probably wasn't using these communications to uncover something sinister, as she knew very well that there were no such incriminating documents. Her main task was to make me look unreliable, or perhaps like I was hiding something. She needed to make the jury question at least *one* of my responses, and by doing that she could work towards making them question *all* my responses.

'It's quite straightforward language Mr Contogoulas, isn't it? *I'm going 90 although 91 is what I should be posting*?' she repeated once again.

'Again, I don't know what he refers to when he says *'should'*. As far as I was concerned, every submission he made was always in accordance to the prevailing proper and honest procedure. I can repeat it twenty more times if needed, but this is the truth, and this is what was on my mind at the time.'

I suggest, Mr Contogoulas that you knew full well that Mr Johnson was doing something wrong or improper at the time.'

'Absolutely not!' I protested.

'You realised, didn't you, that Peter Johnson was accommodating your requests outside of submitting true LIBOR rates?'

'Again, I did not.'

'It was all about profit, wasn't it?'

'Well, when you're working in a bank, a big part of what you do is about profit, yes.'

'And honesty was no concern to you, was it, Mr Contogoulas?'

'Honesty was paramount, Miss Deacon.'

With her questioning, Deacon tried hard to pass certain key messages to the jury. I thought that these messages weren't necessarily selected to highlight aspects of my behaviour that the jurors might have considered to be wrong, instead they were clever tricks to remind them that bankers were particularly hated people at the time. One of these was the concept of *ambition*.

'Mr Contogoulas, would you say that you are an ambitious man?' asked Deacon, while purposely making her voice sound judgemental.

For a second, I went into panic defence mode, trying to figure out where she was going with that question. Instantly, I remembered John's words about answering questions and relaxed.

'Yes, I'd say that I am an ambitious man, Miss Deacon,' came the swift reply. It was probably not the answer she was expecting, but she carried on.

'Yes, you are, Mr Contogoulas,' she said in a near-sarcastic voice. 'You are ambitious, and you would go above and beyond your duties in order to advance, wouldn't you?'

'My goal,' I replied confidently, 'was always to advance professionally and get recognised accordingly, in terms of promotions and compensation. There's no doubt about it, I'm not a person who is content with having the same job for decades. Having said that, I would never do anything improper or illegal to achieve that goal. Throughout my whole life I have worked extremely hard, but I always played by the rules, Miss Deacon.'

'That's what you claim, Mr Contogoulas, but I suggest that you were a man driven by ambition to get promoted and become a very senior and well-paid employee, isn't that correct?'

'That's correct, Miss Deacon. My drive and ambition were identical to those of a person straight out of law school aiming to become a barrister and then a highly-paid QC, don't you think? I snapped, provoking muffled laughter in the courtroom.

Next, Emma tackled my time at Merrill Lynch and my communications with Don Lee. The indictment for the particular charge explicitly specified that the alleged conspiracy involved 'Barclays employees' – so theoretically my time at ML shouldn't have been allowed in the trial. The prosecution had asked for the

ML material to be included in the trial, knowing that there was a good chance that their request would not be granted. To my surprise, the judge allowed it.

'It's not consistent with the indictment,' said Leonard, *'but the jury may hear the evidence and decide whether they can find it useful to gauge Mr Contogoulas's state of mind while he was employed at Barclays.'*

Even though I'm not a lawyer, I felt that this was one of the most absurd things I had ever heard. *How can something done in a future time help with a defendant's state of mind in the past?* It was a blow for me, but I was going to fight it.

Deacon tackled my communications with Don, obviously trying to use them against me in the eyes of the jury. I had stated that I had been a mere conduit while at Barclays, but here I was, making my own requests for my own book. She attacked mercilessly but failed to make any real progress, as I was consistent and disciplined in my answers. I probably frustrated Emma, and in the end, I even managed to turn her whole argument on its head.

'Miss Deacon,' I said, 'You do realise that when I left Barclays and went to Merrill Lynch, I went to an establishment with a totally different setup and procedures, don't you? There were completely new people – traders, compliance officers, legal – whom I didn't know about beforehand, right?' I asked. 'Well, think about it for a second,' I continued. 'If I was indeed in a criminal conspiracy at Barclays, knowing full well that what I was doing was wrong, what would I do at Merrill Lynch? Would I just waltz in, without any consideration of the prevalent structure and controls, and simply continue breaking the law? Would I not first try to ascertain how things work, how to avoid being detected, and who could be party to this conspiracy?'

Suddenly, I realised that I was on a prolonged monologue, but I continued nevertheless.

'My actions were entirely consistent with a person who had absolutely no idea that they were improper or dishonest. You are trying to use my communications at Merrill to incriminate me, but in fact they *prove* that I am being truthful here today. The jury can clearly see this by now, and I'm afraid that you're probably the only person in this room who doesn't. Your agenda and bias may prevent you from seeing the truth, but I urge you to take a step back and re-evaluate all the evidence.'

Not long after, the cross-examination finally came to an end. Deacon had tried everything, but I thought she only managed to score a few points, mostly due to my frustration and tiredness. In the meeting room, the team had a quick debrief to assess the situation:

'Stelios, my man. That was good!' said Karl, the junior barrister.

'Yes, I thought you handled it very well,' added James. 'I've seen many cases where innocent people get overcome by anxiety and stress, and they get absolutely destroyed. You held your nerve well and you made excellent responses to some very tricky questions,' added James cheerfully.

'Good,' I replied. 'I was definitely nervous at times and couldn't really tell how well I was doing.'

'You did well, Stelios,' said John with a confident smile. 'You most certainly did well.'

***

LIBOR Trial: Week Eight

It was Jay Merchant's turn to give evidence, and by now it was obvious that he was the prosecution's main target. He was the most senior person out of all the defendants – the proverbial 'big fish' – and the prosecution were desperate to secure his conviction.

He sat on the designated chair, his grey pin-striped suit in complete matching colour with his hair. He had always been a well-groomed, sharp dressed man, whose dress sense was just as good as his trading skills. Examination-in-chief went according to plan, with Hugh Davis doing a good job demonstrating Jay's character and career progression. He spent extra time tackling a very important point for Jay, and in fact for all the defendants. Throughout the trial, the prosecution had been emphasising that the practice of LIBOR requests had been extremely profitable for the traders. Hines used phrases like 'billions of dollars involved' and 'eye-watering sums of money'. He had used this particular emphasis in order to convince the jury that the traders in question had a huge personal financial benefit from the activity. But was this really the case? The jury were in for a big surprise.

Hugh Davis took Jay step by step through the necessary calculations and assumptions, in order to quantify the amount 'gained' as a result of the LIBOR requests. Together they tried to prove what theoretical maximum effect a LIBOR request had on the final published LIBOR rate.

'Mr Merchant, what was the average size of the trades resetting on any particular day, for the USD Short-Term swaps book?' asked Hugh.

'On average, it was roughly one to two billion US Dollars,' replied Jay. 'We can verify this number because we have the actual data from Barclays. Let's take the aggressive side and say that it was two billion dollars.'

'Thank you, Mr Merchant. Now, mathematically, what is the theoretical maximum effect that one submission can have on the final LIBOR published rate? Is that something that can be quantified?'

'Yes, it can, and we have indeed quantified it. We have done the calculations and the maximum theoretical effect is one eighth of a basis point, or in other words 0.00125%,' replied Jay confidently.

'Taking those two numbers together, what is the actual theoretical maximum dollar value of each LIBOR request, Mr Merchant?'

'That will be 6250 dollars.'

'Thank you, Mr Merchant. Now, how many LIBOR requests were you involved in, during the period in question?'

'Forty-eight,' said Jay.

138

'Right, so please correct me if I'm wrong, but I make the total theoretical benefit to the swaps book from all the requests as being…'

'Let's check your mathematical skills now, Mr Davies,' chuckled Jay.

'…6250 dollars times 48, or in other words a total of 300,000 US dollars.'

'That's correct!'

'Phew,' laughed Hugh, 'It's a simple calculation and I still managed to get really nervous about it. I could never be a trader,' he giggled.

'Yes, you might want to stick with the legal profession,' said Jay.

'Indeed,' said Hugh, bringing the conversation back to a serious note. 'But all jokes aside, let's take a minute to consider this number, 300,000 dollars of theoretical maximum profit for the bank. What was the average pay-out at the time, Mr Merchant, for a trader in your position?'

'Some traders had an explicit percentage deal in their contract, but this was not the norm; for most traders, the year-end bonus was entirely discretionary. The usual discretionary pay-out would have been around four to five percent.'

'OK, so four to five percent. 300,000 dollars times five percent equals 15,000 dollars. That was the theoretical maximum amount for you personally, Mr Merchant, from all the LIBOR requests that you were involved in, is that correct?'

'That is correct.'

'May I remind the court that Mr Merchant's compensation for 2005 was over 800,000 dollars and his 2006 and 2007 numbers were well into seven figures, isn't that right Mr Merchant?'

'That's right,' confirmed Jay.

'So, Mr Merchant, let me get this straight,' said Hugh in a puzzled voice, 'the prosecution is suggesting that you risked everything – your freedom, your career, and seven-figure annual pay-outs, for 15,000 dollars. *Fifteen thousand dollars*. While your annual pay was several orders of magnitude higher, does that make any sense to you?'

'Of course not. No sane person would ever do what the prosecution are alleging, and frankly it's a ridiculous thing to imply.'

The examination in-chief ended with Jay on a high. However, he was about to be brought violently back to the ground by James Hines's cross-examination the following morning. No one knew exactly what happened, but the next day Jay was almost like a different person. From the moment he sat on the chair he looked uncomfortable. Hines started his questioning and Jay's answers were nervous, slow and tense. He inexplicably struggled to give straight answers even for the simplest questions. After every one of Hines's questions, he would gaze forward looking perplexed, taking a particularly long time before answering.

'*What's wrong with you, Jay?*' I asked myself, trying not to show desperation.

The jury were concentrating on Jay but on occasion they would glance at the other defendants. Any sign of weakness could potentially harm all five of us, and we knew it. Jay's cross-examination finished two days later, and frankly it could have gone a lot better. He didn't make any big mistakes and neither did the prosecution manage to score any ground-breaking victories. However, his demeanour was poor and it certainly instilled doubt in the jurors' minds. Hugh Davies was now evidently worried about his client, even though he tried hard not to show it.

***

I had been secretly dreading Alex Pabon's evidence. I was fully aware of his temperament and unpredictable character, as well as his frequently colourful language. This was now 2016 – a decade after the events in question – and there was a hope that he would have softened up. After all, he was no longer a young twenty-something cowboy; he was a stay-at-home dad in his thirties.

Thankfully, Alex performed much better than anyone had anticipated. He was unexpectedly calm and focused, although there were times when his frustration took the upper hand. On several occasions he huffed and puffed, his strong American accent revealing that he was facing difficulty. Putting his hands on his head, visibly swallowing hard and repeating his words, were strong tells that he was struggling.

Deacon took him through some of the messages that he was involved in, both text and audio. In terms of language used, Alex was distinctly different from all the others; he cursed a lot and sometimes used very strong words. Deacon made sure she stressed and repeated all those pieces of evidence, in the hope that she would make the jury dislike Alex. I didn't think that she necessarily needed to prove that Alex was guilty at that moment in time – getting jurors to dislike him could probably be enough for her. Once they did, it would make it much easier for the prosecution to push them towards a guilty verdict.

LIBOR Trial: Week Nine

Ryan Reich was the last of the defendants to give evidence. He was a big, muscular American in his thirties with a clean-shaven head and a distinctly square jaw. He was a tremendously gifted person, both physically as well as intellectually. In college, he was an outstanding student as well as one of the university's baseball stars. He was the first on the training ground and the last to leave, mentoring younger guys and helping them improve their academic and athletic performance. He looked big, strong and tough on the outside, but inside he was a truly gentle and compassionate individual.

After graduation, he entered the banking arena and became one of the high-flying youngsters who shot up the corporate ladder. During his time at Barclays, Ryan was in his mid-twenties and had relatively limited experience, but he quickly caught the eye of senior management. Jay hired him in 2007 onto the New York USD swaps desk, essentially filling the gap that Alex Pabon had created when he left the firm. Ryan quickly earned Jay's respect and his trading performance exceeded all expectations. In the following few years, and up until he was terminated as the LIBOR investigation developed, he generated considerable profits for the bank and in turn he got compensated handsomely.

Ryan's evidence unfolded in quite a neutral way, failing to produce any fireworks. He spoke in an impeccable manner, never losing his temper and being as helpful to the jury as possible. One of the most important pieces of advice given by the defence barristers was perfectly summarised by James one day:

'Your number one priority should be to help the jury. Try to make every answer you give as understandable and helpful as possible for them. A defendant who explains things simply and clearly is most often telling the truth. A person who answers cryptically or overcomplicates things usually has something to hide. Truth is straight as an arrow, while a lie swivels like a snake.'

Ryan's evidence was completed with no problems whatsoever, and that marked the end of the defendants giving evidence. It had been a momentously difficult period, but it was finally over.

***

The trial had now reached the final stretch. First up were the character references where each trader either brought witnesses to testify in person or had prepared statements read out. This was standard procedure by the defendants in order to highlight their positive qualities to the jury. There was a wide variety of people giving character references, which included among others:

- Jonathan's co-worker from the charity he had become involved in, as well as a work ex-colleague.
- Jay's university roommate and tennis partner from the United States.
- Ryan's baseball coach from college and a work associate from his post-Barclays employment.

I had just three references, as my team were confident that they could perfectly bring out my character to the jury.

My first reference was from a good friend of mine and a university classmate, Harry. We had been friends since we were eighteen years old, having spent four very close years at university. Harry had, by now, become a member of the Greek parliament and a greatly respected individual in my country. To his credit, even though he had become a public figure and could potentially incur damage by being associated with a man who was on a criminal trial with such global focus, Harry didn't hesitate. He said straight away that he wanted to help, and I was deeply appreciative of that. They say that you only really know who your true friends are when you are in difficult situations, and Harry certainly turned out to be one of them.

Harry described my good heart and natural tendency to see the good in everyone. He spoke about how humble I was, never becoming arrogant or letting my success get to my head. It was a short and sweet account of our long-time friendship; coming from a respected member of parliament, my team considered it to be a great asset in my defence.

The second reference was from my friend, Georgia. She was a Greek woman in her early forties who up to five years prior had been very successful in her life. She lived in the trendiest area of Athens, had a lucrative finance job and was about to start a family with her fiancé. However, fate had other plans for her. She was infected with a rare disease while on holidays in the US, and her illness was misdiagnosed for almost three years. When her diagnosis was finally made correctly, the damage had already been substantial. She was unable to walk or stand properly, had limited hand movement ability and terrible trouble speaking. She had been transformed from a beautiful, healthy and successful young woman into a person needing constant care.

Georgia described how she had met me through family acquaintances, and how we bonded as friends. As her condition deteriorated, I helped her in any way I could – financially as well as psychologically. She even described how I continued to help her financially even after I had lost my job and my savings were being depleted, and how I never told her about my money problems. I knew that she would have not accepted the help if I had told her that I had been fired, so she only found this out just before the trial began.

The third and final reference was from another of my close friends. Nick was an exceptionally smart and a successful individual, with a great career in consulting and a bright future ahead of him. He had been through a painful divorce a few years earlier, and he described exactly how I had helped him through it. From helping Nick move out of his flat, to giving him emotional support, I was there to look out for my friend in need.

All three witnesses' accounts were emotional and sincere, and they had unquestionably made a positive impact on the jury.

LIBOR Trial: Week Ten

The final part of the trial, and possibly the most significant, was the closing speeches. This part effectively forms an executive summary for the jury, who are presented with a handy recap of all the salient points. It's also the part during which the jury members are most concentrated and alert, therefore the contents of the closing speeches often prove to be crucial. It's also a very useful segment for the judge, who makes notes throughout the course of the trial and can use this opportunity to ensure that they are complete and accurate.

The prosecution was first to make their closing speech, and unsurprisingly it was yet again particularly punchy. Hines summarised their case against the defendants just like he had done in his opening speech, but this time round he incorporated many of the strong points that had arisen from the defendants' cross-examination. He delivered the speech in his usual style, using a sequence of logical steps to strategically move from one concept to the next. It was an effective, if slightly dull process, that he knew exactly how to convey. In his last few sentences, he left no doubt regarding the prosecution's stance.

'Ladies and gentlemen of the jury,' he said seriously, 'I urge you to consider the facts of this case. It's a conspiracy to defraud, and Peter Johnson's guilty plea is a proof positive that a conspiracy actually took place. Your job is to determine which of these five defendants had been a part of the conspiracy. Moreover, to what extent. It's the prosecution's case that all the defendants were part of this conspiracy, their ultimate goal being to maximise their own income at the expense of their unsuspecting clients. These people rigged one of the most important benchmarks in the world, a benchmark which was supposed to be independent and trustworthy. They were driven by greed and stopped at nothing to achieve their hunger for money and success. We strongly urge you to consider all the information and arrive at the only reasonable verdict, which is to find these five men guilty of conspiracy to defraud.'

Hines was finished and the defendants no doubt felt relieved that they wouldn't have to hear his voice again.

***

It was the turn of the defence barristers to take over the closing speeches, having the single goal of ending the trial on a high for the five men in the dock. One by one they defended their clients, doing their utmost to put forward the best possible arguments in their favour. Most of the defence QCs took a day or two to finish their speeches, wanting to carefully take the jurors through the most important pieces of evidence one last time. It had been a long and arduous journey, but the finishing line was now very close.

John had been discussing his closing speech strategy mainly with James and Karl, but he also welcomed the feedback from the rest of the team. There had been a lot of toing and froing, and he hadn't really reached a stage where he was totally comfortable. His main concern was that although he wanted to spend enough time going through all the elements in my favour, he didn't want to make it to a long speech. He wanted to keep it short, in line with my relative importance in the whole trial.

'If I spend too long defending you, it might change the jury's perception of your role within this story,' said John purposely.

'The fact of the matter is that you were the most junior person, and certainly the most insignificant one in terms of knowledge and duties. I want this to be perfectly clear to the jury when they're deliberating,' he concluded, and the rest of the team duly agreed.

As usual, John had made a skeleton draft of his closing speech on his laptop, and he was ready to deliver it. However, in his usual 'Ryder' fashion, he changed his mind literally minutes before he was scheduled to start. He decided that he was going to cut some big chunks of it; he was going to keep it short and sweet.

In his unique style, John captivated the jury and the observers in the public section, from the first instant. He was dead serious and methodical when needed, but he often changed his rhythm and produced some genuinely funny moments too. He handled his audience just like a conductor guides an orchestra, knowing exactly when to raise the tempo or when to slow the pace right down. He joked around, engaging some jury members to the extent that they were actually laughing out loud, but in the very end he became deadly serious.

'Ladies and gentlemen of the jury,' he said, 'you have been through an ocean of information in the past twelve weeks or so. I wouldn't blame you if you never wanted to hear the word LIBOR again in your lives, or if you never wanted to set foot in a bank again.'

The jury laughed once again, no doubt feeling the strain of their continuous efforts of the previous three months.

'However,' John continued very seriously, 'you still have the most important decision ahead of you. You will be asked to decide on the fate of these five men. You will have the power to send each one of these people either back to the arms of their loved ones, or to prison.'

The jurors' faces became very solemn now.

'We have already outlined Mr Contogoulas's position within the alleged crime, and you should now have a comprehensive picture of the situation. Mr Contogoulas was an extremely junior person with no prior experience, doing what his bosses were asking him to do. You have evidence of what Mr Contogoulas did when he did find out about dishonest actions. He had no personal gain from the LIBOR requests, and in fact he had everything to lose. His actions were totally consistent with those of a man who believed he was doing nothing wrong. A man who had never set a foot wrong during his whole life, a man for whom honesty and helping others were paramount. Mr Contogoulas is an honest, hard-working member of the society who deserves to be reunited with his wife and young children. He deserves to be freed from the burden of this horrible and undeserved multi-year adventure that he's been through. Ladies and gentlemen of the jury, you must reach the only fair and objective verdict, and that verdict is *not guilty*.'

LIBOR Trial: Week Twelve

It was a Wednesday afternoon when the trial effectively came to an end. It had been twelve gruelling weeks for the defendants, who had been through an absolute rollercoaster of emotions. Being called a criminal and threatened with imprisonment is not an easy thing to take, especially when you're accused of a crime you didn't commit.

It had also been a very tough and demanding period for the jurors, as they were introduced to a plethora of new concepts and had to assimilate them within a short period of time. The theories behind LIBOR, interest rate swaps and trading were certainly not simple or easy to understand. The jurors knew that they had a huge responsibility, so they had to concentrate hard in order to keep pace with the information they were receiving.

Judge Leonard, having taken a day to summarise the case for the benefit of the jury, was now ready to send them to their designated room for deliberations. He thanked the jury for successfully getting through this particularly demanding trial and informed them that they would need to produce unanimous decisions

144

for each one of the defendants. If they had any questions, or if they needed to see or hear any particular piece of evidence again, he would be at their disposal to help. With those words he released the jury and the court was adjourned.

My team and I found our way to the meeting room and we sat down around the main table.

'So, what do we do now?' I said impatiently.

'Now, we wait,' replied James as he switched on his laptop. 'For me, this is the most frustrating part of any trial. You just have to sit there waiting for the jury to reach a verdict, which may come within a day or which might take weeks. I suggest you find something to do, in order to keep yourself busy. Read a book, play a game on your phone, anything that distracts you. There's nothing more we can do on this case, so personally I'm going to work on some of my other pending tasks.'

'That's good advice,' confirmed John. 'We have done the best we could, and I personally think that, barring suicidal confessions from Bagguley or Harrison, things went as well as we could have hoped for.'

'Right,' I said. 'Well, there's only one thing I really need right now,' I continued, as I stood up and walked over to the desk.

'Coffee, anyone?'

***

I got home a few hours later and the first thing I did was to call Semiramis.

'Hey honey, I'm home,' I said.

'Great! I'm still at work, I will be heading out in an hour or so. How did it go today?'

'Well, the trial is over, and the jury has been sent out to deliberate. I think that we did well, and so does the rest of the team. I have a good feeling about this. The jury have been attentive and engaged throughout, and what I find really encouraging is that a few of them have been making lots of eye contact with me. One lady in particular has smiled at me on several occasions – that can only be a good thing, right?' I said.

'For sure. Remind me – do they have to produce a unanimous verdict?' Semiramis asked excitedly.

'To start with, yes. But if the jury fail to reach a unanimous verdict, from a certain point onwards the judge can allow an eleven-one or ten-two split.'

'Gotcha. Well, we won't be needing that, as we will get a unanimous not guilty verdict!' beamed Semiramis.

'Indeed!' I roared. 'We have ordered it from the universe, and it will be so!'

The first couple of days passed and no unanimous verdicts had been reached. Every morning at 10 a.m. the court would be in session, bringing the jurors and swearing them in. Following that brief five-minute process, they would be sent off to continue their deliberations. Similarly, at around 4:30pm they would be brought in and get released for the day. Thanks to this procedure, the defence teams would get a chance to see the jurors twice a day and try to 'read' their mood.

The first week of deliberations went by and there were still no unanimous verdicts. I had secretly hoped for quick verdicts, something that would have most likely been an indication of acquittals. But the quick verdicts hadn't come, and I was starting to get worried.

'How can anyone not realise that I am not guilty of this charge?' I would ask myself. *'It should be clear as day. Why can't they see that I was just relaying orders? Do they really think that I was a criminal mastermind?'*

I would often express this frustration to John and the others, and naturally they completely understood how I felt.

'It's just how this process works, Stelios,' James would say in order to calm me down. 'The jurors need to be one hundred percent sure of their decision, and as a result they will usually take longer than you would expect to reach it.'

The second week of deliberations kicked off and on Friday afternoon the jury were brought in for the usual five-minute process to release them for the weekend. I took a good look at their faces and I saw twelve drained people. They may have been tired, but they seemed in good spirits and their facial expressions were not hostile in any way. John had told me that when a jury is close to delivering guilty verdicts, it's usually unmistakeably visible in their faces. They will avoid eye contact, they will be serious and look distant. None of these were evident in the jurors right now, so I kept my optimism even though I was worried about the delay in reaching the verdicts.

The following Monday morning, everyone assembled in the courtroom as usual. However, something didn't feel right at all, and all the defence teams noticed it. The jury entered the room and suddenly they seemed completely withdrawn. There was no eye contact, their faces were deadly serious, and it seemed like they couldn't wait to get out of the room. I was instantly taken over by fear – I was on the verge of having a panic attack. *What was happening? What had changed from Friday afternoon until that Monday morning?* The jury were supposed to be at home, not deliberating or working on the case at all. *What – or who – had caused this huge shift?*

The jury was sent to their room and the defence teams gathered together. My feelings were echoed by everyone else; it was not just my impression that things had taken a turn for the worse. Hugh, Jay's QC, was particularly gloomy. He was convinced that the tables had now been turned, and the most likely outcomes were going to be guilty verdicts. He worried for Jay, who had always been the prosecution's number one target. Hugh thought that not guilty verdicts would now be extremely hard to get; the best-case scenario would be a 'hung' jury.

Note: A 'hung' jury is when the jury fail to reach a verdict in a non-resolvable deadlock.

Hearing those words, my heart sank. I later spoke to John in private:

'John, can this really be happening?' I said in distress. 'What's your gut feeling?'

'I know what you want to hear, Stelios,' John replied in his usual calm and steady voice. 'Hugh may be right, but I still believe that we have a good chance. In fact, you still have the best chance out of all the defendants. Juries often want to acquit at least one defendant, and if this happens in this trial, you will be the acquitted one. Stay positive and please don't worry. It will all be fine in the end.'

His words had a magical power, always managing to calm me down when I was on the verge of losing it.

'Thank you, John,' I said, patting him on the shoulder. 'I'm not losing faith. We can win this.'

LIBOR Trial: Week Fourteen

Two days later, there was finally a breakthrough. The jury handed a piece of paper to the court clerk, who in turn gave it to the judge. Soon after, Judge Leonard gave the news to the defence and prosecution teams: they had reached three verdicts but were unable to reach unanimous verdicts on the other two.

There now were two available options for the defence: they could choose to take the three verdicts and let the jury deliberate on the remaining two, or they could wait until all five verdicts were reached and receive them all at the same time. The defence teams wasted no time deciding; they wanted to take the verdicts as soon as possible.

Half an hour later the court doors opened, and the room started filling with people. News of the verdicts had reached the media and they were eager to hear them and record the reactions. There was not an empty seat in the public gallery. The five defendants slowly entered the dock, trying to lift each other's spirits. They knew full well that some of them were likely to receive bad news. I sat in my chair feeling quietly confident, but nervous nevertheless.

The defendants didn't have to wait long to find out. The jury foreman stood up and he had a distinct half-smile on his face. It seemed to me as if he was particularly pleased about the verdicts he was about to hand out. Judge Leonard asked him the standard question:

'Have the jury reached at least one unanimous decision on the defendants?'

'Yes, your honour.'

'Have you reached a verdict in the case of Jonathan Matthew?'

'We have, your honour.'

'What is your verdict?' asked Leonard.

The whole room sat still and held its breath.

'*Guilty*!' said the foreman in a strong voice.

His voice had a strange tone, as if he enjoyed delivering the punishing verdict. I would swear that I even saw a slight smile on his face as he said the dreaded word.

The defendants' hearts sank.

Jonathan dropped his head and let out a deep sigh. Even though he always knew that it was a possible outcome, he couldn't believe it was actually happening. His wife covered her eyes with her hands and started sobbing. Reality started to sink in. For the next few years she would be separated from her husband and raise their baby child on her own. It had been a terribly cruel turn of events, and it was now pretty obvious that the other two verdicts could only also be guilty verdicts. There was no time to relax for the other defendants, as the judge carried on with the standard procedure.

'Have you reached a verdict in the case of Stylianos Contogoulas?' he continued.

I felt as though my heart had stopped beating. I literally held my breath as I waited for the next words to come out of the foreman's mouth.

'We have not,' said the foreman with a slightly disappointed tone.

I felt a huge weight lifted off my shoulders. Even though it was not an acquittal, for now I had avoided conviction. My first instinct was to clench my fist in celebration, but I restrained myself. After all, Jonathan was sitting immediately on my right and had just received terrible news.

'Have you reached a verdict in the case of Jay Merchant?' Leonard proceeded.

'Yes, your honour,' came back the foreman's broadly expected response.

'What is your verdict?'

'*Guilty.*'

Jay shook his head in disbelief. Being the most senior of the defendants, he knew he was in trouble.

'Have you reached a verdict in the case of Alex Pabon?'

'Yes, your honour.'

'What is your verdict?'

'*Guilty.*'

Alex hung his head and whispered: '*shit.*'

'Have you reached a verdict in the case of Ryan Reich?' asked Leonard, in what was actually a pretty pointless question.

'No, we have not,' said the foreman.

'Thank you, you may sit down,' concluded the judge.

After the judge left the room, the five traders stood in the dock, speechless. I slowly walked to Jay and hugged him.

'Be strong, man,' I said. 'This is terribly unfair and makes no sense to any of us. But you will get through it and you will be back with your family once and for all. If there's anything we can do for you and your family, please don't hesitate to ask.'

I then hugged Jonathan and Alex, and made my way straight to the meeting room.

The atmosphere in the room was surprisingly upbeat, given what had just transpired only a few minutes prior.

'Well, let's look at the positives,' said John. 'That could have gone a lot worse. We're still in it and clearly at least one juror is having trouble believing that you are guilty.'

'Yes, that was my initial thought too,' I added. 'I'm convinced that it's more than one juror, too.'

'That's good,' James joined in the conversation. 'But in order to make one hundred percent sure we'll need three jurors to be firmly on your side.'

'Correct,' confirmed John. 'The judge will no doubt reduce the hurdle rate from a unanimous decision to a split.'

John, being frequently a judge himself, knew exactly what he was talking about. The following morning, judge Leonard did precisely what John had predicted – he was now going to allow an eleven-one or ten-two split decision from the jury. This move could yield more verdicts, but it was as far as the judge would go.

***

Three more days passed and there was still no verdict on Ryan and me. The jury had asked to have a couple of audio recordings replayed for them, but they remained in deadlock. The judge eventually asked them if they were any closer to further verdicts and the foreman's distinctive answer was:

'We are absolutely deadlocked on one defendant but are hopeful that we may reach a verdict on the other one.'

Who could the "hopeful" one be? I ran the scenarios in my head and still found the situation encouraging for me. If the closer verdict was an acquittal, then surely it would be for me. If I was the deadlocked one, then it would mean a hung jury. As things stood, a hung jury was just as good a result as an acquittal – I would be able to go straight back home to my family.

The following Friday marked over two weeks of deliberations for the jury. Judge Leonard decided that the jury had had enough time to reach the final two verdicts and asked the foreman one last time if they had reached a verdict on myself or Ryan.

The answer was *no*.

Ryan and I sat in the dock as if we were frozen, initially not realising the magnitude of the result. We were now free men and could take the next flight home. Finally, I stood up and started walking towards the courtroom exit. As I exited the room and reached the second-floor corridor, I bumped into John, James and Karl, who were already out. They all congratulated me, and that's where the realisation hit me.

'Congratulations, Stelios!' exclaimed John.

'For what?' I replied, looking completely lost.

'For getting the best possible result given the circumstances,' continued John with a smile. 'There were never going to be any acquittals on this trial, so we can chalk this one up as a win!'

'Yes, I guess that's right…' I mumbled as I tried to get my thoughts together. 'So, what does this mean now?' I enquired.

'This means that if you want to, you're free to fly back home to your family mate,' stepped in James.

'My family… yes, my family… *my family*!' I said. A huge grin covered my face and I put my arms around James. 'Guys, it's been a pleasure to have met you. Now please don't get this wrong, but I hope I never see any of you ever again!'

The three barristers laughed loudly. They congratulated me once more and then wished me a safe trip back. They fully understood just how badly I wanted to be on the next plane home.

I put my backpack over my shoulder and hurried into the lift. Upon my exit from the building I found yet more reporters and photographers, which I avoided once more, much to their disappointment. I was aware that the SFO still had the option of seeking a re-trial, and I simply couldn't afford to do something stupid that would jeopardise my chances. The SFO was known for being vindictive and if I lashed out against them, it would surely provoke their anger. I wanted to tell my story and show the media just how unfair this whole adventure had been, but I showed restraint for now.

I continued straight on, walking briskly towards the tube station. Five hours later I was at Heathrow airport, ticket in hand, on my way home.

Chapter Sixteen
The Return Home

The next morning, I opened my eyes and looked around. It was the familiar setting of my bedroom. I was lying on my comfortable bed and opposite me was my wooden white closet. I turned to my side and saw my wife lying next to me. I giggled because she was fast asleep and yet she had a perfect smile on her face.

Suddenly it all felt like it had been a bad dream. I started wondering whether all of it had actually happened – the preparation, the trial, and the verdicts. I must have moved a bit more, because I noticed that Semiramis's eyes had opened.

'Good morning my love,' she said as she pulled me towards her. 'What a wonderful day it is to have you back home.'

We spent the next ten minutes kissing and hugging, until the silence was broken by our two young daughters.

'Daddy, daddy!' they both shouted merrily and jumped on the bed. Just like that, the nightmare was over, and our family was finally reunited.

Later that day, I wrote an email to Steve and Roland. I wanted to know what the possibility of a re-trial was, and when the SFO was likely to make decision.

Steve replied shortly after with some encouraging news, as we had managed to acquire some valuable information about the jury split. Apparently, the split for Ryan was nine-three against, meaning that if one more juror had switched sides to *guilty*, he would have been convicted. Now I realised that the foreman's words *"we are hopeful that we might reach a fourth verdict"* referred to Ryan. He had escaped by the skin of his teeth.

The good news was that in my case, the split was the other way, so there were more jurors in favour of an acquittal. This was information that no doubt would have made its way to the SFO as well, and it was one of the reasons why Steve was optimistic. At that moment in time, he genuinely thought that the SFO would not seek a re-trial, because finding a more prosecution-friendly jury for them would be a tall order. Steve told me that the SFO had one week to make their decision, and that he thought they would probably decide not to retry me.

As I finished reading Steve's email, I felt relieved. However, I had learnt not to celebrate prematurely, so I decided to wait patiently. *It ain't over till the fat lady sings.*

I spent that day playing with my daughters and cooking with my wife. It was the perfect no-stress family day, and I felt happy again for the first time in ages.

Sadly, it wasn't to last.

The following day I received the email I was dreading from Steve. The SFO, contrary to all expectations, had swiftly decided to retry both myself and Ryan. The letter of representations sent by Steve on my behalf – outlining the main reasons why it was not in the public interest to retry me – had apparently been largely ignored.

Instantly, my world went dark again. *Why would the SFO want to retry me? What did they really have to gain by going after the most junior guy in the original trial?* They had got their 'win', with the convictions of Jay, Jonathan and Alex, and with PJ's guilty plea. *Why was it in the interest of the average UK citizen to go after me again?* I was still on legal aid, so the millions in legal fees would keep mounting – all on the expense of the UK taxpayer. *Were the people at the SFO so blind and ruthless?*

No way, I thought, *there must be another reason for this. A much deeper and serious reason.*

***

The decision to retry naturally brought sadness and frustration to me and my family, but that didn't last long. Semiramis's character and resolve had always been rock solid, and what happened next was yet more undeniable proof of that.

'So, when is the retrial scheduled for?' Semiramis asked impatiently.

'March 2017,' I replied.

'Good. We have around eight months to prepare,' she continued. 'And this time, there's no way in hell I'm letting you go through it alone.'

'If we can somehow organise that, it would be really amazing!' I exclaimed as my face lit up with hope.

'I'm going to make it happen, honey,' continued Semiramis. 'I'm going to pull some strings and arrange to work from the London office. We just need to find someone who will take care of the girls while we're both busy from the morning until you return in the afternoon. It's very doable.'

'I have a Greek friend who lives in London and whose wife doesn't work. I'll ask them to help us out,' I said enthusiastically.

'There you go! We're going to go there, and this time we're going to *Get. The. Job. Done.*

The emphasis on those last four words really resonated with me. I looked at my beautiful wife, who had already turned her back to me and was busy preparing some food. My two young daughters had scattered a bunch of toys on the living room floor and were joyfully playing with each other. Milly, our dog, was asleep on her mat by the kitchen, making the girls giggle with her soft snoring sounds.

I looked around at our house and realised that it was a really great place to live. It was much bigger than the tiny flats I had been renting when I was in London. I walked over to the door by the kitchen and looked outside at our garden. It had a good-sized lawn in perfect condition, and tall trees all around. I glanced at the swings, the see-saw and the slide that the girls always loved playing with. I remembered trying myself to go down the narrow slide and getting properly stuck, looking totally silly in the process.

Finally, I realised that even though I had been through so much difficulty, I was, in fact, really lucky. I turned around and saw the girls playing with marker pens, having drawn all over their faces and looking quite ridiculous. I let out a small laugh and shook my head.

'What the matter, my love?' asked Semiramis sweetly.

'Oh, nothing,' I whispered. 'I just can't believe how lucky we are.'

***

The next day, it was back to business for me. I shot off an email to my lawyers, asking what the strategy would be for the retrial. This time round I was determined to be prepared better, especially since I knew the prosecution strategy very well by now. John's initial thought was that we needed to take a different approach compared to the first trial, as it would be a very different proposition. I was the junior among five defendants in the first trial; this time round it would be just me and Ryan, a trader whohad only marginally more experience than me, and whose defence had always been very similar.

The long road of preparation for the retrial had well and truly begun, but the big surprise came from a call I received soon thereafter. It was from Andy, the BBC journalist, who had been following the case closely. He expressed his great disappointment for the convictions, and he wished me good luck with the retrial. However, he also shared some very interesting information with me.

'Hi Stelios, thanks for taking the call,' kicked off Andy.

'It's my pleasure Andy,' I said amiably. 'I know that you're probably the only person in the media who hasn't been blindly pushing the prosecution's case. You actually tried to uncover the truth,' I continued.

'Yes, and the truth isn't pretty, Stelios.'

'It sure isn't, Andy. Thank you for all your hard work and persistence.'

'I'm not sure if you've already seen this,' continued Andy, 'but we reported on it yesterday. We have found documents from a past court trial showing the existence of an internal fund within Barclays, called the 'Ricardo fund', during the 2008-2009 global financial crisis,' said Andy in a serious voice. 'Google it, I think you will find it very interesting!'

'I wasn't aware of that, thank you very much for pointing it out Andy.'

A few moments later, I found the article that Andy had mentioned, and started reading. The existence of an internal fund was quite common in banks, so that didn't surprise me at all. The fund's owners and beneficiaries were all Barclays senior managers, including Bob Diamond and some others who were directly or indirectly involved in my trial. This fact was also interesting, but again it was nothing particularly strange, given the time period in question. However, the next thing I read was jaw-dropping: the fund had made huge bets on LIBOR collapsing, only a few days before Lowballing began. Part of the article read as follows:

'Barclays profited from lowballing its sterling Libor rate, according to new allegations that have surfaced as part of a UK civil case brought against the bank by a care home that has cast a shadow over its former top management.

The bank had an offshore fund named Ricardo into which it paid £130m of profits from its interest rate derivatives business, the commercial court in London heard on Friday as part of a case that will call as witnesses Bob Diamond, the bank's former chief executive, and other members of its former executive team.

The Ricardo Master Fund "was an eponymous fund named after Mr Ricci", the court heard, referring to Rich Ricci, the former co-head of Barclays' investment banking business and another witness in the case. Jerry del Missier, Mr Ricci's co-head who will also be called to appear in the case, "described the fund as Barclays' global interest-rate portfolio", Mr Justice Flaux said after reading the claimants' written arguments, before suggesting that authorities in Singapore should be contacted to glean more details about the fund.

Legal arguments filed by the claimants, Graiseley Properties and Graiseley Investments – the owner of Guardian Care Homes – allege that the Ricardo fund "was a direct beneficiary of the manipulation (including downward manipulation) of sterling Libor."

The bank admitted to lowballing its Libor rate submissions to paint a false picture of its financial health during the credit crisis.

"The idea that people in Barclays did not know that there was manipulation of Libor and that it was wrong is simply not true," Mr Justice Flaux said on Friday at the hearing.'

I finished the article and I simply couldn't believe what I was reading. Then, I totally exploded. I rushed to Semiramis and explained what I had just found out.

'It seems to me that these guys *knew* that lowballing instructions had been given, and they *knew* that LIBORs were going to drop. It looked like a coordinated move to make them collapse and show everyone that the markets were returning back to normal,' I exclaimed.

'It sounds like it,' said Semiramis.

'So, let's see if I have this straight,' I continued. 'Unless I'm mistaken, they had inside information and traded on it using their own money, right before the markets started moving. They made a huge deal of money and funnelled it directly to their own pockets! And they have the *nerve* to blame us traders for the LIBOR requests which were neither fraudulent nor false or dishonest in any way?'

I was fuming, but it seemed pretty clear to me. On the face of it, these senior people apparently made millions of pounds, artificially moving the LIBOR rates. Then, when people started asking questions, they threw a few junior traders under the bus. *Could it be true? Could they get away with all the profits and put innocent people in prison?*

154

Straight away, I felt that if this information had been available to the jury, Jay, Jonathan and Alex wouldn't be behind bars right now.

***

The following months leading to the retrial passed relatively quietly. I spent time with my family, enjoying every moment with them. My preparation with the legal team progressed well, and we had already settled on our game plan. It was all plain sailing with the exception of two interesting developments.

Firstly, a book was released which had the LIBOR 'scandal' in its core. The book mainly covered Tom Hayes's story, but it also briefly mentioned a few other related individuals. The book was written by two journalists and it took a deeply one-sided view of the events. It was a blatant attack on Hayes and his family, and it portrayed him as a master criminal who would stop at nothing to fulfil his ambitions.

What surprised me was the fact that the authors had been allowed by the court to actually go ahead and publish it. I had been strongly advised not to speak to the media about the case, as my statements could jeopardise or compromise the upcoming retrial. Andy had been eager to interview me, but my legal team had strongly advised against it.

The publication of this book didn't make any sense to me; how was it that I wasn't allowed to speak to the media, but the prosecution's agenda was freely pushed to the whole world? It didn't seem fair to me. I voiced my anger to the lawyers, but their response was disappointing. Apparently, the authors were allowed to publish the book, as it was about Hayes and not the Barclays traders' trials.

That's pathetic! I thought. *The fact that the book is mainly about Hayes is irrelevant. In my view, the main issue of the book was LIBOR, and how – according to the authors – making LIBOR requests was illegal activity. It would undoubtedly affect my retrial negatively, that's plain to see!*

This was yet another clear sign that the prosecution – and whoever was driving their actions – were going to use every weapon at their disposal to secure as many convictions as possible.

Interestingly, one of the two authors of this book was at the time engaged to Anne, the reporter who had tried to befriend me during the first trial. Furthermore, Anne had published a number of stories relating to the LIBOR trial, and they had all been aggressively negative towards the defendants. She seemed to always adopt the prosecutions' side of the events and used her journalistic position to push the bank's agenda. This was hardly surprising as it was a well-known secret that the major banks controlled the media and had a strong say in what was printed. Anne's employer in particular had a huge part of its earnings coming from bank fees – that made it highly unlikely that the media giant would turn against its paying customers or damage them in any way.

The other interesting – and much more important – development was Jay Merchant's appeal to his conviction. The court of appeals reconsidered his case, taking in some new material that had been made public. This was material that had been kept by the prosecution and which effectively proved that the practice of making LIBOR requests had been established for decades.

The prosecution's case was that the five charged traders had been the proverbial 'black sheep' within a business ruled by integrity and ethical behaviour. It was alleged that Jay Merchant had initiated the practice, even though I had testified that Gourtay was already making requests before Merchant joined the desk. There were emails from Gourtay to Johnson, with the Frenchman making himself direct requests, but they were somehow ignored. Merchant had been adamant that he had seen LIBOR requests being made while he was on the Euro desk.

The court of appeals also gained access to material demonstrating that in fact the whole banking sector – including the BBA – knew of the practice of LIBOR requests. In the documents in question, it was evident that LIBOR requests were seen as standard market practice, just as the five defendants had claimed all along. In light of this new evidence, the arguments put forward on behalf of Jay were powerful and had a strong chance of success.

The court of appeals, after having considered all the arguments, finally delivered their decision after weeks of discussion. In the official statement, it acknowledged the gravity of the new evidence and how it had shed new light on the case. It expressed surprise that such evidence was not put forward by the SFO, when it was clearly relevant information and could potentially cause an important shift in the jurors' decision-making process. The court of appeals said all the right things and checked all boxes required for a successful result. However, it had left the bombshell for the end: astonishingly, it ruled that Jay's conviction was safe.

Jay's sentence was reduced slightly but at that stage, the reduction was only minor. It was a shocking ruling, and one that reinforced my belief that things were not as straightforward as they seemed. In my mind, it was dead simple: some powerful people intended on shifting the focus from the fraudulent lowballing to the largely insignificant, and effectively legal at the time, LIBOR requests. They wanted to give the people blood, by charging a few unsuspecting junior traders. Their unequivocal goal was to send all the junior traders to prison and make sure they stayed there until the whole story was forgotten.

As I read the court of appeals ruling, I felt helpless. That invisible hand had closed yet another door, just as a glimmer of hope had emerged. I was now almost convinced that no matter what I did, this was a fight I couldn't possibly win.

Soon after, however, my gloomy spirits were lifted by an email from Roland. It seemed that the court of appeals had given me and Ryan a lifeline, and Roland was particularly upbeat about it.

In its ruling, it explicitly changed the questions that the jury would have to ask themselves in order to acquit or convict. In the first trial, the jury had to decide whether the defendants were party to a conspiracy to dishonestly procure false or misleading LIBOR rates. However, going forward, the jury had to answer the following question:

"Did the defendant deliberately disregard the proper basis for submission of true and honest LIBOR rates?"

That particular sentence made a world of difference according to Roland, and he was absolutely right. It had become evident during the first trial that none of the traders knew what the proper LIBOR basis for submission was, and neither did Bagguley, Harrison, Bommensath or even Scutt or Ewan. Therefore, the issue had become extremely simple – if a defendant didn't know what the proper procedure is, how could he or she deliberately disregard it? This was a question that jurors should have great trouble answering in the retrial. The past six years had been a veritable rollercoaster of emotions for me, with continuous highs and lows, and I had just reached a significant high.

***

The sentencing for Jay, Peter, Alex and Jonathan took place just a few days after the trial was over. The sentences were particularly harsh, just like in Tom Hayes's case. Johnson was given a four-year sentence, which included a reduction due to his guilty plea. Merchant received six and a half years, the harshest of all sentences. Matthew got four years and finally Pabon received two years and nine months. All very disappointing sentences in my mind, and totally disproportionate to the crime.

For Christ's sake, I thought, *people get less than that for violent crimes or rape!* The sentences were disappointing but at least now I knew what the worst-case scenario was for me, in case I was convicted in the retrial.

'Alex got thirty-three months, right?' asked Semiramis in her usual direct manner.

'Yes,' I replied.

'That means that the worst-case scenario for you is the same, correct?'

'Actually no, it will be less than that. I was more junior than Alex and sentences are always more lenient after a second trial. I think that the theoretical maximum is more like two years.'

'OK, good. Two years. And how much of that would you actually have to serve?' continued Semiramis in a surprisingly upbeat tone.

'One year, with good behaviour.'

'Great!' smiled Semiramis. 'One year. We can handle that,' she exclaimed.

'Actually, my love, it gets even better,' I added. 'The law says that if you're a foreign national you can choose to be deported back to your country six months before your sentence ends. The only catch being that you cannot return the UK during those six final months.'

'Fantastic! If the worst comes to the worst, I will take the kids to London, and your parents will come too. I will work from the London office and your parents will take care of the kids during the day. We will visit you every weekend or as often as we are allowed. It will only be six months. We will get through this!' As always, Semiramis remained solid as a rock.

The final act before the retrial was the confiscation hearing for the four convicted traders. The amounts confiscated were supposed to reflect the damage inflicted to the 'victims', and the gravity of the crime committed. Johnson was ordered to pay £114,000, an amount that he had most likely bargained with the prosecution before pleading guilty. Merchant was ordered to pay £300,000, Matthew £34,000 and Pabon a measly £2,300. Pabon's laughable amount was yet another clear sign that the SFO's decision to retry us was idiotic at best.

Chapter Seventeen
The Retrial

February 2017

The date of the retrial came quick as a flash, and the Contogoulas family was ready for the next and hopefully final step of the adventure. We arrived in London on a wet Saturday night and settled into our rented flat. It was on the first floor of a relatively new riverside development, within easy reach of Southwark Crown Court and Semiramis's workplace.

The following Monday morning, I kissed my wife and kids goodbye, and took the now familiar route to court. I had felt certain that my odyssey was over when I boarded that flight home the previous year, so it felt slightly surreal to be going through the whole process again. I put on my headphones, started my favourite playlist and turned up the volume.

As soon as I went through the revolving entrance doors to the building, I saw the familiar faces of the security personnel. They also recognised me and gave me a cheery 'hello'. I greeted them back, realising that they were totally oblivious to whether I was a lawyer, court employee or person under trial. I had been very polite to them during the first trial, and I wasn't about to change my ways.

The team's new meeting room was, amazingly, even smaller than the one from the previous year. At least it had a window with natural light coming in through it, so that was a minor improvement. John, James and Karl were already there when I entered the room.

'Good morning, Stelios,' said James cheerily.

'Good morning guys,' I replied as I looked around and sat down in the one remaining empty chair.

'We have another battle ahead of us,' said John as he began one of his typical but effective pep-talks. 'The situation will be quite different to last year and you could argue that it will be tougher this time round.'

He took a slight pause and said the next word so loudly that it was not doubt heard well outside the room.

'*However,*' he emphasised, 'we are very well-prepared, and we know the prosecution's approach. It's very unlikely that they will change it dramatically. We're going to stick to our strategy, get out there, and we will get the positive verdict in the end. It's the right verdict, it's the just verdict, and it's the verdict you deserve, Stelios.'

'It is,' I said, as I gained confidence.

'Good!' exclaimed John. 'Let's go.'

As I entered the dock, I greeted Ryan and couldn't help feeling a bit more lonely than last time round. By now, I was fully familiar with the judicial process and every step involved. I looked at Deacon who was sitting just a few feet ahead of me and for a split second she looked back at me. I flashed her a smile, feeling distinctly unsure why I did that immediately after.

Jury selection went very smoothly and at its completion the atmosphere was already starting to feel a lot better than the previous trial. The mix of people was much more balanced; there were men and women from all ages and from what looked like many diverse backgrounds. It was a huge relief for me, as I only wanted one thing all along: a fair and an unbiased jury.

***

The first few days of the trial were a déjà vu experience for both defendants. It was all very familiar, and our calmness was unmistakeable. I felt surprisingly detached emotionally, and the stress and nervousness of the previous year were all but gone. I found myself on occasion wondering whether this was normal, or if there was something wrong with me. It didn't matter, I was pleased that I felt comfortable and recognised that the jury would certainly pick up on that confidence.

On this trial, due to the smaller number of defendants, there was only one prosecution barrister – Emma Deacon. She had a junior barrister to help her – Dominic Lewis, just like in the previous trial – but she was going to do all the work this time round. Deacon seemed to be a very ambitious young barrister who was consistently being ranked among the top QCs in the country. This was her big chance to notch up an important and very public victory. Ryan and I had escaped with a hung jury last time, and she was prepared to use any means possible to secure both convictions. She desperately needed the win.

I expected Deacon's opening speech to be punchy, but what followed surprised me. She pursued a highly aggressive strategy, determined to show the world that she would get the result that Hines couldn't achieve the previous year. Her portrayal of myself and Ryan as greedy criminal masterminds carried huge risk. This 'shock and awe' strategy may have got an immediate negative reaction from the jury towards the defendants, but what would they think when they heard the defence opening speeches? Would reality emerge as being completely at odds with what she was portraying? Nevertheless, she carried on relentlessly, going through every single one of her attacking points, in her usual loud and slightly arrogant voice. When she was finally done, she looked at the jurors with a smile and thanked them for their attention.

The defence opening speeches were the antithesis of Deacon's approach. Both John and Adrian followed a considerably more low-profile approach, depicting the defendants as two decent, hard-working men who had simply been in the wrong place at the wrong time. One of John's main goals was to convince the jurors that this could have actually happened to *them*, if they had been in my shoes. He wanted to make absolutely sure that they had no doubt that the average person would have acted in exactly the same way I had.

John and Adrian completed their opening speeches in a steady and confident manner. It was a flawless performance, managing to get under the jury's skin and showing them just how different reality was, compared to the picture that Deacon had painted previously. I could clearly see surprise and disbelief in the jurors' eyes and body language. The defence had won the first battle.

The real fun began when the time came for the prosecution witnesses to give evidence. John Ewan had initially refused to give evidence, no doubt feeling sick of repeatedly giving evidence and being put in such a terrible position. However, the SFO wouldn't have any of that, and they promptly forced him to do it. On the stand, he was just as bad as he had been during the first trial.

Bagguley, Harrison and Bommensath gave evidence once again and they performed exactly as expected. All three followed the same line, effectively blaming the defendants for everything that had happened while completely distancing themselves from the LIBOR request activity. Whenever they were asked questions that could compromise the prosecution's case, they either found it difficult to answer simple questions, or conveniently had total memory loss. One juror would later very accurately call their performance as *"Playing for Barclays United"*.

McLaughlin was next up, giving his expected laughable answers to John's simple questions regarding the Gourtay/Harrison incident. It had been a sequence of small wins for the defence, but we really hit the home run when it was Saul Rowe's turn.

***

A few days prior, Ryan's team had made a major breakthrough. They had obtained a series of Rowe's emails and mobile phone texts, and they weren't pretty.

It had been made quite clear during the first trial that Rowe was not the 'expert' that the SFO had claimed. He lacked essential knowledge of basic concepts, and as such was probably unable to help the court on his knowledge alone. This time round, Ryan's team discovered a series of emails from Rowe to other market professionals, asking them for help – in many cases paid help – with material he wasn't familiar with. This was in fact allowed by law, as long as it was properly and fully disclosed. However, Rowe had apparently failed to make the appropriate disclosure, making him a completely unreliable witness. To make things worse, he used certain phrases, such as *"I need to show that I know what I'm talking about,"* which demonstrated just how clueless and unsuitable he was.

Adrian's cross-examination of Rowe was absolutely brutal, and it delivered a big blow to the SFO's reliability. In typical style, Adrian left the best for last: a number of newly discovered texts from Rowe's phone. UK law explicitly stated that when an individual is giving evidence in court, he or she is not allowed to discuss the evidence with anyone. Failure to do so is a criminal offence punishable with up to fifteen years imprisonment. Astonishingly, Rowe's texts revealed that he had in fact been asking for help and information *during* his evidence in the first trial.

It was an extremely poor and humiliating performance by Rowe, now at risk of being prosecuted himself. Just as Judge Leonard was about to release Rowe from the stand, he menacingly asked him:

'What part of *you are not allowed to discuss your evidence with anyone* did you not understand, Mr Rowe?'

Leonard didn't expect an answer to his semi-rhetorical question, and of course he never received one.

It was later revealed that Saul Rowe had been paid more than £400,000 between 2014 and 2017 by the SFO to be a court expert on banking, in its LIBOR prosecutions. Four hundred thousand pounds for someone who is clearly not an 'expert' in what he was hired to do. So, if this – admittedly large – payment was not for his expertise, what was it actually for?

Anne, the journalist, had been present during most of the retrial, just like she had done the year before. She had made a few attempts to speak to me and get close to me, but I made it very clear that I wasn't interested. Following her fiancé's aggressive book and her one-sided reporting, I didn't want anything to do with her any more. She had got the message and never even said good morning any more, as there was no reason for her to keep pretending otherwise. Her orders had become crystal clear to me – I was the enemy, and her job was to try and take me down at all costs.

***

The trial had been progressing exceptionally well for Ryan and me. So much so, that when the time came for us to give evidence, we were faced with the same dilemma as the previous year. In the meeting room, a big decision had to be made:

'Stelios, I have good news and I have bad news,' said John teasingly.

'I always like to have the good news first. Lay it on me John,' I replied eagerly.

'The good news is that this trial has been going as well as we could have possibly hoped for, so far. We have managed to score lots of points and the prosecution are really struggling.'

'Agreed! So, what's the bad news?'

'The bad news, my Greek friend, is that you now have to make a huge decision. A decision which could determine whether you are convicted or acquitted.'

'I had a feeling that this was coming,' I confessed. 'I would love to not give evidence – I remember very well how tough that was last year.'

'Exactly,' confirmed John. 'The prosecution has failed on practically every attempt they made to score points against you. Their final opportunity to accomplish this will be if you give evidence. Wouldn't it be wonderful if we denied them that chance?'

I was thrilled that I might not give evidence, but I wanted to make absolutely sure that my refusal wouldn't damage my chances of success. I also wanted to know what each team member's opinion was on this issue.

'OK John, what's your gut feeling? What would you do in my place?' I asked.

'I would strongly recommend you do not give evidence,' said John confidently.

'Team, what do you think?' I asked, as I looked around the room.

'I agree with John,' said Karl assuredly.

'I'm not sure actually,' added James hesitantly. 'There are compelling reasons for either decision. If I absolutely had to make a choice right now, I'd tell you to give evidence.'

'I'm with John on this,' said Steve, 'and we were actually discussing this yesterday with Roland, who also agrees.'

'We have a four to one split decision it seems,' I summarised. 'A unanimous decision would have been better, but this is good enough. Let me sleep on it and we will make our decision tomorrow.'

My dilemma was a simple one: either give evidence and be subjected to three days of relentless attack, or not give evidence and lose the chance of telling my own 'story' to the jury. An unexpected stroke of luck went on to make this choice an extremely easy one.

My 2011 FSA interview was inadmissible to the trial due to its compelled nature, but the prosecution had actually included the material in the main document bundle, even though they couldn't use it. From what I understood at the time, I would not have been able to introduce this material myself, but this blunder by the prosecution had cleared the way.

The decision was made the following day: I was going to include my 2011 FSA interview summary and not give evidence. This way, the jury would get to hear my account and any negative inference from not giving evidence myself would hopefully be reduced.

John proceeded to make the request to include the FSA interview summary to the evidence bundle, and the prosecution's immediate reaction was the perfect sign that we had made the right decision.

It was sheer panic.

Deacon played her final card, perhaps hoping that my Mediterranean temperament might force me into an error. She presented me with an ultimatum: if the FSA interview summary was to be included in the trial, she would herself introduce a summary of my 2016 evidence from the first trial. She claimed that it would essentially amount to a confession, or at best there would be conflicting accounts which would make me appear untruthful. However, if I decided to give evidence after all, she would refrain from introducing that evidence.

It sounded an awful lot like blackmail to me, and I was very sceptical. Close examination of the two summaries actually showed that my accounts were unsurprisingly entirely consistent five years apart.

'This is absolute nonsense!' exclaimed John. 'Deacon is panicking,' he said triumphantly.

'I've read and re-read both summaries and they are entirely consistent,' added James. 'I say we accept the prosecution's suggestion and get them both introduced.'

There would now be two separate accounts of the events available to the jury, one of which was to the very same court and in front of the same prosecuting barrister. What an inspired decision that had turned out to be!

The final hurdle for the defence was Ryan's evidence. Even though, I declined to give evidence, Ryan was still adamant about it. He was convinced that speaking to the jury himself would maximise his chances of acquittal, and he was right.

During his evidence he was calm, collected and extremely helpful to the jury. He answered all the questions in a structured and easy to understand fashion. He focused on simply telling the truth, and as a result he demolished the prosecution's efforts to thwart him. He handled the pressure beautifully and completed the task calmly and flawlessly, much to Deacon's frustration.

And so, it was once again time for the closing speeches. The prosecution closed in the same way they had kicked off, swinging one punch after the other. Deacon produced a lot of aggression and made many bold claims, even though the evidence and witnesses had clearly demonstrated the exact opposite. She was desperate, and she knew that she was losing the battle. Her junior, Dominic, had actually bumped into my team in the elevator a couple of days prior, and he confessed off-the-record that it was not looking good for the prosecution.

The defence closing speeches were clear and to the point. You simply can't get away from the facts and the truth, and the prosecution's case had been murky at best. The jury reacted positively to Adrian and seemed to get all his points across. They had been attentive and engaged throughout the trial, constantly making notes and seemingly grasping all the important aspects. When John took over, the jury absolutely loved him. Ever the entertainer, he kept it serious when he needed to make an important point, but he also often lightened the mood and had the jury laughing at will.

5ᵗʰ April 2017

At 2pm on Wednesday the 5ᵗʰ April, the trial was over, and the jury were sent out to deliberate.

Two hours later, everyone returned to the courtroom for the standard procedure of releasing the jurors overnight, but there was a huge surprise in store for us.

The shock announcement from the judge was that the jury had already produced one unanimous verdict. Leonard asked both defence counsels if they wanted to hear the verdict now or if they preferred to wait to receive both verdicts when they became available. Ryan and I both nodded, indicating that we wanted the verdict delivered immediately.

The foreman stood up and Judge Leonard asked the standard question.

'Have you reached a verdict in the case of Stylianos Contogoulas?'

'We have not, your honour.'

'Have you reached a verdict in the case of Ryan Reich?'

'We have.'

'What is the verdict?'

'*Not guilty.*'

As soon as the verdict was delivered, I turned to my left and looked at my co-defendant. Ryan couldn't believe that his ordeal was finally over. He put his hands on his face and started crying from happiness and relief. I gave him a few seconds and then reached over and hugged him.

'Well done, man!' I exclaimed and patted him on the back.

Ryan was still sobbing and barely managed to utter a 'thank you'. In the public gallery, emotions were running high. Among the various journalists, Andy Verity was also there, and he was visibly delighted. As the emotions subsided and the courtroom slowly emptied, the defence teams exited and chit-chatted in the corridor outside.

Ryan's team were understandably thrilled and were giving me words of encouragement. One of Ryan's solicitors in particular, a young woman, started crying with relief. I found that very strange – surely experienced lawyers were used to winning and losing such cases with no emotional attachment.

I walked over to Adrian and congratulated him. I acknowledged that he had not only done an excellent job for Ryan, but he had also indirectly helped all other defendants during both trials. Adrian thanked me for the kind words and confessed to me that it had been no ordinary case for the whole legal team. Everyone involved had found it extremely unfair that the defendants were scapegoated and had to spend years of their lives fighting to clear their names.

As I walked on, Andy grabbed me in the corridor and expressed his immense relief for Ryan's acquittal. He was optimistic for my chances as well and asked if he could briefly interview me outside the building when the desired acquittal materialised for me as well. I had no reasons to refuse and promised that I'd be there.

When the team met up in the meeting room upstairs, emotions were high. We discussed the verdict and collectively agreed that it was a very good sign for me. Contrary to the previous trial, this jury was not afraid to acquit the junior traders. It seemed that they managed to see the traders' position within the whole story and realised that Ryan couldn't have possibly known that what he did was improper.

'If that's what they think about Ryan, how the hell can they not think the same for me?' I wondered.

John was cautiously optimistic and admitted that a quick acquittal for Ryan was better than no verdict at all.

I went home that day and spent the evening with Semiramis and the girls. The excitement was so great that we had trouble sleeping that day. We stayed up and talked for most of the night, hoping that it would soon be our turn to celebrate.

6th April, 2017

Morning came, and I made my way to court, feeling optimistic. I was now alone in the dock, but there were some familiar faces in the public seating area. Ryan was sitting there in support, even though he had a flight to the US only a few hours later. Adrian was sitting next to him, smiling meaningfully at me.

What amazing people! I thought, as I tried to control my enthusiasm and reminded myself that I wasn't out of the woods yet. The jury were brought in at 10 a.m. in the usual procedure and they looked very calm. There were no signs of hostility or doubt in their eyes.

The jurors were released ten minutes later, and I rushed back to the meeting room. John had a prior out-of-town engagement that morning, so it was up to James and Karl to keep me sane for the rest of the day. The three of us started discussing the situation but we didn't get very far.

At 10:32 a.m., the courtroom clerk rushed to the room and informed us that the jury had just passed an envelope to her, informing her that they had reached a verdict. Everyone knew that it was a good sign, but we couldn't celebrate until we heard the foreman say those two elusive words.

This finally brings us to the point where the judge has received the envelope from the jurors, informing him that they had reached their verdict.

I entered the courtroom and sat in my usual seat at the dock. The judge came in, but before the jury were shown in, something mysterious happened. The court clerk got up and closed the dock's door. That door had been left open throughout the whole trial – *why close it now*? I looked around in fear, not knowing how to interpret that sign. Then things got even worse.

The internal door within the dock – the door that's usually used when transporting dangerous criminals in and out of it – was suddenly opened and a bailiff entered. The bailiff was a heavily built lady with handcuffs around her waist. She came in, closed the door and sat down behind me. I was panicking at this point. I was sweating and kept asking myself if she could possibly know something that no one else did.

I then took a deep breath and thought more clearly. I reminded myself that at that point, the only people who could possibly know the verdict were the twelve jurors. I concluded that this may well have been standard protocol for some cases, and I tried hard to calm my nerves.

The jury entered the room and sat in their designated seats. I couldn't keep my eyes off them, frantically looking for a sign. Suddenly, juror number six – a middle-aged lady – turned to me and smiled.

A few seconds later, Judge Leonard asked me to stand.

'Have you reached a verdict in the case of Mr Contogoulas?' he asked the foreman.

'We have your honour.'
'What is your verdict?'

'*NOT GUILTY.*'

I put my hands on my face and welled up, as I realised that the nightmare was finally over. When I opened my eyes, I looked straight at the jury and saw them looking back at me. I mouthed 'thank you' at them and made the shape of a heart with my hands.

I had dreamed about that moment for years and I had even rehearsed in my mind exactly what I was going to say to the prosecution. I had decided on every single word, carefully chosen to make them know exactly how disgusted I felt about that whole farce of a trial. However, as I was about to exit the dock, none of those people existed as far as I was concerned. As I took those twenty steps or so to the courtroom exit, I felt my heart rate slow right down. It was as though the whole room had gone silent and I was walking in slow motion. I had a vision of my family waiting for me at home. I smiled, finally at peace.

Chapter Eighteen
The Aftermath

The final meeting in the tiny meeting room was a particularly loud one. There were cheers and hugs among the men, finally releasing all those years of trapped emotions. James had already called John and told him the good news, which was greeted by loud cries and celebration from the other end of the line. John was already on the train, on his way back to London.

The debriefing was quick, as there wasn't much of importance to discuss. It was more an opportunity for me to compose myself before exiting the building. I knew that Andy and his BBC crew would be outside, waiting to get a few words out of me.

As I got out of the lift on the ground floor, I looked at the man who ran the canteen, the entrance guards and other building staff. They were all people that I had got to know over the past two years, and I realised that it would probably be the last time I ever saw them. I said goodbye to everyone and exited through the large revolving door.

Andy was waiting just a few metres outside the building, mic in hand, with a big grin on his face. His cameraman and support staff were standing just beside him, ready to capture the much-awaited moment. I walked straight towards him, with Steve and Roland following immediately behind. We stopped in front of the cameras and Andy asked the first question.

Suddenly, I felt the nerves get the best of me and worried that I wouldn't be able to get a coherent sentence out. I composed myself for a few seconds as it was finally starting to dawn on me: I was free and could finally start making long-term plans with my family. This story had taken away from me nearly six years of my life, and it had been a huge burden to bear for everyone involved.

'Stelios, how do you feel?' asked Andy excitedly.

'Delighted,' I beamed. 'I'm extremely pleased that justice has been served and glad that this nightmare has finally ended.'

'What are your plans now?'

'It's been nearly six years of my life and I want to finally move on. I just want to go back to my family now.'

Andy tried to get a few more words out of me, but it was futile. All I wanted to do at that moment was to see my wife. I thanked him and walked on for a few more steps, but then I suddenly stopped. I noticed some of the jurors standing just a few metres further back, looking directly at me.

'Hey Steve, do you see them standing there?' I asked.

'Yes, I see them,' replied Steve calmly.

'What do we do? Can I talk to them?' I enquired nervously.

'You can do whatever the bloody hell you want!' exclaimed Steve. 'You've been acquitted, you're a free man and you can talk to whoever you like.'

'OK, I want to talk to them.'

I stopped in front of the jurors and greeted them with a nervous 'Hi'. One of them – juror number six, the middle-aged lady who turned out to be a teacher – stepped forward and looked at me with a smile. Astonishingly, she asked if she could shake my hand. I wanted to burst out crying but instead I controlled myself and just welled up a bit. I shook her hand and the handshake turned into a warm hug. The other jurors came around to us and the situation soon evolved into one big group hug. Finally, the lady spoke.

'Listen, Stelios, I have to tell you just how incredible I found this case. And it wasn't just me, obviously, we all agreed on this.'

'I can imagine,' I replied, 'I often felt like I was in a bad dream, or a terrible movie.'

'You see,' continued the lady, 'after the prosecution's opening speech we all thought you were both guilty. The story, the prosecution told was aggressive and made you look terrible.'

'Yes,' I agreed, 'she did go out all guns blazing, didn't she?'

'She definitely did. However, when we listened to the defence opening speeches, it all started to change. When the prosecution witnesses started parading in front of us, trying their best to make you look like the black sheep in this whole story, we started getting angry. We couldn't believe our eyes and ears!'

'Imagine how I felt, sitting in the dock listening to these people trying to make me look like a master criminal!' I exclaimed.

'It must have been awful, I can't even begin to imagine what that must have been like. But seriously, we could obviously see that this wasn't some kind of rogue trader situation. It was clearly happening everywhere, at all banks, and spanning all seniority levels. It was unmistakeably standard practice and a junior person could not have known otherwise.'

'I'm really happy that you recognised that, because another jury did not,' I said.

'That's inconceivable. For us, it was clear as day. By the end of the trial, we were actually upset that juniors like you and Ryan were singled out and thrown under the bus.'

'Well, thank you for seeing the truth,' I said, and held her hands in mine. 'But I must ask you, how come you acquitted Ryan before me?'

'Ah,' laughed the teacher. 'We simply decided to start deliberating on him first, solely because he had just given evidence and we had his account fresh in our heads.'

'Phew!' I exclaimed jokingly. 'For a few hours I thought that you may have decided to acquit Ryan and convict me instead.'

169

'Believe me, that was never going to happen,' she said with a smile. 'Right, I think we all need a drink, we're going to the pub just around the corner, perhaps we will see you there.'

I walked on and called my wife. She was screaming and shouting from joy and I couldn't quite make out what she was saying, but she was already on her way to meet me and that was all that mattered. I sat down at the nearby pub with Steve and Roland and we ordered drinks. James and Karl arrived soon after and we all joined on a toast.

'To your freedom, Stelios!' said James.

'To justice!' I joyously responded.

Two pints later, John finally arrived. He had been on a trial in Leeds and had boarded the first train to London when he got the news of my acquittal. He shook my hand and gave me a solid hug. He grabbed a beer and made a toast in his inimitable style.

'Today is a great day. Today, in a world where injustice occurs all around us, we scored a big win. What the bank and the prosecution tried to do to you was terrible. But, as long as we can notch up wins like this one, my faith in the system will remain. Cheers to you, Stelios.'

Semiramis arrived shortly afterwards and joined in the celebrations, just in time to catch a new round of drinks. Emotions were high at some point I noticed some of the jurors sitting just a few tables away. I gestured for them to come and join us, which they happily did. We all spent the next hour or so discussing the case and all the events of the past few weeks.

Finally, it was time for us all to go our separate ways. I thanked everyone individually and finally, I took Semiramis by the hand and we made our way home.

We were out celebrating later that evening, when I received a message from one of my friends, asking me to check Anne's latest post. I reached for my phone and quickly located it, instantly realising that it was a blatant character assassination attempt against me. Anne had been searching through my twitter account and identified a few tweets that I had sent at various points during the trial. Her article title was *"LIBOR trader prefers to tweet rather than testify in court"*. In my view, it was a disgraceful attempt to salvage something, following my emphatic win in court. I read the whole article and then calmly put my phone away. There was nothing these people could do to ruin that night for me.

For a while, Andy Verity had wanted to dedicate an episode of the popular BBC Panorama series to the LIBOR trials. However, the court had forbidden it until the end of our retrial. At that point though, the hurdle had been lifted and he was free to proceed. He had already arranged to air the segment during prime-time BBC television, and I had agreed to speak on camera and finally express my views in public, eager to say exactly what was on my mind.

The documentary was called 'The Big Bank Fix' and it was aired on the BBC on Monday 10th April 2017. Andy revealed a secret recording that implicated the Bank of England in LIBOR 'rigging', raising big questions about evidence given years earlier to the Treasury Select Committee by Barclays CEO Bob Diamond and Paul Tucker, who went on to become the deputy governor of the BoE. The following is part of the BBC article posted the same day:

"In the recording, a senior Barclays manager, Mark Dearlove, instructs LIBOR submitter Peter Johnson, to lower his LIBOR rates.

He tells him: 'The bottom line is you're going to absolutely hate this... but we've had some very serious pressure from the UK government and the Bank of England about pushing our LIBORs lower.'

Mr Johnson objects, saying that this would mean breaking the rules for setting LIBOR, which required him to put in rates based only on the cost of borrowing cash.

Mr Johnson says: 'So I'll push them below a realistic level of where I think I can get money?'

His boss Mr Dearlove replies: 'The fact of the matter is we've got the Bank of England, all sorts of people involved in the whole thing... I am as reluctant as you are... these guys have just turned around and said just do it.'

The phone call between Mr Dearlove and Mr Johnson took place on 29 October 2008, the same day that Mr Tucker, who was at that time an executive director of the Bank of England, phoned Barclays boss Mr Diamond. Barclays' LIBOR rate was discussed.

Mr Diamond and Mr Tucker were called to give evidence before the Treasury select committee in 2012. Both said that they had only recently become aware of lowballing.

Panorama played the October 2008 recording to Chris Philp MP, who sits on the Treasury committee.

He told the programme: 'It sounds to me like those people giving evidence, particularly Bob Diamond and Paul Tucker were misleading parliament, that is a contempt of parliament, it's a very serious matter and I think we need to urgently summon those individuals back before parliament to explain why it is they appear to have misled MPs. It's extremely serious.'

Mr Diamond told the BBC: 'I never misled parliament and... I stand by everything I have said previously.' Mr Tucker did not respond to questions from the BBC. "

This BBC Panorama broadcast caused a real stir and although public opinion will always be divided in such important issues, Andy's programme was – as far as I was aware – the first one to comprehensively bring together the practices of 'trader requests' and 'lowballing'.

Another shocking revelation involved Mark Dearlove, the head of the Barclays Money Markets desk at the time. Apparently, in a previous civil court case involving Guardian Care Homes and Barclays, he was said to have accepted that 'he was involved in and aware of manipulation of LIBOR'. Dearlove was said to have been investigated by the bank regarding this issue, and given a written warning in 2012.

Why were there no charges brought against Mark Dearlove, given that he had effectively given a confession to manipulating LIBOR? Could it be because he happened to be the son of former MI6 head, Sir Richard Dearlove? Was I the only one who could clearly see the pattern here? *Protect the powerful senior people and sacrifice the juniors.*

Chapter Nineteen
Post-Trial Events

My post-trial life in Greece finally returned to normality. I resumed my role as a stay-at-home dad, with my business venture continuing on the side. I took care of the girls and our two dogs. We got a three-month old white male Boxer from an animal shelter a couple of months after I was acquitted. While, Semiramis continued working from her employer's Athens office.

During the following twelve months, a few interesting developments took place, related to the LIBOR trials.

***

Development #1

Alex Pabon appealed his conviction and although it was ultimately unsuccessful, the Appeal Court judges were particularly disapproving of the SFO and their use of Saul Rowe. The judges labelled the situation a "debacle" and rapped the SFO for their lack of proper due diligence.

A number of traders who had been charged by the SFO – including myself – demanded that the SFO prosecute him for doing what appeared to be breaking the law while giving evidence. Surprisingly, the SFO refused to prosecute Rowe, even though they themselves had proof of his crime. We subsequently went to the UK Metropolitan Police with the same request, and their official response came in March 2019:

'...it is not possible to demonstrate that any errors in Rowe's evidence were either material to the proceedings or had a tendency to pervert the court of justice.'

'...there are insufficient grounds to suspect Rowe of having committed a criminal offence.'

And the most absurd part, in my opinion:

'...with regard to alleged offences contrary to the Fraud Act 2006, it is clear that the victim in this case would be the Serious Fraud Office.'

The victim would be the Serious Fraud Office? How about the people whose lives were ruined because of the SFO's inability to secure a knowledgeable and reliable 'market expert'? To me, it looked like the victim was not the SFO, but the people who were sitting behind bars as a result of Rowe's evidence.

The Metropolitan Police's assessment and final decisions looked completely wrong to me. Was Rowe or the SFO being protected? If yes, why and by whom? I'm not a conspiracy theorist by nature, but this case was full of such events which had to be questioned.

***

Development #2

There was also a series of revelations relating to Tom Hayes, his former employer UBS, and the law firm that represented the bank – as described in a scathing piece by a well-known publication.

As the article described, it turned out that Hayes had been the perfect scapegoat for UBS. He was a non-Swiss national, he was no longer working for UBS at the time of the charge, and when he did work for UBS he was as far from their headquarters as possible, enabling them to claim non-awareness. According to the publication, two dozen UBS traders and executives disappeared overnight from the UBS Zurich trading floor, later to be discovered that they had all been suspended over LIBOR but were sworn to secrecy over the matter. Eventually, none of these people were ever sanctioned or suffered any form of penalty, instead they all received golden handshakes to go with a non-disclosure agreement.

However, to me, the most disturbing aspect was how the bank's law firm was said to manage their internal investigation. The piece described how initial investigations were undertaken, then selected traders were forced across the border into Germany where they were harshly grilled by a number of lawyers. There was apparently a simple reason for that: Swiss banking law dictated that any information resulting from interviews undertaken in Switzerland couldn't be disclosed. On the contrary, information gathered from interviews outside of Switzerland were not subject to same secrecy and were eligible for admission in future court cases. The article reported that, unsurprisingly, the only people forced over the border for the LIBOR investigations were lower level employees and not senior executives. The clinical result of all this was that managers ended up being fully protected by the bank, while the juniors were fed to the wolves.

Sarah Tighe Hayes had been for years working tirelessly towards getting Tom out of prison and clearing his name. During the two subsequent LIBOR trials, substantial pieces of information came to light which could potentially have changed the outcome of Tom's trial, had they been available at the time. Sarah continuously pushed for a further appeal, citing this more recent evidence as enough reason to put the conviction in doubt.

***

Development #3

Another UBS junior trader, Arif Hussein, had been dismissed from the bank due to his implication with similar LIBOR requests, and was also handed a lifetime ban from the finance industry by the regulator. During his appeal, the judges were once again particularly harsh against the FCA and the bank involved.

They highlighted the fact that Mr Hussein was *'A junior trader at UBS and was put under investigation in relation to a limited number of chats taking place over a very short period, all against a background of widespread use of LIBOR requests within UBS which senior managers widely condoned and for which they bear ultimate responsibility'.*

The judges even went as far as to point out that senior management at offending banks always escaped punishment while junior employees saw their lives and careers destroyed. They concluded correctly, in my opinion, that such behaviour sent a dangerous message to senior management within banks, encouraging unlawful behaviour with impunity. At the time of writing in March 2019, Arif Hussein has taken the offensive by suing UBS for breach of contract.

***

Development #4

There were evident inconsistencies when it came to regulators pursuing various individuals related to the LIBOR case. While some people went down the SFO route, being either charged (like myself) or named as co-conspirators (like Fred Gourtay or Don Lee), others were handled by the Financial Conduct Authority (FCA). From what I read in the press, there had been individuals directly involved in the LIBOR case, who had been referred for consideration to the FCA's Regulatory Decisions Committee (RDC). This was an option that was never extended to me by the investigating authority. The RDC went on to consider each separate case and it released individuals whose actions it ruled to have not been improper or to have constituted illegal activity.

Let me make it clear that I'm not implying that everyone who was involved in the LIBOR case should have gone the SFO route; in fact, I'm happy that other people didn't have to go through the same nightmare that I did. But why the inconsistent behaviour towards some individuals compared to others? What was the decision-making process that led the SFO to charge someone, name him as a co-conspirator, refer him to the RDC, or simply leave him alone? It would be extremely helpful if the people who made those decisions could provide some explanation.

Don Lee, himself, was treated favourably compared to Hayes and the five LIBOR defendants; having not gone through the gruelling process of a twelve-week trial. In fact, he was reported to have been paid over two million US dollars in damages by Barclays, after being terminated for allegedly engaging 'in communications involving inappropriate requests relating to LIBOR'.

***

Development #5

The US regulator for financial services, FINRA, had a specific process in place for when a registered representative left a firm for any reason. Firms were required to file a form and submit it within thirty days, in which they were asked to provide certain specific items of information. This form, referred to as the 'U5' form, was usually completed shortly after an individual had left the firm.

Jay Merchant voluntarily left Barclays in September 2009, as he had been head-hunted by UBS. Consequently, in completely normal fashion, the 'Termination Type' field on his U5 form was set to *"Voluntary Resignation"*. However, what happened years later was far from normal. Jay's U5 had apparently been edited by the bank and now told a very different tale. The termination type was altered to *"Discharged"* and in the 'Allegations' field they added the text *'Allegations that the individual engaged in communications involving inappropriate requests relating to LIBOR. Allegation that individual failed to properly supervise individuals on his team who were alleged to have engaged in communications involving inappropriate requests relating to LIBOR.'* Why was the U5 filing changed years later to give what seemed to be a false representation?

***

Development #6

The SFO decided to charge a number of Barclays' ex-employees, over the alleged rigging of EURIBOR. EURIBOR is a very similar instrument to LIBOR, with the main difference being that it regarded the EURO currency.

In a very similar pattern to the LIBOR trial, one of the accused traders pleaded guilty, most likely in order to secure a more lenient punishment, making the SFO's task much easier and the defendants' infinitely harder. Another trader, a French national, refused to attend the trial. Given that the particular 'crime' in question wasn't considered to be illegal in France (and many other countries, for that matter), France refused to extradite him to the UK to face trial. He was tried in his absence and was predictably convicted by the jury. The other verdicts were two acquittals and a hung jury for the remaining three defendants.

I knew two of the three traders, Carlo Palombo and Sisse Bohart, from my time at Barclays. I appreciated exactly the situation they were in; after all, I was in precisely the same spot back in 2016. I was practically certain that the SFO would have learnt from the retrial of myself and Ryan, and I thought that they would never choose to retry the three traders. However, the SFO managed to surprise me yet again, deciding to retry the traders.

In March 2019, Carlo was found guilty by the jury, while Sisse was acquitted. I was particularly saddened to hear about Carlo's conviction. I joined Barclays roughly at the same time he did back in 2002, and I always sat relatively close to him during the four years I was there. I got to know him quite well, and I was impressed by his kindness, positive attitude and integrity. I believe that he never acted dishonestly and was simply following instructions, in a very open manner, just like I did. I personally don't think he's done anything wrong, and yet he will be taken away from his wife and unborn baby. It was a sad day when I heard of his conviction, and I hope he and his family find the inner strength required to get through this safely.

Development #7

Jay Merchant, having served half of his sentence and been released from prison, continued on his quest to reveal the truth and clear his name. During the LIBOR trials, one of the main weapons for the prosecution was the high remuneration of the defendants. While it's easy to call someone 'overpaid', it's always worth considering all the effort and hard work that people put, before they manage to reach those levels. In my case, it could be easy for an outsider to see my compensation while at Barclays (peaking at around £200,000 on a single year) and think that I was overpaid. However, it wasn't all just handed to me; it came following decades of hard work, dedication and persistence:

I worked very hard in school every single year without exception, earning high grades in the process.

I studied for hours on end to get good 'A'-level grades, sacrificing the laid-back lifestyle that many of my peers had at the time.

I successfully completed a very demanding university degree and then a follow-up Master's degree.

I started my professional career and worked 12-hour days for years.

I got accepted in a tough MBA course, and completed it with distinction.

I beat thousands of other applicants to earn a place in the bank's summer internship program.

I put in the hard work to earn a full-time trading job and acquired the difficult skills that make someone a successful trader.

Going back to the whole issue of traders being 'overpaid': the prosecution tried hard to remind jurors at every opportunity that the defendants were very handsomely paid by the bank. However, they wanted to absolutely avoid any mention of the three Barclays prosecution witnesses' pay (Bagguley, Harrison, Bommensath). If the numbers were revealed, the jury would see exactly how much better senior managers were being paid, and they would get some much-needed perspective. Jay tried to get this information introduced to the trial, but it was refused by the judge.

In 2019, given that Jay was now a free man, he was able to push his side to the story without any constraints. A UK Times article published in February 2019 revealed the whole truth, as shown in the snippet below:

'A trio of former Barclays bankers shared almost £160m in pay and bonuses over seven years while a key interest rate, Libor, was being rigged, it can be revealed.

Mike Bagguley, Eric Bommensath and Harry Harrison shared the sum between 2005 and 2011. The fixing of the interbank rate saw three junior traders jailed.

The disclosure of their pay came through the efforts of Jay Merchant, a former Barclays trader who was jailed in 2016 for rigging the interest rate benchmark. He is seeking to clear his name. The three bankers were Merchant's superiors; Bagguley was his supervisor.

Merchant, 48, who served half his sentence before being extradited to India — the country of his birth — has accused Barclays and the Serious Fraud Office (SFO) of sharing a common goal: "To cover up the truth and deflect blame on to a handful of low-level traders."

The pay was disclosed to Merchant's legal team during his trial, but was ruled inadmissible as evidence. He claims he always followed orders from superiors and that if the evidence had been heard by the jury, he would have walked free. He said it showed that senior bankers had profited while "traders like me had no personal benefits whatsoever."

One can only guess about the effect that information would have had on the case, and how it could have affected the final verdicts. Once again, some crucial and definitely relevant information for the defence was ruled inadmissible as evidence by the judge.

Development #8

In early 2019, there was a fraud trial related to a 1.8 billion pound investment in Barclays Bank by the Gulf state of Qatar, which was made during the peak of the financial crisis in 2008. In relation to that investment, four former Barclays individuals were charged with conspiracy to commit fraud by false representation: ex-CEO John Varley, along with Roger Jenkins, Tom Kalaris and Richard Boath. As reported by The Guardian, the SFO was heavily criticised over its investigation:

'The judge overseeing the fraud trial of four former Barclays bosses has criticised the Serious Fraud Office for failing to take 'reasonable and appropriate' steps to obtain key evidence.

Mr Justice Jay said the SFO had not done enough on disclosure of key documents from Qatar's lawyers during its six-year investigation into whether Barclays bankers paid secret fees to the Gulf state as it invested £4bn in the bank during the financial crisis.

The jury was told on Thursday that Jay had ruled that the SFO's investigators had "not taken all reasonable and appropriate steps" to obtain documents from Latham & Watkins, a US law firm which represented Qatar and Sheikh Hamad bin Jassem, the Qatari prime minister at the time of Barclays' emergency fundraising in 2008.'

Those were certainly some strong words from the judge against the SFO, and reading that article reminded me of my particular case. The words 'failing to take reasonable and appropriate steps to obtain key evidence' instantly reminded me of what I thought were missing communications between myself and Gourtay. *Coincidence?*

Chapter Twenty
Epilogue

The amount of material and evidence against the SFO, Barclays and UBS have been mounting for years. Their practices have been slowly coming to light, but it's always going to be a near-impossible task for an individual to defeat them in a legal battle. In my mind, I have at this point what I think is the full picture of the events and motivation behind them.

In my view it's all quite simple, and I think it should already be pretty clear by reading this book. It boiled down to just one thing: *Lowballing*. My life – and the lives of many others – had been turned upside down because of Lowballing, but the individuals involved in the practice were much too powerful and could never be publicly identified or prosecuted. When Barclays was fined in the Graiseley trial and its Lowballing practice was uncovered, the individuals involved remained untouched. Even Mark Dearlove's extraordinary admission in the Guardian Care Homes civil court case wasn't enough to bring charges against him.

It has also become obvious from the various trials – both civil and criminal – of the past years that making LIBOR requests was standard practice in many banks, on a number of currencies, for decades. Jerry Del Missier's testimony to the Treasury Select Committee demonstrates exactly why a junior employee would have never thought that there was anything remotely wrong about the practice.

Several banks have already settled with plaintiffs on LIBOR 'manipulation', paying billions of pounds as a result. Lowballing could later become a much more serious issue for banks, so it had to be buried under the carpet and forgotten about.

The convenient LIBOR scapegoats were carefully selected by the banks – in my view most likely by bank lawyers – with no second thought about how their lives and families were going to be destroyed, as a result. The lawyers involved needed to fulfil the senior managers' commands, if they wanted to keep their jobs and get compensated handsomely in return.

Since the beginning of my legal adventure, my view on regulators has become increasingly clear: they need to keep the banks happy, if they want to maximise their chances of going through the elusive revolving door which eventually leads to a highly-paid corporate job in the future.

Over the past couple of decades, it has become a frequent occurrence where individuals move from being a regulator to an institution that they had been responsible for regulating. In such cases, there is a clear ethical barrier which I fear no longer exists. In my simple mind, I believe that there should be a minimum period (perhaps five to ten years, or even more) during which individuals should have to spend away from their regulated market, before being able to take a job position in it. Surely if I, a regular person, can see the evident conflict of interest, it should be clear to everyone?

On the subject of regulators and prosecutors, there is a further issue that is often lost in the debate, and it's that of the "prosecutorial imperative" One of my contacts who is deeply familiar with the legal side of fraud cases once described to me the natural bias that exists here. After a case gets into the system, there is little – other than honourable conduct on the part of the prosecutors – that pushes prosecutors to bring an investigation to a timely close without charges. The assigned prosecutor sees *no reward* in advocating against prosecution. Perhaps the 'system' should correct for this through rigorous supervision on strict timelines and post-mortems on cases that run off the tracks. Hospitals do post-mortems; so should criminal prosecutors.

When the SFO decided to retry me and Ryan, even though they probably knew that they had little chance of getting a conviction, I got the distinct feeling that it was a 'free option' for them. In other words, they would have nothing to lose by taking another shot at us. If they managed to win, they would get all the glory; if they lost, there would be no apparent repercussions.

The sheer speed of the jury's acquittals demonstrated what an illogical and mistaken decision it had been to retry us. My lawyers' letter of representations – outlining exactly why a retrial would have been wrong – had been largely ignored by the SFO. Following our acquittals, the SFO faced no backlash and neither did they have to explain why they made such a seemingly foolish move. Where's the incentive for the prosecutor to seriously consider *not* pursuing a retrial?

The bottom line, as far as I'm concerned, is that the regulators' power against the controlling minds behind the banks has been severely reduced, and frankly, that should really scare the hell out of the average person.

Journalists and media employees always play a big role in stories like the LIBOR "scandal". The media have enormous power when it comes to covering news, and they can certainly use this power to guide the masses. For LIBOR, journalists needed to follow their bosses' orders, which were in my view likely to ensure that the senior bankers escaped unscathed. In return for a job well done, these journalists would in turn get promoted and compensated accordingly.

Is this all a big conspiracy theory, or has everything been carefully planned by the individuals and banks involved? I urge you, the reader, to spend some time considering all the information and evidence presented in this book, and to search for more details online if required. Try to put yourself in my shoes and think about how you would have acted in my place. Put aside any existing prejudice you may have against bankers. Forget the one-sided version of the events that you have been spoon-fed by the media regarding the LIBOR 'scandal', until now. And finally, think about the very senior people involved in this case. How many of them have been imprisoned? How many of them have been charged? How many of them were left alone to continue working in their seven-figure jobs? (*Hint: the answers are 'none', 'none', and 'all of them'*).

Now, think about all the juniors who have gone through the torrid experience of being tried in a UK Crown court – some like myself, twice. Even people like me, who were ultimately acquitted and found not guilty of any crime, had – at minimum – their careers ruined. How is this even remotely fair?

Personally, the more I think about people like Tom Hayes, Jay Merchant, and others who spent time in jail as a result of these prosecutions, the more I get upset. I feel that it's been a total travesty of justice, and that it's entirely wrong that a number of young kids have had to spend years away from their fathers. All this, for an alleged crime that (a) there was no explicit law, rule or regulation against when it happened and (b) which was not considered to be a crime in many western countries at the time. The regulation and operation around LIBOR were subsequently completely overhauled in 2012, introducing explicit clauses against 'manipulation', such as making LIBOR requests. None of us should have ever been charged for this alleged crime!

In my mind, the real LIBOR 'conspiracy' had nothing to do with the defendants in the trials. It was a complex web of participants in various roles and countries, all masterfully orchestrated by a handful of extremely intelligent lawyers. The orders came from very high up in the hierarchy, conspiring to destroy a handful of lower-level individuals, in order to protect senior management and appease the crowds. It was like a modern-day Colosseum, where Julius Caesar had just thrown the religious sacrifice onto the arena, with the lions waiting to tear them apart. Meanwhile, the people were cheering and asking for blood, thinking that justice was about to be done. With the media effectively controlling public opinion with their portrayal of the defendants, it was an easy task to deliver on the banks' agenda. Furthermore, with proper and impartial journalists – like Andy Verity – unable to report the truth until the retrial was over, the damage had already been done.

I knew exactly what the real LIBOR conspiracy was, but there was no way I could take on the banks on my own. As I sat on my garden lawn one summer evening, I took a minute to look around me.

My kids were playing on their swings, moving back and forth and laughing merrily, their soft brown hair flowing in the air. My wife was a few feet further away, watering the plants and humming one of her favourite tunes. The dogs were chasing each other around the garden, frequently stopping to catch a few breaths.

The past seven years had been a veritable rollercoaster of emotions. The events had brought my family very close, as we all worked as a unit in pursuit of the ultimate goal, which was to bring the truth out for the world to see, and to set me free from this heavy burden.

One of this story's useful side-effects for me was that I found out exactly who my real friends were. There were individuals whom I'd known since I was very young, who abandoned me. Some simply stopped interacting with me until my acquittal, at which point they nervously admitted that they did so because they didn't know what to say while I was front page news. Others, astonishingly, went on to bad-mouth me behind my back.

But it wasn't all bad. There were people like my London-based friend Jason, whom I had only known for a relatively short time, who supported me like a brother. It was an amazing "safety net" feeling to have, knowing that I had a few people who were there for me in London during the incredibly tough times of the trials. The end result was that my circle of friends and family shrunk considerably, and that was a great thing. Just like spring-cleaning your house, this "de-cluttering" of one's social circle is a process that should probably be performed every few years.

As I was sitting on my garden, I took a sip of my ice-cold coffee and realised that my own personal victory had begun many years before my acquittal. I had been fortunate enough to spend most of my time raising my girls, from the day they were born. Before the first trial, my father had characteristically told me that I was the luckiest man on the planet, and I had struggled to understand the meaning at the time. On that day, however, it was crystal clear. Financially, I had lost everything, going from a handsomely-paid trader to a part-time entrepreneur struggling to make ends meet. But at that very moment, I was the wealthiest man in the world.